See the **WIDER** picture

Houses in Holambra, Sao Paulo, Brazil

The name of the city of Holambra comes from the words Holland, America and Brazil: Hol-Am-Bra. The city is famous for growing flowers and plants and every year, in the spring, the city welcomes thousands of visitors to the Expoflora. This amazing event is the largest exhibition of flowers, plants and garden design in South America.

Do you have a favourite plant or flower?

Course Map

Your Student's Book comes with access to:

▶ The Student's eBook

 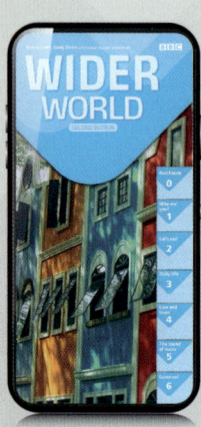

Audio, video and interactive activities with instant marking bring the content of the Student's Book to life in the eBook. It includes everything you need to participate in online lessons.

▶ Online Practice

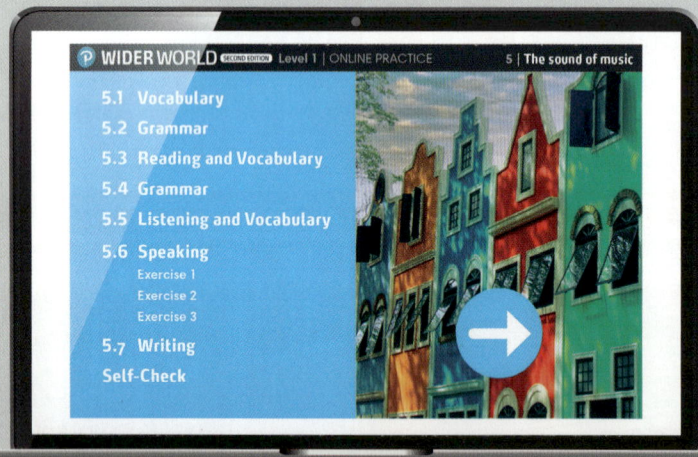 

Online Practice includes Workbook tasks and Extra Practice Activities, with instant marking. You can also find homework tasks and tests assigned to you by your teacher.

> *Wider World Second Edition* is fully accessible on your computer, tablet and mobile phone. You can enjoy the full functionality of your course wherever you are.

You can access your digital components through the Pearson English Portal.
See the inside front cover for access details.

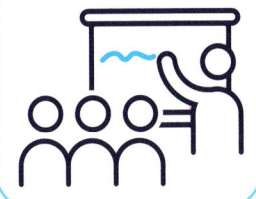

Classroom Lessons

Student's Book

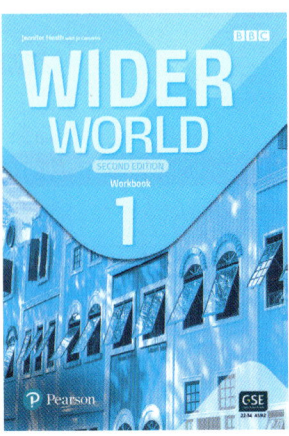
Workbook

Online Lessons

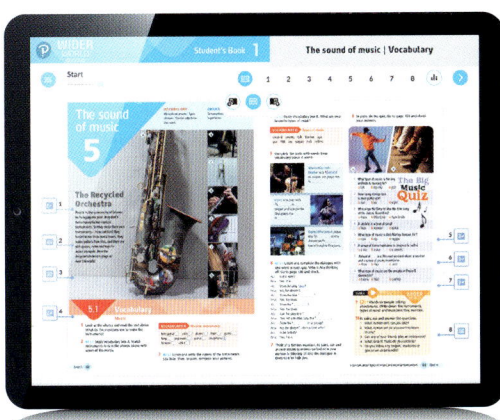
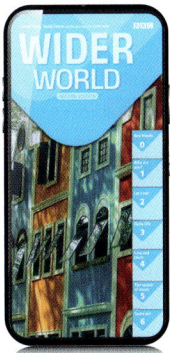
eBook

Homework

Workbook

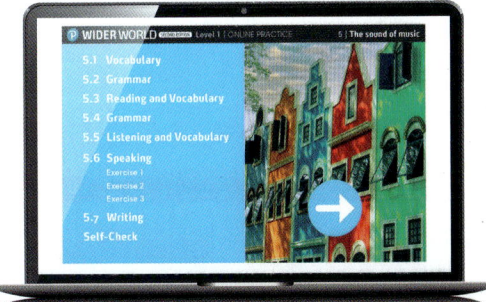

Online Practice

Contents

0 Best friends

0.1 Hello!
Subject pronouns | To be | Possessive adjectives | The alphabet | Spelling
pp. 6–7

0.2 My things
Possessions | Plural nouns | Demonstrative pronouns | Colours
p. 8

	Vocabulary	Grammar	Reading and Vocabulary	Grammar
1 Who are you?	Family and people: • Family • Countries and nationalities • Adjectives to describe people pp. 12–13	• Can BBC VIDEO Wider World p. 14	*A world of imagination* An article about role playing games BBC VIDEO Wider World p. 15	• Have got VIDEO *The surprise party* SET FOR LIFE Collaboration p. 16
	BBC CULTURE *Young geniuses*	VIDEO *Child prodigies*	Visible Thinking: See, Think, Wonder	
2 Let's eat!	Food and drink • Food and drink • Meals pp. 24–25	• There is/There are + some/any p. 26	*A teenage chef* An article about a teenage chef BBC VIDEO Wider World p. 27	• Countable and uncountable nouns • Quantifiers VIDEO *The picnic* BBC VIDEO Wider World p. 28
	SET FOR LIFE Collaboration and teamwork: Plan a project in a group *Let's work together* pp. 34–35			
3 Daily life	Routines • Describing routines • Adverbs of frequency • Verb + noun collocations pp. 36–37	• Present Simple: affirmative and negative BBC VIDEO Wider World p. 38	*My new home* An article about living in a new country BBC VIDEO Wider World p. 39	• Present Simple: questions and short answers VIDEO *Do you play bowling?* SET FOR LIFE Leadership p. 40
	BBC CULTURE *Same lives, different lives*	VIDEO *A typical day?*	Visible Thinking: Take a different view	
4 Live and learn	School • Classroom objects • Prepositions of place • School subjects BBC VIDEO Wider World pp. 50–51	• Present Continuous p. 52	*Problem? Ask Ella!* Online posts about making friends BBC VIDEO Wider World p. 53	• Present Simple and Present Continuous VIDEO *Don't panic!* SET FOR LIFE Self-management p. 54
	SET FOR LIFE Self-management: Be a smart student *My study routine* pp. 60–61			
5 The sound of music	Music • Musical instruments • Types of music BBC VIDEO Wider World pp. 62–63	• Comparatives p. 64	*The Teenage Challenge* An article about a music challenge p. 65	• Superlatives VIDEO *The coolest guitar* SET FOR LIFE Self-management p. 66
	BBC CULTURE *Don't stop the music!*	VIDEO *Feeling the music*	Visible Thinking: Think, Puzzle, Explore	
6 Game on!	Sport • Sports • Sportspeople • Sports collocations BBC VIDEO Wider World pp. 74–75	• Was/Were • There was/There were p. 76	*Sports fun facts* Short texts about sports facts p. 77	• Past Simple affirmative: regular and irregular verbs VIDEO *The running competition* SET FOR LIFE Social responsibility p. 78
	SET FOR LIFE Initiative and mindset: Be strong in difficult situations *Don't give up!* pp. 84–85			
7 The digital age	History and technology • Computers and technology • Dates in history pp. 88–89	• Past Simple: negative BBC VIDEO Wider World p. 90	*What can you do to help the planet?* An article about everyday technology p. 91	• Past Simple: questions and short answers VIDEO *How strange!* p. 92
	BBC CULTURE *Museums of the future*	VIDEO *Museums in the UK*	Visible Thinking: Think, Pair, Share	
8 Our world	Geography • Compass points • Continents • Countries • Nature BBC VIDEO Wider World pp. 100–101	• Modal verbs: have to/don't have to, mustn't p. 102	*Talking about world languages* An article about world languages BBC VIDEO Wider World p. 103	• Articles: first and second mention VIDEO *The culture vlog* p. 104
	SET FOR LIFE Social responsibility: Understand people from different cultures *Doing things differently* pp. 110–111			
9 On the go	Transport and travel • Means of transport • Getting around • Travel collocations BBC VIDEO Wider World pp. 112–113	• Present Continuous for future arrangements p. 114	*It's almost holiday time!* An article about holidays p. 115	• Be going to for future plans VIDEO *Summer plans* SET FOR LIFE Self-management p. 116
	BBC CULTURE *Who needs planes?*	VIDEO *Get on board*	Visible Thinking: Why do you say that?	

GRAMMAR TIME pp. 126–134   **IRREGULAR VERBS** p. 135   **STUDENT ACTIVITIES** pp. 136–139

0.3 In my class Imperatives | Classroom language | Object pronouns p. 9	**0.4 When is your birthday?** Days | Months | Seasons | Cardinal and ordinal numbers | Dates p. 10	**0.5 What is the time?** Telling the time | Wh- questions | Saying phone numbers p. 11

Listening and Vocabulary	Speaking	Writing	Revision	Progress Check
An interview about fashion p. 17	VIDEO *Nice to meet you* Greeting and introducing people p. 18	A description of a person • *and*, *but* p. 19	Vocabulary Activator p. 20 Revision p. 21	**1-3** pp. 48–49 • **Vocabulary and Grammar:** multiple-choice cloze, transformations, open cloze • **Speaking:** role play • **Listening:** multiple choice • **Reading:** note completion • **Writing:** a blog post
Project: a wiki about a famous talented person pp. 22–23				
Conversations about buying food p. 29	VIDEO *Anything else?* Ordering food and drink SET FOR LIFE Communication p. 30	A recipe • Sequence words p. 31	Vocabulary Activator p. 32 Revision p. 33	
A radio programme about feelings p. 41	VIDEO *What's your perfect job?* Talking about likes and dislikes p. 42	A blog post • *so* and *because* p. 43	Vocabulary Activator p. 44 Revision p. 45	
Project: a video about daily life around the world pp. 46–47				**1-6** pp. 86–87
A radio programme about a boarding school p. 55	VIDEO *The new video game* Polite requests p. 56	An announcement • Time expressions p. 57	Vocabulary Activator p. 58 Revision p. 59	• **Vocabulary and Grammar:** open cloze, transformations • **Speaking:** describe a picture • **Listening:** note completion • **Reading:** multiple choice • **Writing:** a report
A radio programme about live music BBC VIDEO Wider World p. 67	VIDEO *What do you suggest?* Suggestions p. 68	Text messages • Eliminating words in messages p. 69	Vocabulary Activator p. 70 Revision p. 71	
Project: a survey about music pp. 72–73				
A radio programme about sports BBC VIDEO Wider World p. 79	VIDEO *What are your hobbies?* Talking about hobbies and interests p. 80	A report • Adverbs of degree p. 81	Vocabulary Activator p. 82 Revision p. 83	
				1-9 pp. 124–125
An interview about childhood BBC VIDEO Wider World p. 93	VIDEO *I don't agree* Agreeing and disagreeing SET FOR LIFE Communication p. 94	An email • Past time expressions p. 95	Vocabulary Activator p. 96 Revision p. 97	• **Vocabulary and Grammar:** multiple-choice cloze, open cloze, transformations • **Speaking:** discussion task with visual stimulus • **Listening:** multiple choice • **Reading:** matching • **Writing:** an email
Project: a digital presentation about a museum pp. 98–99				
A conversation about communication problems p. 105	VIDEO *Do you understand?* Checking understanding and clarifying SET FOR LIFE Collaboration p. 106	'How to' tips • Verbs and prepositions p. 107	Vocabulary Activator p. 108 Revision p. 109	
Conversations about the weather BBC VIDEO Wider World p. 117	VIDEO *Lost in the city* Asking for and giving directions p. 118	An invitation email • Future time expressions p. 119	Vocabulary Activator p. 120 Revision p. 121	
Project: a travel plan for a school trip pp. 122–123				

CLIL ART p. 140 LITERATURE p. 141 HISTORY p. 142 SCIENCE p. 143

Best friends

0

VOCABULARY
The alphabet | Possessions | Colours | Classroom language | Days | Months | Seasons | Cardinal and ordinal numbers | Dates | Telling the time

GRAMMAR
Subject pronouns | *To be* | Possessive adjectives | Plural nouns | Demonstrative pronouns | Imperatives | Object pronouns | *Wh-* questions

0.1 Hello!

Subject pronouns | *To be* | Possessive adjectives | The alphabet | Spelling

1 ▶ 1 🔊 0.1 **Watch or listen and read the texts. In pairs, match descriptions 1–4 with photos A–D.**

Lena, Noah, Mateo and Mia are good friends. They're fourteen years old. They are in Year 9 at West Green High School in England. They are all in the same class.

1 ☐ This is Mateo. He's from the USA, but he's in the UK now with his parents. His dad is a musician and his mum is a vet. His hobbies are music and video games. This game is very exciting!

2 ☐ This is Lena. The people in her family are her mum, her dad and her ten-year-old brother, Adam. Adam is a good brother – most of the time. Lena's favourite hobby is music. Is she good? Yes, she is. She's really good! Her other hobbies are films and TV – lots of TV.

3 ☐ Here's Noah. His hobbies are art, video games and board games. This board game is his idea. Good job, Noah!

4 ☐ This is Mia. Her dad is from the UK and her mum is from Jamaica. Mia is very sporty. Her favourite hobby is fashion. Mia's clothes are always nice!

2 Study Grammar box A. Which pronouns are not in the texts in Exercise 1?

GRAMMAR A — Subject pronouns

I you he she it we they

3 Study Grammar box B. Find examples of *to be* in the texts in Exercise 1.

GRAMMAR B — To be

+	−
I'm (am) Noah. He/She's (is) my friend. You/We/They're (are) good friends.	I'm not (am not) a musician. He/She isn't (is not) sporty. You/We/They aren't (are not) sixteen years old.
?	
Are you sporty? Is she good? Are they from the USA?	Yes, I am./No, I'm not. Yes, she is./No, she isn't. Yes, they are./No, they aren't.

4 Complete what the people in Exercise 1 say with *am/'m not, is/isn't* and *are/aren't*.

1 Lena: Mia *is* very sporty but I _____ . I _____ good at music.

2 Mia: Lena and I _____ in the same class at school.

3 Mateo: **My mum and dad** _____ from the UK. **My mum** _____ from Los Angeles and **my dad** _____ from Mexico.

4 Noah: **Mia** _____ very good at sports. **Mateo and I** _____ good at video games.

5 Replace the words in bold in Exercise 4 with subject pronouns.

1 *She is very sporty …*

6 Make questions with *to be*. Then, in pairs, ask and answer the questions.

1 you / from the UK / ?
2 your sister / fourteen / ?
3 you and your friends / in the same class / ?
4 your dad / a musician / ?
5 your friends / good at sports / ?

7 Study Grammar box C. Choose the correct option.

GRAMMAR C — Possessive adjectives

I	you	he	she	it	we	they
my	your	his	her	its	our	their

1 A: What's *my / your* name?
  B: *It's / My* name's Catherine.
2 Look at the girls in the photo. *They're / Their* my friends. *They're / Their* names are Lucy and Tess.
3 This is a photo of my friend Joanna and *she's / her* dog. *Its / Their* name is Luckie.
4 Nico is from the UK. *His / He's* mum is from Italy.
5 A: Is this *your / you* new friend?
  B: Yes, it is. *His / Her* name's Anna.

8 🔊 0.2 Listen to the alphabet and repeat. Say the alphabet round the class from A to Z. Then from Z to A!

9 🔊 0.3 Study the Watch out! box. Listen and choose the correct name. Then write and spell your first name and your surname.

WATCH OUT!
Jessica = J-E-double S-I-C-A   Freddie = F-R-E-double D-I-E

1 *Ellie / Eli*
2 *Geri / Jerry*
3 *Vikki / Vicky*
4 *Mr Davies / Mr Davis*
5 *Kailee / Kylie*
6 *Hanson / Hendon*

I'm _____ .

YOUR WORLD

10 Make questions with *to be*. Then, in pairs, ask and answer the questions.

1 how old / you / ?
2 you / from the USA / ?
3 what / the names of your friends / ?
4 how old / your best friend / ?
5 your school / big / ?

A: *How old are you?* B: *I'm …*

0.2 My things

Possessions | Plural nouns | Demonstrative pronouns | Colours

1 In pairs, look at the pictures and read the text. Choose the correct option.

The fight is about their *things / room*.

2 🔊 0.4 Study the Vocabulary box. Tick (✓) the things you can see in the pictures.

VOCABULARY Possessions

☐ bag ☐ bike ☐ book ☐ camera ☐ diary
☐ key ☐ mobile phone ☐ mug ☐ skateboard
☐ T-shirt ☐ wallet ☐ watch

3 Study Grammar box A. Write the plural form of the words in the Vocabulary box.

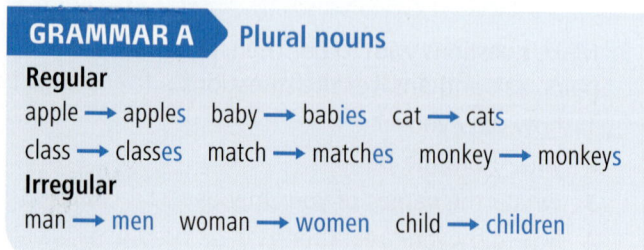

GRAMMAR A Plural nouns

Regular
apple → apples   baby → babies   cat → cats
class → classes   match → matches   monkey → monkeys
Irregular
man → men   woman → women   child → children

4 Study Grammar box B. Choose the correct option.

GRAMMAR B Demonstrative pronouns

Singular   Plural
this ↓ that →   these ↓ those →

1 That / **Those** books are very good.
2 Is *this / these* your watch?
3 *That / Those* boy is in our class.
4 *This / These* mobile phones are new.
5 Are *this / these* our desks?
6 *That / Those* T-shirts are very big!

5 In pairs, look at the pictures in Exercise 1 and find something:

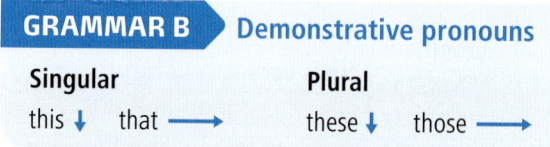

1 ● red.   5 ● brown.
2 ● yellow.   6 ● black.
3 ● blue.   7 ● orange.
4 ● green.   8 ○ white.

This T-shirt is blue. This …

6 In pairs, ask and answer about your things. Use the ideas below and add your own.

YOUR WORLD

bike   mobile phone   school bag   watch

A: *What colour is your school bag?*
B: *It's blue.*

0.3 In my class

Imperatives | Classroom language | Object pronouns

1 🔊 0.5 Match sentences 1–6 with pictures A–F. Listen and check.
1 ☐ Open your book.
2 ☐ Don't talk.
3 ☐ Sit down!/Stand up.
4 ☐ Don't write in your textbook.
5 ☐ Look at the board.
6 ☐ Put your hand up.

A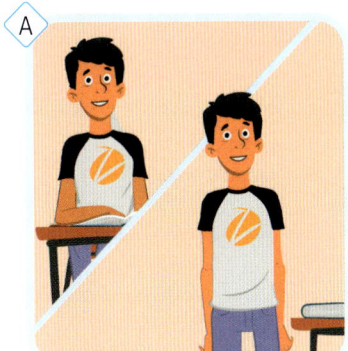
B
C
D
E
F

2 Study Grammar box A. Find another example of a negative imperative in Exercise 1.

GRAMMAR A — Imperatives

+	–
Sit down.	Don't talk.
Close your book.	Don't look at the answers.

3 Complete the class rules with the verbs below.

be   do   ~~look~~   ~~talk~~   talk   write

Class rules: English

✓ 1 *Talk* in English, please.
✓ 2 _____ in your notebook.
✓ 3 _____ your homework.
✗ 4 *Don't look* at your phone in class.
✗ 5 _____ late.
✗ 6 _____ in your language.

4 🔊 0.6 Listen and follow the instructions.

5 🔊 0.7 Match questions 1–4 with answers a–d. Listen and check.
1 ☐ What is the English word for 'amigo'?
2 ☐ Excuse me, which page are we on?
3 ☐ What's the spelling of 'exercise'?
4 ☐ What's the homework?

a Exercise 5 on page 6.   c E-X-E-R-C-I-S-E.
b Friend.   d Page 7.

6 Study Grammar box B. Complete the sentences with object pronouns.

GRAMMAR B — Object pronouns

I	you	he	she	it	we	they
me	you	him	her	it	us	them

1 Wow! Listen to *her*! She's a fantastic singer!
2 Pierre is from Paris. Talk to _____ in French.
3 Give _____ the key, please.
4 Mum and I are on holiday, but Dad isn't with _____ .
5 Thanks for your help. This present is for _____ !
6 Don't look at your phone in class! Put _____ in your bag.
7 Those are my sandwiches. Don't eat _____ !

YOUR WORLD

7 Ask your teacher two questions from Exercise 5.

What is the English word for 'muzika'?

0.4 When is your birthday?

Days | Months | Seasons | Cardinal and ordinal numbers | Dates

1 🔊 0.8 Complete the days of the week with the missing letters. Listen and check.
1. M o nd a y
2. T _ _ sday
3. We _ _ esday
4. _ _ _ _ rsday
5. F _ _ day
6. S _ t _ rday
7. S _ _ day

2 🔊 0.9 Complete the calendar with the months below. Listen and check.

August   February   May   November

3 In pairs, write the months for each season. Use the pictures in Exercise 2 to help you.
Summer: _June_ , _____ , _____
Autumn: _____ , _____ , _____
Winter: _____ , _____ , _____
Spring: _____ , _____ , _____

4 Count around the class.
1. Count backwards from 30 to 0: 30, 29, …
2. Count to 30 in twos: 2, 4, 6, …
3. Count to 36 in threes: 3, 6, …
4. Count to 50 in fives: 5, 10, …

5 🔊 0.10 Study the Watch out! box. Listen and write the numbers you hear in words and numbers.

> **WATCH OUT!**
> 300 = three hundred (**not** three hundreds)
> 511 = five hundred and eleven
> 4,000 = four thousand (**not** four thousands)
> 8,921 = eight thousand, nine hundred and twenty-one

a _thirteen – 13_   e _____
b _____   f _____
c _____   g _____
d _____   h _____

6 Write the ordinal numbers in words.

1st _first_   9th _____
2nd _____   12th _____
3rd _____   20th _____
4th _____   21st _____
5th _____   26th _____
8th _____   30th _____

7 🔊 0.11 Study the Watch out! box. Listen and choose the date you hear.

> **WATCH OUT!**
> In British English, we write *1 November*. We say 'November the first' or 'the first of November'.

1 a 1 January   b 11 January
2 a 13 March   b 30 March
3 a 29 July   b 20 July
4 a 13 October   b 30 October
5 a 21 December   b 23 December

YOUR WORLD

8 In pairs, ask and answer the questions.
1. What day of the week is it today?
2. What is today's date?
3. What's your favourite day of the week?
4. What's your favourite month and season?
5. When's your birthday?

0.5 What is the time?

Telling the time | Wh- questions | Saying phone numbers

1 🔊 0.12 Look at the clocks in photos 1–6 and complete the times. Listen and check.
   1 It's *eleven* o'clock.
   2 It's half past _____ ./
      It's seven thirty a.m.
   3 It's a quarter to _____ ./
      It's _____ forty-five p.m.
   4 It's ten _____ one.
   5 It's _____ to _____ ./
      It's five fifty-five p.m.
   6 It's twenty-five _____ _____ .

2 🔊 0.13 Listen and write the times.
   1 3.00 p.m.   4 _____
   2 _____   5 _____
   3 _____   6 _____

3 Order the words to make questions.
   1 your / what / name / is / ?
      What is your name?
   2 where / you / from / are / ?
      _____
   3 is / when / birthday / your / ?
      _____
   4 who / best friend / your / is / ?
      _____
   5 are / how old / you / ?
      _____
   6 your / what / favourite thing / is / ?
      _____
   7 phone number / is / what / your / ?
      _____

4 🔊 0.14 Complete the interview with questions from Exercise 3. Listen and check.
   A: ᵃ *What is your name?*
   B: I'm Lucy.
   A: ᵇ _____
   B: I'm fourteen.
   A: ᶜ _____
   B: Dundee, a city in Scotland.
   A: ᵈ _____
   B: It's on 18 February.
   A: ᵉ _____
   B: 032744 6519.
   A: ᶠ _____
   B: A girl called Becca. She's in my class at school.
   A: ᵍ _____
   B: Probably my phone.

5 Study the Watch out! box. Then, in pairs, take it in turns to say the phone numbers.

> **WATCH OUT!**
> We write *032744 6519*.
> We say 'oh three two seven double four, six five one nine'.

   1 07855 6693   3 020 583 714
   2 883 295 041   4 912 447 653

6 In pairs, ask and answer the questions in Exercise 3. Tell the class three interesting things about your partner.

Who are you?

1

VOCABULARY
Family | Countries and nationalities | Adjectives to describe people | Personality adjectives | Clothes and footwear

GRAMMAR
Can for ability | *Have got*

My amazing family!

Hi, I'm Julia. I'm fourteen and I'm Brazilian American. Here are some of my favourite family photos.

That's me in the middle with my little sister Lara. My mum's name is Marcia. She's from Brazil. My dad's name is Chris. He's American.

My mum's side of the family are all crazy about football – or perhaps they're just crazy. 😀 This is my uncle João and my cousin Gabriel.

You're never too old to try something new! This is my my grandpa Bill and my grandma Betty (my dad's parents) on holiday in France.

My auntie Emma (my dad's sister), her British husband Ed and my little cousin Leo. Leo: 'Look, daddy, I'm an aeroplane!'

1.1 Vocabulary

Family and people

1 Look at the photos and read the texts above. How many people are there in Julia's family? What are their names?

2 🔊 **1.1** Write the words from Vocabulary box A in the correct column. Listen and check.

VOCABULARY A ▸ **Family**

aunt brother cousin daughter father grandfather
grandmother husband mother parents sister son
uncle wife

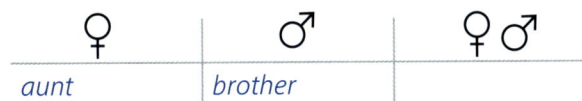

♀	♂	♀♂
aunt	brother	

3 Find other words in the texts in Exercise 1 for these words.
1 aunt _auntie_
2 mother _____
3 father _____
4 grandfather _____
5 grandmother _____

4 Study the Watch out! box. Then make sentences with 's or '. Who says these sentences?

> **WATCH OUT!**
> We use 's and ' to talk about possession.
> **Singular:** *Julia's mother is Brazilian. Her uncle's hair is brown.*
> **Plural:** *Her grandparents' home is in Los Angeles.*
> *Her cousins' names are Leo and Gabriel.*

1 our mum / name / is / Marcia
   Our mum's name is Marcia. (Julia and Lara)
2 my husband / name / is / Chris
3 my son / favourite team / is / São Paulo FC
4 my parents / names / are / Emma and Ed
5 our son / costume / is / funny
6 our grandparents / favourite country / is / France

5 Ask your classmates about their family.

What Who When	brother sister dad mum	name favourite TV show favourite singer birthday	?

A: What's your brother's favourite TV show?
B: My brother's favourite TV show is …

6 🔊 **1.2** **I KNOW!** Complete Vocabulary box B with countries and nationalities from the texts in Exercise 1. Listen and check. Can you add more countries and nationalities?

VOCABULARY B ▸ **Countries and nationalities**

¹_Brazil_ – Brazilian   Italy – Italian   the UK – ³_____
China – Chinese   Japan – Japanese   the USA – ⁴_____
²_____ – French   Poland – Polish   Turkey – Turkish
Germany – German   Spain – Spanish

7 In pairs, ask and answer the questions. Then think of more questions to ask your partner.
1 What nationality is the actor Daniel Radcliffe?
2 What nationality is the singer Rosalía?
3 What nationality is the tennis player Serena Williams?
4 Where is pizza from?
5 Where is sushi from?
6 What's your favourite food? Chinese? Turkish? Something else?

8 🔊 **1.3** **WORD FRIENDS** In pairs, check you understand the words below. Then write them in the correct column. Some words can go in more than one column. Listen and check.

~~big~~ ~~blonde~~ blue brown dark green
grey long ~~old~~ red short slim small
tall young

Eyes	Hair	General appearance
big	blonde	old

9 Look at the photos and texts in Exercise 1 and correct the sentences.
1 Gabriel's eyes are blue.
   Gabriel's eyes aren't blue. They're brown.
2 Julia's hair is short.
3 Leo is old.
4 Betty's hair is dark.
5 Ed is short.
6 Bill is young.
7 Leo is tall.
8 Lara's hair is blonde.

10 In pairs, ask and answer questions about the people in your class. Use the words in Exercise 8 to help you.
A: She's tall. Her eyes are green and her hair is very long.
B: Is it Elif?
A: Yes, it is.

YOUR WORLD

11 In pairs, take it in turns to say sentences about people in your family. Your partner guesses if your sentences are true or false.
A: My aunt's name is Susanna. She's Spanish.
B: True.
A: No, it's false. She isn't Spanish. She's Italian.

I can talk about families and nationalities.

1.2 Grammar

Can

1 🔊 1.4 In pairs, match each of the photos A–D in the blog with one of the words or phrases below. Read and check.

> fly   jump   play tennis   run   stay under water
> sing   speak a foreign language   swim

2 Study the Grammar box. Read the text again and complete the sentences below with *can* or *can't*.

GRAMMAR *Can*

We use *can* and *can't* to talk about abilities.

+	–
They can dance.	She can't fly.
?	

Can he speak English? Yes, he can./No, he can't.
How many languages can you speak?

GRAMMAR TIME > PAGE 126

1 Miralem _can_ speak Italian.
2 Tom _____ stay under water for a long time.
3 Aniek _____ walk, but she _____ play tennis.
4 Tara _____ fly, but she _____ jump.

3 🔊 1.5 Guess what these famous people can or can't do. In pairs, make sentences with *can* or *can't*. Listen and check.
 1 Katy Perry / sing / fly a plane
   Katy Perry can sing, but she can't fly a plane.
 2 Beyoncé / speak Japanese / dance
 3 Mo Salah and Kylian Mbappé / play football / jump six metres
 4 Leonardo DiCaprio / speak Chinese / speak German
 5 Lady Gaga / cook Italian food / stay under water for twenty-two minutes

4 Write six questions with *can* and the words/phrases in A and B below.

> A   you   your brother/sister   your friend   your parents

> B   dance   jump three metres   sing   speak English
>   speak three languages   swim one kilometre
>   stay under water for one minute

Can you dance?
Can your parents speak English?

AIDA'S BLOG
Amazing people

Tara Davis is a young Californian athlete. She can't fly, but she can jump 6.73 metres!

A

B

Tom Sietas is from Germany. He can stay under water for twenty-two minutes and twenty-two seconds.

C

D

Aniek van Koot is from the Netherlands. She can't walk, but she can play tennis in her wheelchair.

Miralem Pjanić is a Bosnian footballer. He can play football really well, and he can also speak six languages, including French, German and Italian.

Comments

Marilo, 19.17:   Hi, Aida. Can you sing?
REPLY Aida, 19.20:   No, I can't. ☹
Amal, 19.39:   Can Miralem Pjanić speak English?
REPLY Aida, 19.50:   Yes, he can.
Amal, 19.54:   How many languages can you speak, Aida?
REPLY Aida, 19.58:   I can speak two languages – English and Arabic.

VIDEO ▶   **WIDER WORLD**

5 ▶2 Watch four people talking about the things they can or can't do. Write down the things they mention.

6 In pairs, ask and answer the questions in Exercise 4.
 A: *Can you dance?*   B: *No, I can't, but I can sing.*

Unit 1   14   I can talk about things people can do.

1.3 Reading and Vocabulary
A world of imagination

A WORLD OF IMAGINATION

It's Saturday morning. I'm in a forest. It's full of people in strange costumes. Who are they and why are they here? Fifteen-year-old Megan from Manchester is here to answer my questions.

So Megan, who are these people?
They're LARPers. LARP, or Live Action Role Play, is a type of game. You can be a character from a film or create your own character, and then act in an exciting story with other people.

Who is your character?
My character today is called Dragora. She's a forest queen with long grey hair. She's 100 years old, but her face is young. She's clever and brave, and she can ride dragons.

Are you like Dragora?
Ha ha, very funny! No, I'm not! In real life, I'm quiet and nervous. And my hair isn't grey – it's brown!

Why is LARP popular?
It's popular because you can leave the real world and enter a new world – a world of imagination. It's a great way to make friends – young and old. Everybody is friendly and kind.

Who is it popular with?
It's popular with people of all ages and all over the world!

1 Who is your favourite book or film character? Discuss in pairs.

2 🔊 1.6 Look at the photos and read the article quickly. Choose the correct answer.
LARP is a type of
a film.   b game.   c character in stories.

3 Read the article again. Mark the sentences T (true) or F (false).
1 ☐ Megan is a teenager.
2 ☐ Dragora's hair is short.
3 ☐ Dragora is a young girl.
4 ☐ Megan is different from Dragora.
5 ☐ It's easy to make friends at a LARP.
6 ☐ LARP is popular only in the UK.

4 🔊 1.7 Study the Vocabulary box. Find six of the adjectives in the article. Then write sentences to describe you and people in your family.

VOCABULARY	Personality adjectives
brave clever confident friendly funny	
kind nervous quiet relaxed shy	

I'm quiet and friendly.
My uncle Sam is funny. He isn't quiet!

VIDEO **WIDER WORLD**

5 ▶ 3 Watch eight people talking about their appearance and personality. Write down the personality adjectives they mention.

6 In pairs, take it in turns to describe your favourite book or film character. Use adjectives from the Vocabulary box. Can your partner guess your character?
A: His hair is black and his eyes are green. He's brave and clever. He's in films and books.
B: Is it Edward Cullen?
A: No, it isn't. One of his friends is called Thalia Grace.
B: Is it Percy Jackson?
A: Yes, it is!

I can understand an article about role-playing games.

1.4 Grammar

Have got

VIDEO ▶ **THE SURPRISE PARTY**

Mia: Hello, Mrs Taylor.
Mrs T: Hi, come in! Have you got everything for the party?
Mia: Yes, we have. Where's Lena?
Mrs T: She's at her guitar lesson. She's usually back by six, so you haven't got much time. Oh, and she hasn't got her key with her, so listen for the doorbell!
Mia: OK. I've got the present. Have you got the drinks, Noah?
Noah: Yes, I have. I've got the balloons too.
Mia: Great!
Noah: What about food?
Mia: Mateo's got an app for a pizza delivery restaurant.
Mateo: Pizza-To-Your-Door. Their pizzas are amazing! So, one extra large Margherita … to 14 Park Street. Ready in twenty minutes. Perfect!
Mia: Good teamwork, guys!
Later …
Mia: That's Lena. Quick, everybody, get ready.
Noah: I'm nervous!
Mateo: Shh, be quiet.
All: Surprise!
Lena: Hello, everybody.

Mateo: Oh. Hi, Lena. Happy birthday!
Mia: Sorry about the pizza!
Lena: Never mind – I've got my friends! What a lovely surprise!

1 ▶ 4 🔊 1.8 Watch or listen and answer the questions.
1 Where are Mia, Noah and Mateo? Why?
2 What's the problem at the end of the story?

SET FOR LIFE

2 What is important for good teamwork? Discuss in groups. Look at the ideas below and choose your top two. Are you a good team player?
• listen to others   • share the work
• ask questions   • work hard

3 Study the Grammar box. Find more examples of *have got* in the dialogue.

GRAMMAR Have got

+	−
I've got (have got) the balloons.	I haven't got (have not got) the present.
He's got (has got) an app.	She hasn't got (has not got) a pizza.

?
Have they got food? Yes, they have./No, they haven't.
Has Lena got a piano lesson? Yes, she has./No, she hasn't.
What have you got?

GRAMMAR TIME ▶ PAGE 126

4 🔊 1.9 Complete the text with the correct form of *have got*. Listen and check.
Lena Taylor ¹*'s got* blonde hair and blue eyes. She ²_____ a sister, but she ³_____ a brother, Adam. The Taylors ⁴_____ a nice house. Her friends are there now because it's Lena's birthday today. They ⁵_____ a cake, but they ⁶_____ a present for her.

5 Make questions with *have got*. In pairs, ask and answer the questions.
1 Lena / a guitar lesson / ?
   Has Lena got a guitar lesson?
2 Lena / her key / ?
3 Noah / the drinks / ?
4 Mateo / the balloons / ?
5 Lena's friends / a present for Lena / ?

YOUR WORLD

6 In pairs, ask and answer questions about what your partner and his/her best friend have got. Use the ideas below. Then tell the class three facts about your partner.

a bike   a camera   a key to your home
a lot of cousins   a pet   brothers or sisters
friends in another country

Unit 1 — I can talk about things people have got.

1.5 Listening and Vocabulary

Fashion

1 Look at the photos and read the blog. In your opinion, which person (A–D) has got great style?

2 🔊 1.10 Listen and match the names with photos A–D.
1 ☐ Duncan   3 ☐ Elisa
2 ☐ Marc   4 ☐ Donna

3 🔊 1.10 Listen again and choose the correct answer.
1 Donna's sunglasses are from
   a a shop.   b a market.   c a friend.
2 Elisa's boots are
   a Spanish.   b Italian.   c British.
3 Duncan is
   a an actor.   b a singer.   c a student.
4 Marc's bike is from
   a Germany.   b France.   c the USA.

4 🔊 1.11 Study the Vocabulary box. Look at the photos in the blog and choose the correct option.

VOCABULARY Clothes and footwear

Clothes
dress jacket jeans shirt shorts skirt sweater
sweatshirt T-shirt tracksuit trousers

Footwear   **Other**
boots shoes trainers   hat (sun)glasses

1 Duncan has got a blue *sweater* / *jacket*, a white *T-shirt* / *tracksuit* and a dark green *shirt* / *hat*.
2 Donna has got a red and black *skirt* / *shirt*, blue *sunglasses* / *trainers* and black *boots* / *shoes*.
3 Elisa has got a black *jacket* / *sweatshirt* and black *trainers* / *boots*.
4 Marc has got a white *T-shirt* / *hat*, blue *trousers* / *shorts* and white *trainers* / *glasses*.

5 🔊 1.12 Listen to Chrissy. Listen again and write down what you hear. Then make similar sentences about yourself.

6 🔊 1.13 Order the words to make compliments. Listen and check.
1 trainers / your / are / really cool / !
2 style / you / great / 've got / !
3 fantastic / your shirt / is / !
4 colour / really nice / it's a / !

7 In pairs, make compliments about your partner's clothes. Use Exercise 6 to help you.
A: Your glasses are great!
B: Thanks! Your sweater is really nice!

1.6 Speaking
Greeting and introducing people

VIDEO ▶ NICE TO MEET YOU

Lena: Hey, Adam. I've got tickets for a basketball game on Saturday. It's my favourite team, the Shooting Stars, against the Flying Tigers. Are you interested?
Adam: The Flying Tigers? Yes, of course! They're awesome!
Lena: No, Adam. The Stars are awesome! … Oh, here's Mia.
Mia: Hi, Lena. How's it going?
Lena: I'm fine, thanks. And you?
Mia: I'm good.
Lena: Dad, this is my friend, Mia. Mia, this is my dad.
Dad: Hi, Mia. Good to meet you.
Mia: Nice to meet you too, Mr Taylor.
Lena: This is Adam, my brother.
Adam: Hi, Mia.
Mia: Hi.
Lena: Mia, are you free on Saturday? I've got tickets for a basketball game.
Adam: Hey! What about me?
Lena: It's OK, Adam. I've got three tickets. So Mia? It's the Shooting Stars …
Adam: … against the Flying Tigers.

Mia: Wow! Yes, please. The Tigers are awesome!
Adam: Yes!
Lena: Nooo!

SOUNDS GOOD! Are you free? • Wow!

1 What is your favourite thing to do at the weekend? Compare with your classmates.

> go to a football game   go to a shopping centre
> go to a sports centre   go to the cinema   go to the park

2 ▶ 5 ◀)) 1.14 Watch or listen and choose the correct option.
1 Lena's got tickets for a *basketball / football* game.
2 Adam *is / isn't* free on Saturday.
3 Mia *can / can't* go to the game.

3 Study the Speaking box. Find examples of the phrases in the dialogue.

SPEAKING — Greeting and introducing people

Hello!   Hi!
How are you?   How's it going?
I'm fine/good, thanks.
And you?
My name's …   I'm …
Good/Nice to meet you.
This is my brother/my friend.
Bye.   Goodbye.   See you (later).

4 ◀)) 1.15 Complete the dialogue with the words below. Listen and check.

> bye   fine   hi   how   meet   name   nice   see   this

Becca: Hello, Ajay!
Ajay: ¹*Hi*, Becca. How's it going?
Becca: I'm good, thanks. ² _____ are you?
Ajay: I'm ³ _____ .
Becca: ⁴ _____ is my mum.
Ajay: Hi, Mrs Porter. Good to ⁵ _____ you. My ⁶ _____ 's Ajay.
Mrs P: Hi, Ajay. ⁷ _____ to meet you too.
Becca: Sorry, we can't stop. We're late for our train.
Ajay: Oh, OK. ⁸ _____ !
Becca: Goodbye!
Mrs P: ⁹ _____ you, Ajay!

5 In groups of three, practise the dialogue in Exercise 4.

YOUR WORLD

6 In groups of three, have a conversation. Follow the steps below. Then swap roles.
- You meet at the park.
- Student A: greet Student B.
- Student B: introduce Student C to Student A.
- Student B: say that you're late for … (dinner/your music lesson/school).
- Say goodbye.

Unit 1   18   I can greet and introduce people.

1.7 Writing

A description of a person

1 Read the texts. In pairs, tick (✓) the things Robert and Sandra mention.
1 ✓ personality
2 ☐ nationality/languages
3 ☐ hobbies
4 ☐ appearance
5 ☐ age/occupation
6 ☐ family

2 Study the Writing box. Find examples of the phrases in the texts.

WRITING A description of a person

PARAGRAPH 1
1 **Introduce the person**
My hero is …
My favourite sports star/actor is …

2 **Age/Occupation**
He's thirteen and he's a student.
She's a famous TV presenter.

3 **Nationality/Languages/Family**
She's from Sweden.
She can speak two languages.
He's married and he's got two children.

4 **Appearance**
She's got fair hair and blue eyes.
He's tall and slim.
He's got glasses.

PARAGRAPH 2
5 **Personality/Positive things about the person**
He's got a difficult life, but …
She's brave/clever/friendly.
He's a great person.

3 Study the Language box. Find examples of *and* or *but* in the texts. Then combine the sentences with *and* or *but*.

LANGUAGE and, but

She can dance. She can sing too.
She can dance **and** she can sing.

He can dance. He can't sing.
He can dance, **but** he can't sing.

1 She can run. She can't swim.
She can run, but she can't swim.
2 He's got dark hair. He's got brown eyes.
3 She's quiet. She's very funny.
4 His mother's Italian. He can't speak Italian.

My hero by Robert

1 My hero is my friend Joel.
He's thirteen years old and
2 3 he's a student at my school.
He's English, but his mother's
from Spain. Joel is tall and
4 slim, and he's got dark hair.

5 Life is very difficult for Joel. He's a good student, but he's got big problems with his health and he's often not at school. But Joel is very brave and he's always very happy, friendly and funny. That's why he's my hero.

My hero by Sandra

1 My hero is Greta Thunberg. She's a student from Sweden, but she can speak English
2 really well. Her mother is a famous opera singer and her
3 father is an actor. She's got a younger sister, but she hasn't got a brother. Greta is quite
4 small and she's got fair hair and blue eyes.

5 Greta is my hero because she's very brave and she can talk about the future of our planet to important people. She's the leader of School Strikes for Climate – millions of schoolchildren from all continents are part of it. Now we've all got a voice – that's why she's a great person.

WRITING TIME

4 Write a description of your hero.

1 **Find ideas**
Make notes for your description. Think about:
• age, occupation and nationality.
• family, languages and appearance.
• personality.

2 **Plan**
Organise your ideas into paragraphs. Use the texts in Exercise 1 to help you.

3 **Write and share**
• Write a draft description. Use the Language box and the Writing box to help you.
• Share your description with another student for feedback.
• Write the final version of your description.

4 **Check**
• Check language: are *and* and *but* correct?
• Check grammar: are the forms of *to be*, *have got* and *can* correct?

I can write a description of a person. 19 Unit 1

Vocabulary Activator

WORDLIST 🔊 1.16

Family
aunt (n)
brother (n)
cousin (n)
daughter (n)
father (n)
grandfather (n)
grandmother (n)
husband (n)
mother (n)
parent (n)
sister (n)
son (n)
uncle (n)
wife (n)

Countries and nationalities
American (adj)
Brazil (n)
Brazilian (adj)
British (adj)
China (n)
Chinese (adj)
France (n)
French (adj)
German (adj)
Germany (n)
Italian (adj)
Italy (n)
Japan (n)

Japanese (adj)
Poland (n)
Polish (adj)
Spain (n)
Spanish (adj)
the UK (n)
the USA (n)
Turkey (n)
Turkish (adj)

Word friends (appearance)
Eyes
big (adj)
blue (adj)
brown (adj)
dark (adj)
green (adj)
small (adj)

Hair
blonde (adj)
brown (adj)
dark (adj)
grey (adj)
long (adj)
red (adj)
short (adj)

General appearance
big (adj)
old (adj)
short (adj)

slim (adj)
small (adj)
tall (adj)
young (adj)

Personality adjectives
brave (adj)
clever (adj)
confident (adj)
friendly (adj)
funny (adj)
kind (adj)
nervous (adj)
quiet (adj)
relaxed (adj)
shy (adj)

Clothes and footwear
boots (n)
dress (n)
hat (n)
jacket (n)
jeans (n)
shirt (n)
shoes (n)
shorts (n)
skirt (n)
(sun)glasses (n)
sweater (n)
sweatshirt (n)
T-shirt (n)

tracksuit (n)
trainers (n)
trousers (n)

Extra words
age (n)
auntie (n)
birthday (n)
children (n)
cool (adj)
dad (n)
favourite (adj)
friend (n)
grandma (n)
grandpa (n)
home (n)
house (n)
jump (v)
mum (n)
name (n)
nice (adj)
party (n)
people (n)
person (n)
speak a foreign language
walk (v)

1 Use the wordlist to find these things.
1 six pairs of family members
   mother and father, …
2 the opposites of *big*, *old* and *tall*
3 three words for footwear
4 five hair colours
5 two things you wear on your head

2 Complete the sentences in the quiz with a country or nationality from the wordlist. Go to page 136 and check your answers.

Around the world
1 São Paulo is in *Brazil*.
2 Ankara is the capital of _____ .
3 *Paella* and *tortilla* are types of _____ food.
4 Beyoncé is an _____ singer from Texas.
5 Milan and Naples are _____ cities.
6 Pandas are from _____ .

3 Choose the odd one out.
1 jeans	trousers	(glasses)	shorts
2 blonde	brown	dark	kind
3 aunt	daughter	husband	sister
4 young	quiet	brave	clever
5 shirt	wife	sweater	jacket
6 shy	short	slim	small
7 boots	shorts	shoes	trainers
8 big	long	tall	nervous

4 🔊 1.17 **PRONUNCIATION** Listen to how we pronounce the /ɪ/ sound. Listen again and repeat.
b**i**g   l**i**ttle   **E**nglish   ch**i**ldren   **I**taly

5 🔊 1.18 **PRONUNCIATION** In pairs, say the sentences. Listen, check and repeat.
1 My l**i**ttle s**i**ster **i**s s**i**x.
2 **I**t's fantast**i**c **i**n **I**taly **i**n the spr**i**ng.

Revision

Vocabulary

1 Complete the sentences.
1 My mother's father is my *grandfather*.
2 My dad's brother is my _____.
3 My dad's sister is my _____.
4 My dad is my mum's _____.
5 My brother is my mum's _____.
6 My aunt's daughter is my _____.

2 Look at the photo of Akari below. Complete the words in the description.

Akari   Leon

Akari is fourteen years ¹o*ld*. She's
²J_____ and her home is in Tokyo.
She's got ³l_____ brown hair and
brown ⁴e_____. Akari is a good friend.
She's very ⁵k_____. Today she's got
a black and white ⁶s_____, blue
⁷j_____ and red and white ⁸t_____.

3 Leon is from Berlin. Look at his photo above and write a description. Write about his age, nationality, clothes, appearance and personality. Use the description in Exercise 2 to help you.
Leon is … years old. He's …

4 Imagine you are in these situations. What clothes have you got? Write sentences. Then, in pairs, compare your answers.
1 You're in Spain. It's summer.
   A: *I've got shorts, a T-shirt and sunglasses.*
   B: *I've got a dress and a hat.*
2 You're in Moscow. It's winter.
3 You're at a friend's party.
4 You're at school.

Grammar

5 Order the words to make sentences. Add 's or ' where necessary.
1 name / English teacher / our / Mrs Andrews / is
   Our English teacher's name is Mrs Andrews.
2 best friend / in August / birthday / is / my
3 home / my / is / grandparents / in New York
4 favourite actor / is / Tom Hanks / my / mum
5 names / my / cousins / Cora and Rosie / are

6 In pairs, say if the sentences in Exercise 5 are true for you. If not, make the sentences true for you.
Our English teacher's name isn't Mrs Andrews. It's …

7 Make sentences about Maria. Use *can/can't*.
1 swim ✓ / play tennis ✗
   Maria can swim, but she can't play tennis.
2 dance ✓ / sing ✗
3 speak Spanish ✓ / speak Polish ✗
4 run ✓ / jump six metres ✗

8 Write true sentences about you and your family. Use the correct form of *have got*.
1 I / a brother / a sister
   I've got a brother, but I haven't got a sister.
2 my mum / dark hair / blue eyes
3 my dad / a black sweater / white trainers
4 my grandparents / a house / a car

9 In pairs, ask and answer questions about your best friend. Use *can*, *have got* and phrases from Exercises 7 and 8.
A: *Can your friend swim?* B: *Yes, he can.*
A: *Has he got blue eyes?* B: *No, he hasn't.*

Speaking

10 In groups of three, role play the situation. You meet in a café. Follow the instructions. Use the phrases below and your own ideas.

> Hello!   Hi!   How's it going?   How are you?
> I'm good, thanks.   This is my friend, …
> Nice to meet you.   Good to meet you too.
> See you later.   Bye!

Student A: Say hello to Student B. Ask how he/she is.
Student B: Reply. Introduce Student C to Student A.
Student C: Greet Student A.
Student A: Reply and say goodbye.

Dictation

11 🔊 1.19 Listen. Then listen again and write down what you hear during each pause.

21 Unit 1

BBC CULTURE
Young geniuses

The Junior Memory Championship
Some people are very clever and have got a very good memory. But can you learn to be a memory champion?

In the UK there's a memory competition for children. It's the National Junior Memory Championship. The children's schools are a bit different. They have reading lessons and writing lessons, but there are also memory lessons!

This year the competition is at London Zoo. The children have different tests. They've got a list of numbers. They've got a list of words. They've got a list of names and they've got information about London Zoo. And they've only got five minutes.

Joachim can remember forty-seven words – that's fantastic! Iris can remember forty names – that's fantastic too. But the winner is Lily-Rose. She can remember thirty numbers, thirty-five names and ninety percent of the information. Wow!

champion (n) a person who is the best at a sport, game, etc.
competition (n) a game or test that people try to win
memory (n) the ability to remember things
winner (n) a person who wins a game, competition, etc.

1 In pairs, discuss the questions.
1 Have you got a good memory?
2 What things are easy to remember?
3 What things are difficult to remember?
4 What special talents have you got? What are you good at?

2 🔊 1.20 Read the article. Mark the sentences T (true) or F (false). Correct the false sentences.
1 ☐ The National Junior Memory Championship is for people over eighteen.
2 ☐ The children do memory lessons at school.
3 ☐ The competition is at a school.
4 ☐ The children have got fifteen minutes to do the tests.
5 ☐ Joachim is the winner.

3 Follow the instructions.
1 Make a list of ten numbers and a list of ten English words.
2 Work in pairs. Give your lists to your partner to study for three minutes. How many numbers and words can he/she remember?

BBC Child prodigies

4 VISIBLE THINKING In pairs, look at the photo and answer the questions.

SEE
1 How many people are there in the photo?
2 Where are they from?
3 What can they do?

THINK
4 Where are the people?
   a at school
   b at a music competition

WONDER
5 What would you like to know about the people?
   a Are they very good at music?
   b Are they happy?

5 ▶ 6 Read the dictionary definition. Then watch Part 1 of a TV programme about child prodigies. Check your answers to questions 2–4 in Exercise 4.

> **child prodigy** (n) a very clever child. He/She can do something very well at a very young age.

6 ▶ 7 Watch Part 2 of the video and complete the fact file about the girl.

Name: _Anushka_
Age: _____
Name of club: _____
Hobbies: _____
Dream job: _____

7 Read the statements and choose the options that show your opinions. Then, in pairs, compare your answers.
1 Memory lessons at school *are / aren't* a good idea.
2 Competitions for children *are / aren't* a good idea.
3 Child prodigies *are / aren't* always happy.

PROJECT TIME

8 In groups of three, create a wiki webpage about a famous talented person. Follow these steps.

1 In your group, choose a famous person and decide who can find the answers to these questions.
- What is his/her full name? How old is he/she?
- What is his/her job? Where is he/she from?
- What can he/she do? What is special about him/her?

2 Individually, create your part of the wiki.
- Find the answers to your questions.
- Write full sentences about the person.
- Find some photos of him/her.

3 In your group, create your wiki webpage. You can use a website creator.
- Put the information together.
- Choose the photos to add to your wiki.
- Read and check your wiki.

4 Share your wiki with the class.
- Answer other students' questions.
- Ask questions and comment on the other wikis.

Let's eat!

2

VOCABULARY
Food and drink | Meals |
Places to eat | Cooking |
Popular supermarket foods

GRAMMAR
There is/There are + some/any |
Countable and uncountable nouns |
Quantifiers

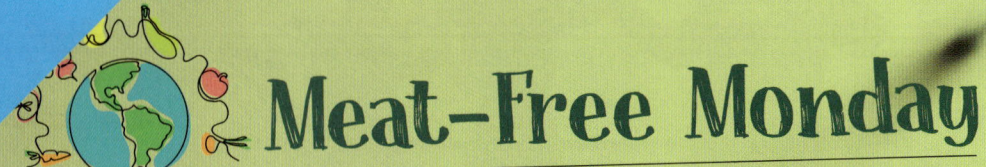

Meat-Free Monday

What is Meat-Free Monday?

It's a simple idea: one day a week without meat and fish (and ideally, without other animal products)! From Tuesday to Sunday, you can eat all your favourite meat and fish recipes. On Monday, you can try a delicious vegetarian or vegan meal. Meat-Free Monday is popular in many countries – in schools, homes and restaurants!

One day a week can make a big difference!

Have MORE of these

Have LESS of these

Why have one day without meat?
- It's good for the planet!
- It's kind to animals!
- It's healthy!
- It's cheaper: eat less meat and more vegetables = save money!

2.1 Vocabulary

Food and drink

1 Read the poster above. Answer the questions.
1. What is Meat-Free Monday?
2. What can you eat? What can't you eat?
3. Is it a good idea? Why?/Why not?

2 🔊 2.1 Study Vocabulary box A. Match photos A–N above with the words. Listen and check.

VOCABULARY A — **Food and drink**

☑ M burger ☐ butter ☐ carrots ☐ cereal ☐ cheese
☐ chicken ☐ eggs ☐ fish ☐ milk ☐ mushrooms
☐ orange juice ☐ pasta ☐ rice ☐ strawberries

3 Write the words from Vocabulary box A in the correct group. Some words can go in more than one group.

Fruit	strawberries
Vegetables	
Meat	
Dairy products	
Drinks	
Other	

4 **I KNOW!** Write the words below in the correct group in Exercise 3. Can you add more words?

apples bananas beef biscuits bread cake
chips ice cream lemonade lemons potatoes
sugar toast tomatoes yoghurt

5 What is your favourite food? Your favourite drink? Are they good or bad for you? In pairs, compare your answers.

My favourite food is cake, but it isn't very good for you.
My favourite drink is orange juice. It's good for you.

6 2.2 Study Vocabulary box B. Order the words from morning to evening.

VOCABULARY B ▶ **Meals**
breakfast dinner lunch

7 2.3 Listen to Josh's video blog. What day is it? Choose the correct time for each meal.
1 Breakfast: *7.15 a.m. / 7.30 a.m.*
2 Lunch: *12.45 p.m. / 1.15 p.m.*
3 Dinner: *6.00 p.m. / 7.00 p.m.*

8 2.3 Listen again and complete Josh's food diary for Meat-Free Monday.

Breakfast: ¹ *toast* with a ² _____ and orange juice
Lunch: vegetarian ³ _____ with ⁴ _____
Dinner: pasta with ⁵ _____ and ⁶ _____

9 In pairs, ask and answer the questions.
1 What time is breakfast/lunch/dinner in your house?
2 What is a typical breakfast/lunch/dinner for you?

Breakfast in my house is at seven o'clock.
A typical breakfast for me is …

10 2.4 Look at the photos and complete the school menu with the words below. Listen and check.

fish fruit rice salad ~~tomato~~

SCHOOL LUNCH MENU

MONDAY
- Cheese and ¹ *tomato* pizza
- Rice pudding

TUESDAY
- Vegetable lasagne with ² _____
- Chocolate cake

WEDNESDAY
- Chicken curry with ³ _____
- Fruit: apple or banana

THURSDAY
- Spanish omelette with salad
- ⁴ _____ salad with yoghurt

FRIDAY
- ⁵ _____ and chips
- Fresh strawberries with ice cream

YOUR WORLD

11 Write a lunch menu for your school – one for Meat-Free Monday, and one for Tuesday. Use Exercise 10 to help you. Then, in pairs, take it in turns to ask and answer about your menus. Which day is your favourite menu?

A: What's for lunch on Monday?
B: On Monday, it's …

I can talk about food, drink and meals.

2.2 Grammar
There is/There are + some/any

1 🔊 **2.5** Study the Vocabulary box. Have you got these places in your country? Vote for your favourite place to eat.

VOCABULARY > Places to eat

burger bar   café   fast food restaurant   pizzeria
restaurant   sandwich bar   vegetarian café

My favourite place to eat is a …

2 🔊 **2.6** Read the blog post. Which places from the Vocabulary box are in Brixton Village Market?

Bibi's Brixton
Eating out

London is an expensive city, but in Brixton Village Market there are some cheap restaurants. There are two fantastic pizzerias. My favourite is Franco Manca – the pizzas are fantastic. There's a good burger bar, Honest Burgers – the cheeseburgers are great. And there's a cool café called Burnt Toast Café. The cakes are delicious, there's free wi-fi and the people are really friendly.

FAQs

Q: Is there a McDonald's in Brixton Village Market?
A: No, there isn't, but the burgers at Honest Burgers are delicious!

Q: Are there any vegetarian cafés in Brixton?
A: Yes, there are. There's a vegan café called Eat of Eden in the market. There are some other vegetarian and vegan cafés nearby.

3 Study the Grammar box. Find more examples of *there is/there are* in the blog post.

GRAMMAR > There is/There are + some/any

	Singular	Plural
+	There's a sandwich bar.	There are some burger bars.
–	There isn't a vegetarian café.	There aren't any pizzerias.
?	Is there an Italian restaurant? Yes, there is./ No, there isn't.	Are there any cafés? Yes, there are./ No, there aren't.

GRAMMAR TIME > PAGE 127

4 Complete the sentences about restaurants in Brixton with the correct form of *there is/there are*.
1 *There's* a café called Black and White. ✓
2 _____ some excellent burger bars. ✓
3 _____ a German sandwich bar. ✗
4 _____ an African restaurant – its name is Asmara. ✓
5 _____ any Turkish restaurants. ✗
6 _____ any good pizzerias?

5 🔊 **2.7** Read the text and choose the correct option. Listen and check.

In my town there are ¹(some)/ any great restaurants. ²There / There's a café with delicious cakes. It's called The Savoy. ³There / They are three Indian restaurants – they're all good. There ⁴aren't / isn't a Japanese restaurant, but ⁵it's / there's a Chinese place called the Red Dragon. There ⁶are / is two pizzerias, Mario's and Pomodoro. Mario's pizzas are brilliant. There's ⁷a / some vegetarian café, Vegatastic. There aren't ⁸any / some burger bars, but there ⁹are / 's a sandwich bar – Slices. It's cheap and the sandwiches are good.

6 Cover the text in Exercise 5. In pairs, take it in turns to ask and answer questions from the prompts. Use *there is/there are*. Then look at the text and check.
1 an Indian restaurant?   4 any pizzerias?
2 a Japanese restaurant?   5 any burger bars?
3 a Chinese restaurant?   6 any sandwich bars?

YOUR WORLD

7 In pairs, take it in turns to play the role of a tourist in your town. Ask about places to eat. Your partner answers your questions.

2.3 Reading and Vocabulary
A teenage chef

Meet Omari, the teenage chef!

According to a study, half of all twelve- to eighteen-year-olds can't boil an egg or bake a potato. But here's one young man who can certainly cook! Omari McQueen is only thirteen, but he's already a famous chef! He's got a cooking channel on YouTube, and he's often on TV with his delicious recipes, including curries, cakes, soups and pizzas!

Omari is a vegan, so there isn't any meat in his recipes. His favourite recipe is vegetable curry. Omari's dream is to have a 'food bus' and travel to different countries. 'My dad can drive it and we can sell my meals all over the world.' What an amazing idea! Good luck, Omari!

Vegetable curry — RECIPE

Cut an onion and fry it in a pan with some curry powder. Add vegetables, coconut milk and water, and mix everything together with a spoon. Cook for twenty to twenty-five minutes. Boil some rice, then put it on a plate with the curry.

Enjoy!

1 In pairs, ask and answer the questions.
  1 Can you cook? 2 What can you cook?

2 🔊 2.8 Read the article and complete the notes with a word or a short phrase.

> Name: ¹_____   Age: ²_____
> Hobby: ³ cooking   Can't eat: ⁴_____
> Dream: to travel the world by ⁵_____
> Favourite thing to cook: ⁶_____
> Eat it with: ⁷_____

3 🔊 2.9 **I KNOW!** Study the Vocabulary box. Match the words with A–F in the photos above. Listen and check. Can you add more words to the box?

VOCABULARY Cooking
☐ bowl ☐ fork ☐ knife ☐ pan
☐ plate ☐ spoon

4 🔊 2.10 **WORD FRIENDS** Complete the phrases with the highlighted verbs in the article. Listen and check.
  1 <u>boil</u> an egg/water
  2 _____ an onion/bread
  3 _____ vegetables/salt
  4 _____ everything together/eggs with milk
  5 _____ an onion/an omelette
  6 _____ a potato/a cake

5 🔊 2.11 Complete the recipe with words from Exercises 3 and 4. Listen and check.

Spaghetti with chicken and mushroom sauce

¹C<u>ut</u> an onion and some mushrooms with a ²k_____ . ³F_____ them in a ⁴p_____ with some chicken, then ⁵a_____ cream. ⁶B_____ the spaghetti and ⁷m_____ it with the sauce. Serve with cheese and eat with a ⁸f_____ and ⁹s_____ . Delicious!

VIDEO — **WIDER WORLD**

6 ▶ 8 Watch nine people talking about their favourite recipes with eggs. Write down the food items they mention.

7 In pairs, talk about your favourite recipes and what you can/can't cook.

My favourite recipe is cheese and tomato pizza. I can also bake cakes, but I can't fry an omelette.

I can understand an article about a teenage chef.

2.4 Grammar
Countable and uncountable nouns | Quantifiers

VIDEO **THE PICNIC**

Mrs G: Right, boys, have you got everything?
Noah: I've got the drinks and the picnic blanket.
Mrs G: Good. The food's in a backpack in the hall, Mateo. There are some sandwiches, there's some fruit, …
Mateo: How many sandwiches are there?
Mrs G: Don't worry, Mateo. There are lots of sandwiches!
Mateo: Great! Are there any strawberries?
Mrs G: No, there aren't any strawberries, but there are some apples and bananas.
Noah: Cool!
Mateo: Is there any cake?
Mrs G: No, but there's lots of chocolate!
Noah: Thanks for the picnic, Mrs Garcia.
Mateo: Yes, thanks, Mum. So, where's the backpack again?
Mrs G: It's in the hall. Bye now. Have fun!

Later …

Mateo: Let's stop here for our picnic.
Noah: Good idea! I'm really hungry.
Mateo: Oh no!
Noah: What's the matter?
Mateo: There are some trainers, a water bottle and some socks, but there isn't any food. This isn't the picnic bag! It's my mum's gym bag!
Noah: Oh no!

1 ▶ 9 🔊 2.12 Watch or listen. Why are the boys unhappy at the end of the story?

2 Study Grammar box A. Mark the words below C (countable) or U (uncountable).

GRAMMAR A	Countable and uncountable nouns		
Countable nouns		**Uncountable nouns**	
Singular	Plural	bread	~~breads~~
a tomato	tomatoes	milk	~~milks~~
an egg	eggs		

GRAMMAR TIME > PAGE 127

- [C] apples
- [ ] bananas
- [ ] cake
- [ ] chocolate
- [ ] fruit
- [ ] sandwiches
- [ ] strawberries
- [ ] water

3 Study Grammar box B. Find examples of quantifiers in the dialogue.

GRAMMAR B	Quantifiers	
	Countable nouns	**Uncountable nouns**
+	There's **an** egg/**a** tomato. There are **some** eggs. There are **a lot**/**lots of** tomatoes.	There's **some** milk. There's **a lot**/**lots of** milk.
–	There aren't **any** eggs. There aren't **many** tomatoes.	There isn't **any** cola. There isn't **much** water.
?	**How many** tomatoes are there? Are there **any** eggs?	**How much** milk is there? Is there **any** milk?

GRAMMAR TIME > PAGE 127

4 🔊 2.13 Choose the correct option. Listen and check.

Freya: Have you got ¹a /(any) food in your bag, Lily?
Lily: I've got ²any / some biscuits.
Freya: How ³many / much biscuits are there?
Lily: Just two!
Freya: How ⁴many / much water have you got?
Lily: I've got ⁵lots of / much water – two bottles. I've got ⁶any / some cake, but it's a bit old and hard. It's from my school lunch last Monday. Do you want it?
Freya: Erm, no, thanks! I don't want ⁷any / much cake!

VIDEO **WIDER WORLD**

5 ▶ 10 Watch five people talking about the food and drink in their kitchen. Write down the things they mention.

6 Write about the food and drink in your kitchen. Then, in pairs, ask and answer to find out what is in your partner's kitchen.

In my kitchen there's some milk, but there isn't any …
Is there any … in your fridge?
How much … is there?

I can talk about quantities of food.

2.5 Listening and Vocabulary
Shopping for food

A 26p B ____ C ____ D ____ E ____

1 Look at photos A–E. Which things can you name?

2 🔊 2.14 Match photos A–E with the words in the Vocabulary box. Listen and check. Which of the foods come in packets? Which come in tins?

> **VOCABULARY** ▸ Popular supermarket foods
>
> ☐ beans ☐ brownies ☐ cheese and onion crisps
> ☐ chocolate chip cookies ☐ fish fingers

3 🔊 2.15 Listen to Greg and his parents. Complete the shopping list with words from the Vocabulary box.

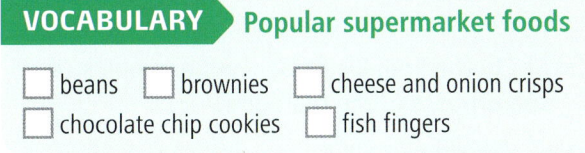

Shopping list
tea   apples   1 _____
bread   ice cream   2 _____
milk   yoghurt   3 _____

4 🔊 2.16 Study the Watch out box. Listen to how we say prices. Then write the prices below in words.

> **WATCH OUT!**
> 35p = thirty-five p/pence
> £1.56 = one pound fifty-six (pence)
> £2.70 = two pounds seventy (pence)

1 26p   _twenty-six p/pence_
2 60p   _____
3 £1.40   _____
4 £2.28   _____
5 £3.15   _____

5 🔊 2.17 Greg and his parents are at a supermarket. Listen and match the prices in Exercise 4 with photos A–E above.

6 🔊 2.18 Greg and his friend Oscar are at the supermarket. Complete their conversation with the words below. Listen and check.

> about ~~buy~~ cheap expensive get good much

Greg: Let's ¹_buy_ some fruit.
Oscar: Yes, ² _____ idea. I like bananas. How ³ _____ are they?
Greg: They're ⁴ _____ . A kilo of bananas is only 64p!
Oscar: OK, let's ⁵ _____ some bananas.
Greg: What ⁶ _____ chocolate biscuits?
Oscar: No, they're ⁷ _____ .

7 🔊 2.19 Listen to the whole conversation and complete the leaflet. Which things do Greg and Oscar buy?

> ### FANTASTIC prices!
> - 1 kg of bananas: ¹ _____ p
> - chocolate biscuits: ² £ _____
> - ³ _____ : £1.95
> - muffins: ⁴ £ _____
> - bottle of ⁵ _____ : £1.25
> - cola: ⁶ _____ p

8 In groups, look at the prices in photos A–E and in Exercise 7. **YOUR WORLD** You have ten pounds. Use these phrases to make a shopping list for a party. Then compare your list with another group.
- Let's buy/get …
- What about … ?
- How much is it/are they?
- Yes, good idea./No, it's/they're expensive.
- It's/They're cheap.
- They're only one pound twenty.

I can understand conversations about shopping for food.

2.6 Speaking

Ordering food and drink

VIDEO **ANYTHING ELSE?**

2.7 Writing

A recipe

1 Read Josie's recipe. Is it easy or difficult?

2 Read the recipe again. Match sections 1–4 with their descriptions a–d.
   a ☐ serving suggestion
   b ☐ instructions
   c ☐ personal comment
   d ☐ ingredients

3 Study the Writing box and check your answers to Exercise 2. Find examples of the phrases in Josie's recipe.

Five-minute Chocolate cake

① " This is my favourite recipe. It's quick and easy to make and it's really delicious! " Josie

②
- 4 tbsp of flour
- 2 tbsp of cocoa
- 4 tbsp of sugar
- 1 egg
- 3 tbsp of milk
- 3 tbsp of vegetable oil
- 30 g of dark chocolate
- 1/4 tsp of vanilla

③ First, put the flour, cocoa and sugar in a large cup. Then add the egg, milk, oil and vanilla. Mix everything together with a spoon. Next, cut the chocolate into pieces. Add them to the cup. Finally, put the cup in a microwave and bake for two to three minutes. Leave the cake to cool. Then take it out of the cup and put it on a plate.

④ Serve it warm with some cream or some fresh fruit.

WRITING — A recipe

① **Start with a personal comment**
This is my favourite recipe.
This is my grandmother's recipe.

② **List the ingredients**
tablespoon (tbsp)   teaspoon (tsp)   gram (g)
a tin of …   a packet of …   a bottle of …

③ **List the cooking instructions**
First, put the flour in a large cup.
Then add the egg.
Next, cut/fry/mix/cook/boil/bake …

④ **Give a serving suggestion**
Serve it warm/cold/hot with some ice cream.

4 Study the Language box. Find examples of sequence words in Josie's recipe.

LANGUAGE — Sequence words

Use sequence words to order ideas.
First, cut the …
Then fry the …
Next, mix the …
After that, cook the …
Finally, add the …
Use a comma after most sequence words, but not after *then*.

5 Order the recipe for potato salad. Number the instructions and add sequence words.
   a ☐ _____, mix the potatoes with two tablespoons of mayonnaise and the onion.
   b ☐ _____, add some salt and pepper to your salad and serve it!
   c ☐ *First*, boil four small potatoes in water for fifteen minutes. Leave the potatoes to cool.
   d ☐ _____ cut an onion into small pieces.

WRITING TIME

6 Write a recipe.

① **Find ideas**
Make notes for your recipe.
- Why is it your favourite recipe?
- What are the ingredients?
- What are the instructions?

② **Plan**
Organise your ideas into four sections. Use Josie's recipe to help you.

③ **Write and share**
- Write a draft recipe. Use the Language box and the Writing box to help you.
- Share your recipe with another student for feedback.
- Write the final version of your recipe.

④ **Check**
- Check language: are the sequence words correct?
- Check grammar: are the verb forms correct?

I can write a recipe.

Vocabulary Activator

WORDLIST 🔊 2.22

Food and drink
apple (n)
banana (n)
beef (n)
biscuit (n)
bread (n)
burger (n)
butter (n)
cake (n)
carrot (n)
cereal (n)
cheese (n)
chicken (n)
chips (n)
egg (n)
fish (n)
ice cream (n)
lemon (n)
lemonade (n)
milk (n)
mushroom (n)
orange juice (n)
pasta (n)
potato (n)
rice (n)
strawberry (n)
sugar (n)
toast (n)
tomato (n)
yoghurt (n)

Meals
breakfast (n)
dinner (n)
lunch (n)

Places to eat
burger bar (n)
café (n)
fast food restaurant (n)
pizzeria (n)
restaurant (n)
sandwich bar (n)
vegetarian café (n)

Cooking
bowl (n)
fork (n)
knife (n)
pan (n)
plate (n)
spoon (n)

Word friends (cooking)
add salt/vegetables
bake a cake/a potato
boil an egg/water
cut an onion/bread
fry an onion/omelette
mix eggs with milk
mix everything together

Popular supermarket foods
beans (n)
brownies (n)
cheese and onion crisps (n)
chocolate chip cookies (n)
fish fingers (n)

Extra words
buy (v)
cheeseburger (n)
chef (n)
chocolate (n)
cook (v)
cream (n)
cup (n)
dairy products (n)
delicious (adj)
dessert (n)
flour (n)
fruit (n)
healthy (adj)
hungry (adj)
ketchup (n)
kitchen (n)
lasagne (n)
meat (n)
oil (n)
omelette (n)
picnic (n)
pizza (n)
price (n)
recipe (n)
rice pudding (n)
salad (n)
sauce (n)
smoothie (n)
spaghetti (n)
soup (n)
spicy (adj)
tea (n)
vegan (n)
vegetable (n)
vegetable curry (n)
vegetarian (n)
water (n)

1 Use the wordlist to find these things.
  1 eight types of fruit and vegetable *apple, …*
  2 three drinks
  3 eight animal products

2 Look at the picture. Name the ten things in the fridge. Use words from the wordlist.

3 Complete the recipe with words from the wordlist.

SPANISH OMELETTE: RECIPE

- ¹C*ut* the potatoes and onions with a ²k_____ .
- ³F_____ them in a pan.
- ⁴M_____ the eggs, salt and pepper in a bowl with a ⁵f_____ .
- ⁶A_____ the potatoes and onions to the bowl.
- Cook everything together in the ⁷p_____ .
- Put your omelette on a ⁸p_____ and eat!
Enjoy!

4 🔊 2.23 **PRONUNCIATION** Listen to how we pronounce the /ɪ/ and /iː/ sounds. Listen again and repeat.
/ɪ/: f*i*sh and ch*i*ps   /iː/: thr*ee* m*ea*ls

5 🔊 2.24 **PRONUNCIATION** In pairs, say the phrases. Listen, check and repeat.
  1 Your d*i*nner *i*s *i*n the fr*i*dge.
  2 V*e*gans can't *ea*t m*ea*t.
  3 Th*e*se ch*i*ps are ch*ea*p.
  4 Ch*ee*se and b*i*scu*i*ts, t*ea* w*i*th m*i*lk.

Unit 2 32

Revision

Vocabulary

1 Read the definitions and complete the words.
1 It's a long orange vegetable. ca**rr**ot
2 It's a drink you can make with fruit. _u_ _ e
3 You can make toast with it. _r_ _d
4 It's another word for 'biscuit'. _o_ _ _ e
5 You can do this when you want to cook an egg. b_ _l
6 You can go there to drink coffee or tea. c_ _é

2 Complete the sentences with the words below.

> add   bake   burgers   cut   fast food   ~~knife~~
> lunch   sandwich   spoon   sugar

1 Can I have a _knife_ and fork, please, and a _____ for my soup?
2 There's a new _____ restaurant in town. You can get _____, chips and lots of other quick meals.
3 We've got eggs, flour, _____ and butter. We can _____ a cake!
4 To make chips, first _____ some potatoes, then fry them in a pan. _____ some salt.
5 For my _____ today I've got a cheese and tomato _____ and an apple.

3 Complete the menu with the words below. There are two extra words. Then write your own menu.

> bowl   fingers   ice cream   juice   ~~milk~~
> plate   rice   strawberries   toast

Today's menu

Breakfast
- Cereal with ¹_milk_
- ² _____ with butter and marmalade
- Orange ³ _____

Lunch
- Fish ⁴ _____ and chips
- Fresh fruit: ⁵ _____, apple or banana

Dinner
- Vegetable curry with ⁶ _____
- Chocolate brownie with ⁷ _____

Grammar

4 Look at the picture in Exercise 2, page 32. Write sentences about it. Use *there is/there are*.
There are five tomatoes. There's …

5 Choose the correct option.
Boy: ¹*Are there* / *Are they* any good restaurants near your house?
Girl: Yes, ²*it is* / *there are*. ³*There's* / *It's* a Turkish restaurant and ⁴*there is* / *there are* two Spanish restaurants.
Boy: ⁵*There is* / *Is there* a burger bar?
Girl: No, ⁶*it isn't* / *there isn't*, and ⁷*there isn't* / *there aren't* any cafés. But ⁸*there's* / *it's* a really good pizzeria.

6 In pairs, ask and answer about restaurants and cafés near your house/in your town.
A: Are there any good restaurants near your house?
B: No, there aren't any restaurants, but there's a great café.

7 Complete the dialogue with one word in each gap.
A: Let's make a cake. Are there are ¹_any_ eggs?
B: Yes, ² _____ are.
A: ³ _____ many eggs are there?
B: There aren't ⁴ _____ eggs – only two.
A: That's OK. How ⁵ _____ sugar is there?
B: There's a ⁶ _____ of sugar – about 500 g.
A: Great. Is there ⁷ _____ chocolate?
B: No, there isn't, but there are ⁸ _____ lemons.
A: OK, a lemon cake! Cool!

8 In pairs, imagine you are at the supermarket. Write a list of six things in your basket. Do not show the list to your partner. Ask questions to find out what is in your partner's basket.
Are there any bananas? How many … ?

Speaking

9 Work in pairs. Student A, follow the instructions below. Student B, go to page 136. Student B starts. Then swap roles.
Student A, you are in your favourite restaurant. Student B is your waiter.
- Order a meal with drinks and a dessert.
- Ask for extras (e.g. ketchup or another drink).
- Ask how much it is.

Dictation

10 2.25 Listen. Then listen again and write down what you hear during each pause.

SET FOR LIFE

Let's work together

International Day Competition
Friday 24 February, 2 p.m.

Prepare a presentation about another country. You can learn some interesting things, have fun with other students and win amazing gadgets for your group!

In your presentation:
1 talk about the country's flag, population and capital city.
2 make some food from that country.
3 say *Hello!*, *How are you?* and *Goodbye!* in that country's language.
4 present a song or a dance from that country.

Open to small groups of students from any year!

1 Choose the correct option to make the sentences true for you. Then, in pairs, compare your answers.
   1 Project work is *fun / boring*.
   2 It's *easy / difficult* to think of ideas for projects.
   3 Working in a group is *fun / difficult*.

2 Read the information about the International Day Competition above. Answer the questions.
   1 When is the International Day Competition?
   2 What can students win?

3 Match photos A–D with tasks 1–4 in the competition.

4 The students in a group have all got different skills. Look at the table below and answer the questions. Write the correct name(s) next to each question.
Who:
1 can dance very well? _____
2 is good at singing? _____
3 isn't very good at cooking? _____
4 can cook very well? _____
5 can't sing very well? _____
6 is good at searching the internet? _____

What can you do well?	Zack	Holly	Ed	Yasmin
find information online	★★★	★★★	★★★	★★★
cook	★★★	★★	★★★	★★
speak different languages	★	★	★	★★
sing	★★★	★	★	★
dance	★★	★★★	★★	★★

A

B

C

D

Units 1–2 | 34 | I can plan a group project.

Plan a project in a group

5 In pairs, decide which student from Exercise 4 can do each of the tasks (1–4) in the competition.

1 *All the students can talk about the country's flag, population and capital city.*

6 🔊 2.26 Listen to the students discussing the competition and answer the questions.
1 What country is their presentation about?
2 Which task for the presentation isn't on their list?

7 🔊 2.26 Listen again and check your answers to Exercise 5. Write the names of the students for each of the tasks (1–4).
1 ___
2 ___
3 ___
4 ___

8 In pairs, discuss which activities in the table in Exercise 4 you can or can't do. Use expressions from the Useful Phrases box.
I can speak German quite well, but I'm not good at dancing.

9 Read the Useful Tips. In pairs, discuss the questions.
1 Are the tips easy or difficult to follow?
2 Can you add one more tip?

SET FOR LIFE

10 In groups, make plans for the International Day Competition. Choose a task for everyone. Follow these steps.

1 Choose a country for the competition. Decide what food, song or dance you can prepare.

2 Draw a table like the one in Exercise 4 and complete it for your group. Write which activities each person can and can't do.

3 In your group, choose a person for each task.
- Say which tasks you would like to do and why. Use expressions from the Useful Phrases box.
I'd like to sing the song because I can sing very well.
- Decide which tasks two students can do together and how you can help each other.

4 Present your plan to the class.

USEFUL TIPS

When you work on a project, it's important to plan your work. Think of the things you are good at. Find a task for everyone in the group.

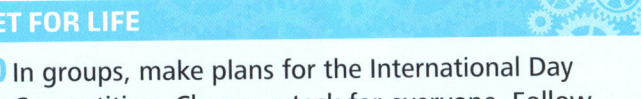
Make a list of tasks before you start.
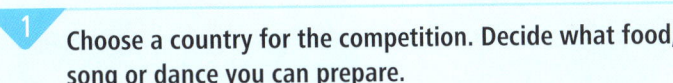
Listen to what people would like to do.
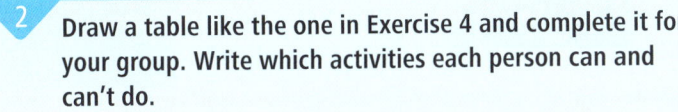
Match people with tasks they can do well.
Share tasks.
Help other people.

USEFUL PHRASES

- Who would like to … ?
- I can … quite well/well/really well.
- I can't … very well.
- I'm (quite/not very) good at …ing.
- I'd like to …
- It's OK. You can do it.
- We can do it together.

Daily life

3
THIS IS MY LIFE
BY MARK BOWER

VOCABULARY
Describing routines | Adverbs of frequency | Verb + noun collocations | Free-time activities | Adjectives to describe feelings

GRAMMAR
Present simple: affirmative and negative | Present Simple (questions and short answers)

A **5 a.m.** Oh no! It's so early!

B **7.30 a.m.** I'm really hungry after my swim.

English, Maths, Science … and four hours of swimming. That's my typical day. My dream is to swim in the Olympics.

C **8.00 a.m.** I can't be late for school!

D **1 p.m.** Lunch in the school canteen.

E **6 p.m.** Home after a long day and another swim!

F **6.30 p.m.** Mmm, pasta. My favourite!

G **9.30 p.m.** Time for a break!

H **10 p.m.** I'm so tired!

3.1 Vocabulary
Routines

1 Look at the photos and read Mark's blog above. What is his main activity outside school? Is his daily routine healthy? Why?/Why not?

2 🔊 3.1 Study Vocabulary box A. Match eight of the verbs/phrases with photos A–H in Mark's blog.

VOCABULARY A Describing routines

exercise   get dressed   get up   go home   go to bed   go to school
have a shower   have breakfast   have lunch/dinner   relax   wake up

Unit 3   36

3 🔊 **3.2** Read more about Mark's day. Complete his routine with the verbs below.

| exercise | ~~get up~~ | go to school | relax | swim (x2) |

Morning: ¹*get up* → get dressed → ² _____ → have breakfast → ³ _____

Afternoon: have lunch → ⁴ _____ in the gym → ⁵ _____ → go home

Evening: have dinner → do my homework → ⁶ _____ → go to bed

My day

I get up at 5 a.m. and I get dressed. I have a banana, then I leave the house. At the pool, I swim for two hours. After that I feel really hungry! I have a shower and then I have breakfast: cereal, eggs and toast.

I always go to school by bus. I often meet my friends at the bus stop. I have lunch at one o'clock and I sometimes exercise in the school gym. After school, I go swimming for another two hours. Then I go home.

We usually have dinner at about half past six. After dinner, I do my homework. Then finally, I can relax! I check my social media, message my friends or play a video game. I go to bed at 10 p.m. I never stay up late!

At the weekend, if I haven't got a competition, I sometimes go to the cinema with friends. I often sleep during the film because I'm still tired after my busy week! I never go shopping – life's too short!

4 🔊 **3.3** Study Vocabulary box B and find the adverbs of frequency in the text in Exercise 3.

VOCABULARY B — Adverbs of frequency

| ♦♦♦♦♦ | ♦♦♦♦ | ♦♦♦ | ♦♦ | |
| always | usually | often | sometimes | never |

5 Write five sentences about your school day or weekend, three true and two false. Use words from Exercises 2 and 4. Read your sentences to a partner. Can he/she guess which sentences are false?

A: On Saturday, I always get up early.
B: I think it's false.

6 🔊 **3.4** **WORD FRIENDS** Match verbs 1–5 with phrases a–e. Use the text in Exercise 3 to help you. Listen and check.

1 ☐ go   a friends (on social media)
2 ☐ meet   b homework/housework
3 ☐ message c swimming/shopping/to the cinema
4 ☐ check   d social media/emails
5 ☐ do   e a friend (at the park/bus stop)

7 Complete the quiz with verbs from Exercises 3 and 6.

How healthy is your life? QUIZ

Do our quiz to find out! Choose a or b.

1
a I always ¹*have* breakfast before I go to school.
b I ² _____ up late, so I never have breakfast.

2
a I ³ _____ to school by bike or on foot.
b I take the bus to school or go by car.

3
a At break, I usually have an apple or a banana.
b At break, I have some sweets or chocolate.

4
a To relax, I ⁴ _____ friends outside.
b To relax, I ⁵ _____ my social media or play video games.

5
a I usually go to bed before 10.30.
b I never go to bed before midnight.

6
a I always ⁶ _____ my homework before I ⁷ _____ to bed.
b I usually do my homework in bed.

8 Do the quiz in Exercise 7. In pairs, compare your answers. Go to page 136 and check your results. **YOUR WORLD**

I can talk about daily routines.

3.2 Grammar

Present simple: affirmative and negative

1 **I KNOW!** In groups, study the words below. How many more pets can you think of in two minutes? Have you got a family pet?

> budgie   guinea pig   hamster   pony   tortoise

2 🔊 3.5 Read Lowri's post. Who is perfect in her family?

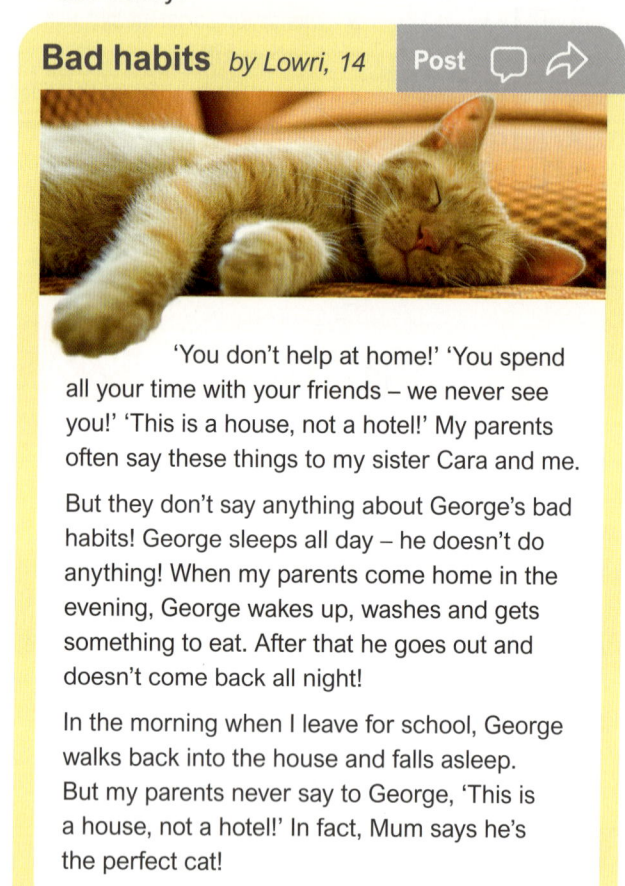

Bad habits by Lowri, 14   Post

'You don't help at home!' 'You spend all your time with your friends – we never see you!' 'This is a house, not a hotel!' My parents often say these things to my sister Cara and me.

But they don't say anything about George's bad habits! George sleeps all day – he doesn't do anything! When my parents come home in the evening, George wakes up, washes and gets something to eat. After that he goes out and doesn't come back all night!

In the morning when I leave for school, George walks back into the house and falls asleep. But my parents never say to George, 'This is a house, not a hotel!' In fact, Mum says he's the perfect cat!

3 Study the Grammar box. Find more examples of the Present Simple in the text in Exercise 2.

GRAMMAR — Present simple: affirmative and negative

+	–
I eat a lot.	We don't listen.
He goes to bed late.	She doesn't help us.

GRAMMAR TIME > PAGE 128

4 🔊 3.6 Study the Watch out! box. Listen and repeat.

WATCH OUT!
play → plays   wash → washes   cry → cries

5 🔊 3.7 Write the third person form of the verbs below in the correct column. Listen, check and repeat.

> finish   go   ~~help~~   kiss   make   miss   stay
> study   tidy   worry

/s/	/z/	/ɪz/
helps	plays	washes

6 Choose the correct option.
1. I really *love* / loves my family, but I don't *like / likes* their bad habits!
2. In the evening Dad *fall / falls* asleep in his chair. He never *go / goes* to bed.
3. My baby brother *cry / cries* at night. Sometimes we *don't / doesn't* sleep at all!
4. Our grandparents often *phone / phones* us when there's something good on TV.
5. My big sister often *take / takes* my laptop and she doesn't *give / gives* it back!

7 Complete the texts with the Present Simple form of the verbs in brackets.

My cat Petra sometimes ¹*tries* (try) to sleep on me and I ²_____ (wake up). After that I ³_____ (not sleep) all night. She ⁴_____ (not want) to sleep on my bed at weekends. She only ⁵_____ (do) it on the night before an exam!

We ⁶_____ (have) a problem with our hamsters, Ben and Gerry. During the day, they're quiet and they ⁷_____ (not come) out. But at night they ⁸_____ (have) a big party!

VIDEO — WIDER WORLD

8 ▶ 12 Watch eight people talking about bad habits. How many people mention pets?

9 In pairs, take it in turns to tell your partner about any bad habits your pets/people in your family have. Use Exercises 6 and 7 to help you.

A: *Our dog eats my mum's shoes!*
B: *My dad talks a lot!*

Unit 3   I can use the Present Simple to talk about things which happen regularly.

3.3 Reading and Vocabulary
My new home

TODAY'S ARTICLE

My new home

My name is Min-jun. I'm from South Korea, but my home now is in Berkeley, USA. My parents work at the university. My grandparents are still in Korea, but we chat online two or three times a week.

Life here is very different from Korea. In Korea, students work very hard. They usually get up at 6.30 a.m. School starts at 8 a.m. and finishes at 10 at night. That's because most students go to private night school after normal lessons to study for exams.

Can you imagine fourteen hours of school a day? There isn't always time to play sport, watch movies or have fun with friends. Students sometimes sleep in class!

In the USA, I have more free time. School finishes at 3.30, then I usually play football with my friends. We sometimes listen to music or play video games. A lot of things are still new to me. Everything is so big: meals, cars, distances (there are six time zones in the USA!). But American people are kind and friendly and I love it here.

1 Have you got family or friends in a different country? Where do they live?

2 🔊 3.8 Read the article. Where is Min-jun from? Where is his new home? Is he happy there?

3 Read the text again. Choose the correct answer.
1 Min-jun ___ talks to his family in Korea.
  a never   b often   c always
2 The school day in Korea is ___ .
  a long   b short
  c the same as in the USA
3 In Korea, students ___ .
  a often watch movies
  b don't have much free time
  c often play sport
4 In the USA, Min-jun ___ .
  a doesn't have any free time
  b sleeps in class
  c does more exercise

4 In pairs, talk about your school day.
School starts/finishes at …
After school, I sometimes/often/usually …

5 🔊 3.9 **WORD FRIENDS** Find the highlighted phrases in the article and complete the sentences. Listen and check.
1 In the evenings I listen *to* music.
2 How often do you _____ TV or movies?
3 I often _____ video games to relax.
4 I always _____ a lot of fun with my cousins.
5 I often _____ with my friends online.

VIDEO ▶ **WIDER WORLD**

6 ▶ 13 Watch seven people talking about their free time. Write down the things they often/sometimes/never do.

7 In pairs, say what you often/sometimes/never do. Use the phrases in Exercise 5 or your own ideas. Then tell the class about your partner.
I often watch a film at the weekend.
I sometimes play games with my sister.
Dan sometimes reads books, but he never listens to music.

I can understand an article about living in a new country.

3.4 Grammar

Present simple: questions and short answers

VIDEO ▶ DO YOU GO BOWLING?

Mateo: Wow! Lena, you're really good at bowling. Do you come here a lot?
Lena: Yes, I do. I really like it.
Noah: You're good too, Mateo! How often do you play?
Mateo: Once or twice a year, perhaps. Your turn now, Noah!
Noah: Wow, these balls are heavy! Oh, that's a terrible throw.
Lena: Never mind.
Mateo: Another good throw, Lena! Does your brother like bowling too?
Lena: Yes, he does. We often play together.
Mateo: What other sports do you do?
Lena: I'm not very sporty, but I like watching basketball. Nice one, Mateo!
Mateo: Right, Noah, it's your turn again. Noah?
Lena: What's the matter, Noah?
Noah: Nothing. I'm not very good at bowling.
Lena: It doesn't matter, Noah. It's only a bit of fun. Do you want some help? We can give you a lesson.
Noah: OK, thanks.
After the lesson …
Lena: Right, are you ready for your turn now, Noah?
Noah: OK … Yes!
Mateo: Great throw, Noah!
Lena: Well done!
Noah: Thanks for your help, guys!

1 ▶ 14 🔊 3.10 Look at the photo. Where are Mateo, Lena and Noah? Is Noah happy? Why?/Why not? Watch or listen and check.

2 What does Lena do when she sees Noah needs help?

SET FOR LIFE

3 What do you do when you see that someone needs help? Discuss in pairs. Use the ideas below to help you. Which idea is the best?
- ask if they want help
- listen to them
- leave them alone
- tell a parent or teacher

4 Study the Grammar box. Find examples of Present Simple questions and short answers in the dialogue.

GRAMMAR — Present simple: questions and short answers

?	
Do you *go* bowling?	Yes, I *do*./No, I *don't*.
Does she *like* bowling?	Yes, she *does*./No, she *doesn't*.
When *do* they *play*?	They *play* on Sundays.
How *does* she *relax*?	She *watches* basketball.

GRAMMAR TIME ▶ PAGE 128

5 Complete the questions with *do* or *does*. Then, in pairs, ask and answer the questions.
1 *Do* you go bowling?
2 When _____ you watch TV?
3 Where _____ your best friend live?
4 What time _____ you get up?
5 _____ your mum and dad chat online?
6 _____ your best friend have a pet?

6 Order the words to make questions.
1 relax / do / how / you / ?
   How do you relax?
2 classmates / watch / your / TV / do / ?
   _____
3 any pets / have / your grandma / does / ?
   _____
4 do / do / when / your homework / you / ?
   _____
5 go / you / what time / do / to bed / ?
   _____
6 you / often go / to the cinema / do / ?
   _____

7 **YOUR WORLD** In pairs, ask and answer the questions in Exercise 6.

I can use the Present Simple to ask and answer questions about routines.

3.5 Listening and Vocabulary
Feelings

1 What can you see in photos A and B? In pairs, match the photos with comments 1–4.
1. ☐ I'm not a fan of winter. I feel tired and sad, and I'm often ill.
2. ☐ Winter's great – I feel happy when I see the first snow of the year.
3. ☐ Winters here are cold, dark and grey. It often snows.
4. ☐ Winter is my favourite season – I'm a big fan of winter sports!

2 🔊 3.11 Listen to Part 1 of a radio programme and choose the correct answer.
1. In winter, many people
   a enjoy the short days.
   b get tired and ill.
   c have a lot of energy.
2. 'To get the blues' means to feel
   a cold.   b ill.   c sad.
3. The topic today is
   a how to feel good about life.
   b the weather.   c energy.

3 🔊 3.12 Listen to Part 2 of the radio programme. Match speakers 1–4 with ideas a–f. There are two extra ideas.
1. ☐ Cody   3. ☐ Lisa
2. ☐ Tim   4. ☐ Zara

a eat something delicious
b do something nice for another person
c have a shower
d drink hot chocolate
e read a book
f watch a sad film

4 🔊 3.13 Study the Vocabulary box. Are the words positive or negative? How do you say them in your language?

VOCABULARY Feelings

bored   excited   happy   relaxed   sad   tired
unhappy   worried

5 Complete the sentences with words from the Vocabulary box. Sometimes more than one answer is possible.
1. Sam is *worried*. He's got a lot of problems.
2. I'm really _____ . I've got tickets to see my favourite hip hop band.
3. Tom often feels _____ . He says there's nothing to do here.
4. They feel _____ . Everything in their life is great.
5. Sarah is really _____ . She doesn't have much energy.
6. I'm _____ . I want to cry.

6 In pairs, say how you feel right now. Use an adjective from the Vocabulary box.

YOUR WORLD

7 In pairs, talk about what you do when you are bored or unhappy. Use the ideas below and Exercise 3 to help you.

go for a walk   go to the shops   listen to music
phone a friend   play with a pet

A: *What do you do when you're bored?*
B: *I go for a walk in the park.*

I can understand a radio programme about feelings.

3.6 Speaking
Talking about likes and dislikes

VIDEO — **WHAT'S YOUR PERFECT JOB?**

Mia: Mateo, what job do you want to do in the future?
Mateo: I'm not sure. Maybe a vet?
Mia: There's a questionnaire here called 'What's your perfect job?' Do you want to do it?
Mateo: Sure.
Mia: OK, first question. Do you like getting up early?
Mateo: Er, yes, I don't mind getting up early.
Mia: Cool. Next question. Do you enjoy being outside?
Mateo: Yes, I love it.
Mia: Question 3. Do you prefer people or animals?
Mateo: Animals. I mean, people are OK, but I prefer animals!
Mia: Question 4. Do you like being busy?
Mateo: Yes, I really like being busy. I can't stand doing nothing.
Mia: Right, last question. Do you enjoy travelling?
Mateo: Yes, I really like travelling.
Mia: OK, let's look at your results. Just a minute … Your perfect job is …
Mateo: Yes?
Mia: … a llama farmer in Peru!
Mateo: What? That's crazy! Right, it's your turn to answer the questions now!

SOUNDS GOOD! Sure. • Just a minute.

1 ▶ 15 🔊 3.14 Watch or listen. What does the questionnaire say is the perfect job for Mateo? What does he think?

2 Study the Speaking box. Find examples of the phrases in the dialogue.

SPEAKING — **Talking about likes and dislikes**

What do you think of … ?   Do you like/enjoy … ?
What kind of … do you like?

| 🙂 | It's my favourite!   I like … , but I prefer …
I love …   I really like/enjoy …   I like … (a lot). |
| 😐 | I quite like …
I don't mind …   It's OK. |
| 🙁 | I don't like …   I don't enjoy …
I hate …   I can't stand … |

---

3 Complete the dialogues with phrases from the Speaking box. Then, in pairs, compare your answers.
1   A: Do you like travelling?
     B: 🙂 *I don't mind it*.
     C: 🙂 _____
2   A: What do you think of online questionnaires?
     B: 🙁 _____
     C: 🙂 _____
3   A: Do you like getting up early?
     B: 🙂 _____
     C: 🙁 _____

4 In groups of three, practise the dialogues in Exercise 3.

5 YOUR WORLD In pairs, take it in turns to ask and answer about the things below. Use phrases from the Speaking box.

> Cardi B   cats   grammar exercises
> Harry Styles   Indian food   listening to jazz
> opera   pizza   playing tennis   rap
> snow   tidying your room
> watching basketball

A: What do you think of Cardi B?
B: I don't mind her. What about you?

⚠️ **WATCH OUT!**
After *enjoy, like, love, hate, don't mind* and *can't stand*, we use the *-ing* form.
I love/can't stand dancing.
We also often use these verbs and phrases with pronouns (*it, him, her, them,* etc.).
A: Do you like dancing?   B: I love it!

I can talk about likes and dislikes.

3.7 Writing
A blog post

1 Read Karabo's blog post. In pairs, say what things are different in your lives.

Karabo starts school at 7.30. I start school at 8.00.

1 Hi! My name's Karabo and I'm fourteen years old. I come from Cape Town in South Africa. This is my typical day.

2 I wake up at six o'clock, I have a shower and then I have breakfast – toast with cheese or cereal. After that I go to school. It's a school for girls. Lessons start at 7.30 every day and finish at two o'clock. We don't have lunch at school, so I always take some sandwiches and fruit with me. After lessons I often stay at school because I'm in the school netball team.

3 I come home at three or four o'clock and do my homework. I'm in Year 9, so there's a lot of homework. Then my parents come home and we have dinner – chicken with potatoes or pizza. After that I've got time to relax. I watch TV or chat with my friends online. I go to bed at 10.30 p.m.

2 Read Karabo's post again. Match paragraphs 1–3 with descriptions a–c.
  a Karabo's typical day
  b Karabo's typical evening
  c About Karabo and her hometown

3 Study the Writing box and check your answers to Exercise 2. Find examples of the phrases in Karabo's post.

> **WRITING** A blog post
>
> **1** Introduce yourself and your home town
> My name's Karabo and I'm fourteen/fourteen years old.
> I'm from/I come from Cape Town in South Africa.
>
> **2** Describe your daytime routine
> I wake up/get up at six o'clock.
> Then/After that I go to school.
>
> **3** Describe your evening routine
> Then my parents come home and we have dinner.
> I go to bed at 10.30 p.m.

4 Study the Language box. Complete the sentences below with *so* or *because*.

> **LANGUAGE** *so* and *because*
>
> Use *so* and *because* to link ideas in sentences.
>
> Use *because* to give a reason.
> After lessons I often stay at school **because** I'm in the school netball team.
>
> Use *so* to explain a consequence.
> I'm in Year 9, **so** there's a lot of homework.

  1 I haven't got a laptop, _____ I borrow my sister's.
  2 I don't play chess _____ I don't like it.
  3 I get up early _____ my dog needs his walk.
  4 I'm tired in the evening, _____ I go to bed early.

WRITING TIME

5 Write a blog post about your daily routine.

1 Find ideas
Make notes for your post. Think about:
• your school day.   • your evening.
• what you do in summer/winter.

2 Plan
Organise your ideas into paragraphs. Use Karabo's post to help you.

3 Write and share
• Write a draft post. Use the Language box and the Writing box to help you.
• Share your post with another student for feedback.
• Write the final version of your post.

4 Check
• Check language: are *so* and *because* correct?
• Check grammar: are the verbs in the Present Simple?

I can write a blog post about a daily routine.

Vocabulary Activator

WORDLIST 🔊 3.15

Describing routines
exercise (v)
get dressed
get up (v)
go home
go to bed
go to school
have a shower
have breakfast
have lunch/dinner
relax (v)
wake up (v)

Adverbs of frequency
always (adv)
never (adv)
often (adv)
sometimes (adv)
usually (adv)

Word friends
(verb + noun collocations)
check emails/social media
do homework/housework
go shopping/swimming
go to the cinema

meet a friend
message a friend

Word friends
(free-time activities)
chat (with friends) online
have (a lot of) fun
listen to music
play video games
watch TV/movies

Feelings
bored (adj)
excited (adj)
happy (adj)
relaxed (adj)
sad (adj)
tired (adj)
unhappy (adj)
worried (adj)

Extra words
at night
at the weekend
bad habit
be good at something
budgie (n)

busy (adj)
buy a present
come back (v)
come home
dream (v, n)
early (adj, adv)
early bird (n)
fall asleep
feel hungry
finish (v)
free time (n)
go bowling
go for a walk
go out (v)
guinea pig (n)
hamster (n)
have a party
help (v, n)
in the evening
in the morning
it's your turn
late (adj, adv)
leave the house
night owl (n)
phone a friend

play sport
play with a pet
pony (n)
private school
put on clothes
read a book
ready (adj)
school gym (n)
sleep (v, n)
spend time
sporty (adj)
start (v)
stay at home
study for exams
swim (v)
tidy your room
tortoise (n)
travel (v)
wash (v)
work (v)

---

1 Use the wordlist to find these things.
   1. four things you do at home to relax
      listen to music, …
   2. four things you usually do on a school day morning, after you wake up
   3. six things you can do on a computer
   4. two words that are the opposite of *happy*
   5. one phrase that is the opposite of *get up*

2 Match the sentence halves.
   1. ☐ I go
   2. ☐ I meet
   3. ☐ I watch
   4. ☐ I chat
   5. ☐ I have
   6. ☐ I check

   a. with my grandparents online.
   b. fun in my English lessons.
   c. my friends at the park.
   d. social media before I get up.
   e. shopping on Saturday.
   f. TV in bed.

3 In pairs, say how often you do the things in Exercise 2. Use the words below.

   always   usually   often   sometimes   never

   A: *I always go shopping on Saturday.*
   B: *I sometimes go shopping on Saturday.*

4 Replace the words in bold with words from the wordlist to make sentences with the opposite meaning. Then, in pairs, say which sentences are true for you.
   1. I often feel **happy** in winter.
      I often feel sad in winter.
   2. I **always** get up early at the weekend.
   3. The night before my birthday, I'm usually really **bored**.
   4. I usually feel **relaxed** before an exam.
   5. I often **get up** late in the holidays.

5 🔊 3.16 **PRONUNCIATION** Listen to how we pronounce the /æ/ sound. Listen again and repeat.

   a̲pple   h̲a̲ppy   c̲a̲t

6 🔊 3.17 **PRONUNCIATION** In pairs, say the sentences. Listen, check and repeat.
   1. My gra̲nda̲d's ca̲t is always rela̲xed.
   2. I ha̲ve an a̲pple when I'm sa̲d.
   3. My ha̲mster can't sta̲nd ca̲rrots.
   4. A̲nn has a sa̲ndwich in her ba̲g.

Revision

Vocabulary

1 Complete the text with the words below. Then, in pairs, say if you are an early bird or a night owl and why.

> bed   dinner   exercise   games   have   tired   ~~up~~   wake

I'm a night owl because I don't get up early!

Are you an early bird or a night owl?

Early birds:
- always get ¹*up* early.
- ² _____ a big breakfast.
- usually ³ _____ in the morning.
- often feel ⁴ _____ in the evening.

Night owls:
- don't ⁵ _____ up early.
- are hungry and have a big ⁶ _____ at night.
- like playing ⁷ _____ at night.
- go to ⁸ _____ late.

2 Complete the words in the text.

> It's the weekend! After a week of school, I can finally ¹*relax*! What do I do? On Saturday, I usually go ²s_____ at the pool. I have ³l_____ and then I meet my ⁴f_____ . We ⁵s_____ go to the cinema to watch a movie. On Sunday, I ⁶l_____ to music in my bedroom or I play with my pet hamster. She's called Apple – it's her favourite fruit! Then it's time to do my ⁷h_____ – it's school again on Monday!

3 Choose the correct option.
1. You aren't very (*happy*) / *sad* today. Is everything OK?
2. I can't find my wallet. I'm *worried* / *bored*.
3. I'm *sad* / *tired* because Rosie can't come to my party.
4. There's nothing to do. I'm *bored* / *happy*.
5. Ezra's *excited* / *relaxed* because he's got a new bike.
6. She swims two kilometres every day, but she's never *tired* / *excited*.

Grammar

4 Complete the text with the Present Simple form of the verbs in brackets.

An unusual day

Lucy ¹*wakes up* (wake up) at 5 p.m. She ² _____ (have) breakfast at 7 p.m. After breakfast, she often ³ _____ (meet) her friend, Jessica, and they ⁴ _____ (watch) a movie together. At 10 p.m., Lucy and Jessica ⁵ _____ (start) work, and they ⁶ _____ (finish) at 7 a.m. What's their job? They're police officers and they ⁷ _____ (work) at night!

5 Order the words to make questions about the text in Exercise 4. Then, in pairs, answer the questions.
1. Lucy / does / what time / wake up / ?
   What time does Lucy wake up?
2. who / meet / she / does / after breakfast / ?
3. Lucy and Jessica / do / in the morning / start work / ?
4. finish work / what time / do / they / ?
5. Lucy and Jessica / what job / do / do / ?

6 Correct the sentences to make them true for you.
1. I wake up at six o'clock in the afternoon.
   I don't wake up at six o'clock in the afternoon. I wake up at seven o'clock in the morning.
2. I have breakfast at six o'clock in the evening.
3. After breakfast, my friends and I watch movies.
4. We start school at ten o'clock at night.
5. I go to bed at nine o'clock in the morning.

Speaking

7 Write three true sentences and one false sentence about you. Use the words and ideas below. Then, in pairs, read your sentences to your partner. Can he/she guess the false sentence?

> can't stand   don't like   don't mind   enjoy   hate   love   quite like

- getting up early
- going to parties
- going shopping
- helping at home
- playing video games
- tidying my room

A: *I can't stand playing video games.*
B: *I think it's false.*
A: *No, it's true!*

Dictation

8 🔊 3.18 Listen. Then listen again and write down what you hear during each pause.

45   Unit 3

BBC CULTURE

Same lives, different lives

Life near the North Pole

The town of Longyearbyen is in the Arctic. There is no other town so close to the North Pole. The school there has around 200 students. They start lessons at eight o'clock and finish in the afternoon. They have a summer holiday in July and August. That's probably like your routine! But there are some big differences.

It's very, very cold in Longyearbyen. It's never more than about seven degrees. And it can be difficult to remember what time it is! There's no sun from November to January, so it's dark for twenty-four hours a day. And from May to September, it's never dark!

At school, the students have lessons in survival. They learn what to do if there is an avalanche or if they see a polar bear. There are more polar bears than people in this part of the world!

There aren't many places for teenagers to go in Longyearbyen, but in the summer they can cycle or walk in the mountains, and in the winter they can drive snowmobiles.

Would you enjoy life in the Arctic?

avalanche (n) a disaster when snow falls down a mountain
polar bear (n) a big white bear that lives in the Arctic
snowmobile (n) a small vehicle that can travel over snow
survival (n) living in a difficult, dangerous situation and not dying

1 In pairs, look at the photo and discuss the questions.
  1 Who do you think the people are?
  2 Where in the world do you think this is?

2 🔊 3.19 Read the article and check your answers to Exercise 1.

3 Read the article again and answer the questions.
  1 How many students are there at Longyearbyen School?
  2 When does their school day start?
  3 When is their summer holiday?
  4 What is unusual about summer in that part of the world?
  5 What can teenagers do there in the winter?

4 (VISIBLE THINKING) In pairs, role play the interview below. Then swap roles and role play the interview again.

TAKE A DIFFERENT VIEW

Student A
Student B lives in Longyearbyen. Ask five questions about his/her life. Use the ideas below to help you.

| get up | go to bed | go to school | like your life here |
| spend your free time | start lessons | | |

Student B
You live in Longyearbyen. Answer Student A's questions.

A: *What time do you get up?*
B: *I get up at seven o'clock.*

BBC ▶ A typical day?

5 Look at the photo and answer the questions.
   1 Which country do you think this is?

   England   Japan   Papua New Guinea   Wales

   2 How is the classroom different from your classroom?

6 ▶ 16 Watch a TV programme about a typical day for schoolchildren in the countries in Exercise 5. Check your answers to question 1 in Exercise 5. Are the children's lives the same as yours or are they different? How?

7 ▶ 16 Watch the video again. Tick (✓) the activities you see in the video.

☐ cook dinner ☐ do homework ☐ get up
☐ go to bed ☐ go to clubs ☐ have breakfast
☐ have lessons ☐ have lunch ☐ walk to school
☐ watch TV

8 In pairs, talk about your ideal day. Say what you would like to do from morning to evening.

On my ideal day, I get up late and then I have pizza for breakfast. After that …

PROJECT TIME

9 In groups of three, create a video about the daily life of people your age in a different part of the world. Follow these steps.

1 In your group, choose a part of the world that you are interested in. Decide who can find the answers to these questions.
- What days do children go to school there? When does their day start? When does it finish?
- What lessons do students study? Do they do other activities at school?
- What are their hobbies? What sports and free-time activities do they do?

2 Individually, create your part of the video.
- Find information online and write the script for your section.
- Find photos to illustrate the information.

3 In your group, record your video. You can use a video app.
- Put all the parts of the video script together and decide who can read it.
- Record the script and add photos.
- Check and edit your video.

4 Share your video with the class.
- Answer other students' questions.
- Ask questions and comment on the other videos.

Progress Check Units 1-3

Vocabulary and Grammar

1 Choose the correct answer.

My ¹____ Natalie, my aunt Emily's daughter, is eighteen and ²____ at a café during the holidays. She's kind and friendly – all the customers like her. She gets up really early because she starts work ³____ 7 a.m. The café is very busy at lunchtime. She ⁴____ gets home at 3 p.m., but she sometimes gets home later. The café isn't big, but ⁵____ is some good food like burgers, pasta and cakes. Natalie can speak ⁶____ and German. It really helps because the café is popular with foreigners. I would also like to work at a café. Maybe next summer!

1 a sister   b uncle   c cousin
2 a works   b work   c does works
3 a on   b in   c at
4 a never   b usually   c always
5 a they   b there   c this
6 a France   b French   c the French

2 Complete the second sentence with the word in bold so that it means the same as the first one. Use no more than three words.

1 Have you got a gym at your school? **THERE**
  Is *there a gym* at your school?
2 Carlos is Spanish and he's a student in my class. **FROM**
  Carlos _____ and he's a student in my class.
3 There's only a small bottle of water. **MUCH**
  There _____ water.
4 He knows three different languages. **CAN**
  He _____ three different languages.
5 I put on my clothes after I brush my teeth. **DRESSED**
  I _____ after I brush my teeth.
6 He doesn't worry about exams. **WORRIED**
  He _____ about exams.

3 Complete the text with one word in each gap.

Many teens say they don't have breakfast every day. They wake ¹*up* late, wash and get ready for school. And they haven't ²_____ the time to make something to eat. ³_____ you have breakfast every day? I always have breakfast in the morning! Here is a very simple recipe for a healthy breakfast bowl. I'm sure there is ⁴_____ cereal in the kitchen. Is there ⁵_____ fruit? What about milk? Yes? So, you can start! ⁶_____ , put the cereal in a bowl. Then add milk and strawberries or bananas. You can also add some nuts. It's ready. Yum!

Speaking

4 Complete the dialogues with the words below. There are two extra words.

| else | favourite | ~~going~~ | how | nice |
| prefer | stand | what |

1 A: Hi. How's it *going*?
  B: I'm fine, thanks.
  A: This is my sister, Sue.
  B: Hi, Sue. _____ to meet you.
2 A: _____ would you like?
  B: I'd like a cheese sandwich, please.
  A: Anything _____?
  B: That's all, thank you.
3 A: Do you like dancing?
  B: I love it!
  A: I can't _____ it. But I love running.
  B: Running is OK, but I _____ dancing.

5 In pairs, do the speaking task.
Student A: Go to page 136.
Student B: Go to page 138.

Listening

6 🔊 PC1–3.1 Read questions 1–4 in Exercise 7. Match them with topics a–d below. Listen and check.

1 ☐ 2 ☐ 3 ☐ 4 ☐

a popular supermarket food
b animals at home
c weekend routines
d clothes and footwear

7 🔊 PC1–3.1 Listen again and choose the correct answer.
1 What pet has Maya got?
   a a hamster   b a pony
   c a guinea pig
2 What does Ada buy?
   a brownies   b cheese and onion crisps
   c chocolate chip cookies
3 What do Finn and his dad both like?
   a the trainers   b the tracksuits
   c the T-shirt
4 What time can Brad go shopping on Saturday?
   a twelve o'clock   b two o'clock
   c four o'clock

8 In pairs, ask and answer the questions.
1 What is your favourite pet animal?
2 What kind of party food do you like?
3 How often do you go shopping for clothes?
4 What do you often do at the weekend?

Reading

9 In pairs, describe the photo and answer the questions below.

1 Who's in this family?
2 How many children are there? How old do you think they are?

10 Read the article and complete the notes below with a word or a short phrase.

My big family story

Hi, I'm Peter and I'm thirteen. I've got four sisters and three brothers. Rob is twenty, so he's the first child, and Tammy is the little one – she's four. We are American, but we live in England.

Getting up and ready for school in my house is team work! I wake up at 6 a.m. so I can have a shower and get dressed before my brothers and sisters. I sometimes make breakfast with Dad or I help Tammy with her shoes and socks. We all eat at 7 a.m. and we leave for school at 7.30.

We're a very happy family. My mum is a teacher at a primary school, and my dad is a vet. We spend a lot of time together. We usually have picnics on Saturdays and Sundays, and on weekdays we often go to the park after school.

We also have pets. Our cat's name is Vicky. Tammy's got a guinea pig, Fluffy. And I've got a hamster. It's brown and really brave! For my birthday I'd like to get a pair of budgies. I love birds.

1 Number of sisters in the family: *four*
2 Nationality: _____
3 First person in the bathroom in the morning: _____
4 Breakfast time: _____
5 Weekend activity: _____
6 Family pets: cat, _____

Writing

11 What time do you do these things? In pairs, compare your answers.
- wake up
- get up
- have breakfast
- go to school
- do my homework
- have dinner

12 Write a blog post about the routine of someone in your family. Write about these things.
- what he/she does in the morning/afternoon/evening
- what time he/she goes to school/work and what time he/she gets home
- what time he/she has meals

Live and learn 4

VOCABULARY
Classroom objects | Prepositions of place | School subjects | Making friends | Learning

GRAMMAR
Present Continuous | Present Simple and Present Continuous

Rider Wood School

Home | **Lost property** | About | News | Contact

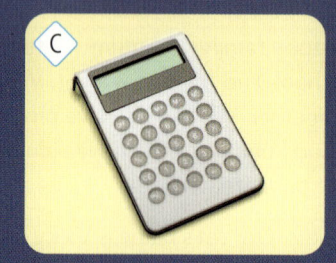

Item	Colour/Other info
1 pencil case	red
2 sports bag	blue
3 calculator	grey
4 dictionary	Spanish
5 poster	animals
6 rubber	purple, crocodile
7 notebook	green, new
8 ruler	yellow

Some **Dos** and **Don'ts** to help us all.

Do:
- check your desks for any pens, pencils, rubbers, rulers, etc. before you leave the classroom.
- give things you find to Mrs Carney or your class teacher.

Don't:
- forget to put your name on all your school things.
- pick up your things during class time. Only come to the teachers' room during the break.

4.1 Vocabulary

School

1 Look at the photos and read the texts above. What is the webpage for?

2 In pairs, discuss the questions.
1. Do you often lose things at school?
2. What things do you sometimes lose?
3. What do you do when you lose something?

3 🔊 4.1 In pairs, study Vocabulary box A. Match eight of the words with photos A–H above.

VOCABULARY A Classroom objects

☑ C calculator ☐ dictionary ☐ notebook
☐ pencil case ☐ poster ☐ rubber ☐ rubbish bin
☐ ruler ☐ sports bag ☐ textbook ☐ whiteboard

4 **I KNOW!** In pairs, add more items to Vocabulary box A. Compare your list with another pair.

5 🔊 4.2 Study Vocabulary box B. In pairs, use objects from your bag to show the meaning of the prepositions.

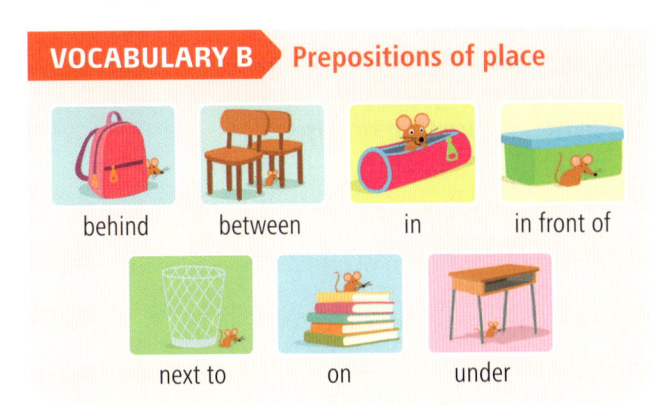

VOCABULARY B — Prepositions of place

behind   between   in   in front of
next to   on   under

6 Look at the picture and complete the sentences with the correct prepositions.

1 The glasses are <u>on</u> the teacher's head.
2 The notebook is _____ the school bag.
3 The pencil case is _____ the school bag.
4 The rubbish bin is _____ the desk.
5 The rubber is _____ the pen and the ruler.
6 The calculator is _____ the books.
7 The teacher is _____ the board.
8 The school bag is _____ the desk.

7 🔊 4.3 Study Vocabulary box C. Tick (✓) the subjects that you do at your school. Which is your favourite?

VOCABULARY C — School subjects

☐ Art ☐ Biology ☐ Chemistry ☐ English
☐ Geography ☐ History
☐ Information Technology (IT) ☐ Maths ☐ Music
☐ PE ☐ Physics

8 🔊 4.4 Listen and complete the school timetable for Class 8A.

	Monday	Tuesday	Wednesday
09.00–10.00	¹<u>History</u>	³_____	Maths
10.00–11.00	English	Chemistry	Biology
11.00–11.20	Break		
11.20–12.20	English	⁴_____	English
12.20–13.20	Lunch		
13.20–14.20	²_____	Music	French
14.20–15.20	IT	⁵_____	⁶_____

9 🔊 4.4 Listen again and answer the questions.
Where is:
1 the laptop? <u>on the chair</u>
2 Switzerland? _____
3 Sophie? _____
4 the chocolate bar? _____
5 Dylan? _____
6 the apple? _____

10 In pairs, talk about days you like/don't like at school. Say why.

I love Mondays because we have Art.
I don't like … because …

VIDEO **WIDER WORLD**

11 ▶ 17 Watch eight people talking about where they keep things. Tick (✓) the places they mention.
1 ☐ in their pocket 4 ☐ on a bed
2 ☐ in a safe place 5 ☐ in a handbag
3 ☐ on a desk

12 In pairs, take it in turns to guess what things your partner has got in these places. Say if your partner's guesses are correct.
• in his/her school bag
• under his/her bed
• next to his/her bed
• on his/her desk at home

A: *I think you've got four textbooks, a red pen and an apple in your bag.*
B: *I haven't got an apple, but I've got a red pen and four textbooks!*

I can talk about classroom objects and school subjects.

4.2 Grammar

Present Continuous

1 Look at the photo. Do you think the girls know each other?

2 🔊 4.5 Read and listen. Then look at Alice's message on page 136 to find out why she doesn't want to talk to her friends.

Sara: Hi, Alice. How are things?
Alice: *silence*
Sara: Alice? Hello! I'm talking to you!
Alice: *silence*
Sara: You aren't speaking to me. Why?
Alice: *silence*
Sara: Are you feeling OK, Alice?
Alice: *silence*
Caitlin: Hi, you two! How's it going?
Sara: I'm fine, but Alice isn't speaking to me. Is she speaking to you?
Caitlin: I don't know. Are you speaking to me, Alice?
Alice: *silence*
Caitlin: No, she isn't! What's wrong, Alice?
Alice: *silence*
Sara: We're wasting our time! Let's go to the snack bar, Caitlin.
Caitlin: Wait a minute. Now she's writing something. And why is she smiling?

3 Study the Grammar box. Find more examples of the Present Continuous in the dialogue.

GRAMMAR	Present Continuous	
+	**−**	
I'm talking. You're talking. He's talking.	I'm not talking. They aren't talking. She isn't talking.	
?		
Are they talking? Is she talking?	Yes, they are./No, they aren't. Yes, she is./No, she isn't.	
How's it going?	Why are they smiling?	

GRAMMAR TIME > PAGE 129

4 Make sentences in the Present Continuous. Then look again at the dialogue in Exercise 2 and Alice's message on page 136 and decide if the sentences are true or false.
1 Alice / speak / to Sara
  Alice is speaking to Sara. It's false!
2 Sara / feel / fine
  _____
3 Caitlin / not speak / to Alice
  _____
4 Sara / write / a message
  _____
5 Sara and Caitlin / pay / Alice 60p an hour
  _____
6 all three girls / go / to the snack bar
  _____

5 🔊 4.6 What is happening? Listen and write sentences in the Present Continuous. Use the verbs and phrases below.

| cry | have a shower | laugh | run | sleep | type |

Somebody is … Some people are …

6 Complete the questions and short answers. Use the Present Continuous. Then, in pairs, ask and answer the questions.
1 A: *Are you feeling* (you/feel) hungry?
  B: *No, we aren't.* My grandmother always gives us a big breakfast!
2 A: _____ (your sister/study)?
  B: _____ Her exam is tomorrow.
3 A: _____ (your dad/cook) dinner?
  B: _____ He's making tea.
4 A: _____ (your parents/watch) TV?
  B: _____ They're at work!
5 A: _____ (you/use) your calculator at the moment?
  B: _____ You can take it.

YOUR WORLD

7 In pairs, take it in turns to ask and answer about what the people/pet(s) in your life are doing now. Use the ideas below to help you.
- your best friend
- your brother/sister
- your grandparents
- your parents
- your pet(s)
- your teacher

A: What's your cat doing now?
B: She's sleeping on Dad's favourite chair.

I can use the Present Continuous to talk about things that are happening now.

4.3 Reading and Vocabulary
Making friends

1 🔊 4.7 Read the posts. What do Ben and Ella have in common?

Problem? Ask Ella!

Ben: Hi, Ella! Have you got any advice on how to make friends with someone? I'm new in town and I haven't got any friends here yet. Maybe it's because I'm shy – when I meet someone for the first time, I don't know what to say. I usually try to be funny and tell terrible jokes. I'm not that bad when I get to know people!

Ella: I know how you feel, Ben! My family and I are in Scotland at the moment because my dad has a work contract for two years here, at the University of Edinburgh. Back home, in London, I have a great group of friends. I know they are always there for me when I need them, but I also need someone here! My two new friends, Mary and Alex, are not school – they're from my drama club. Maybe you can join an after-school club too. It is easy to talk to other people about something you all like.

2 Read the posts again and choose the correct answer.
1 Why is Ben writing to Ella?
   a to ask her to be his friend
   b to talk about his friends
   c to ask for help
2 Ben tells terrible jokes when he
   a feels relaxed.
   b meets new people.
   c is with people he knows well.
3 Ella is
   a from Scotland.
   b in London.
   c in Edinburgh.
4 Ella, Mary and Alex
   a are in London.
   b are in the same class at school.
   c have one thing they all like.

3 🔊 4.8 **WORD FRIENDS** In pairs, check you understand the phrases below. Which of the phrases can you find in the posts in Exercise 1?
1 be there for someone
2 get to know someone
3 make new friends
4 meet someone for the first time
5 best friend
6 group of friends
7 make friends with someone

4 Complete the sentences with words from Exercise 3. Then, in pairs, say which sentences are true for you.
1 My friends *are* always *there* for me when I need them.
2 My _____ friend and I spend all our free time together.
3 When I _____ someone for the _____ time, I feel excited.
4 I have a very small _____ of friends.
5 Before I get to _____ someone well, I don't talk much.
6 I can't make friends _____ people I don't like.
7 It's very easy for me to _____ new friends.

VIDEO — WIDER WORLD

5 ▶ 18 Watch seven people talking about their friends. How many people mention these things?
It's important that my friends:
1 are kind.
2 are there for me.
3 listen to me.

6 In pairs, decide how important these things are in a friendship (5 = very important, 1 = not so important). Compare your list with other pairs.
☐ be there for each other
☐ laugh a lot
☐ like the same things (e.g. music, fashion, sports)
☐ do the same activities
☐ see/call each other every day
☐ live near each other

I can understand online posts about making friends.

4.4 Grammar
Present Simple and Present Continuous

VIDEO ▶ DON'T PANIC!

Mum: Ah, it's raining! Why does it always rain at the weekend?
Dad: Would you like a cup of hot chocolate?
Mum: Yes, please. Wait, why are you making chocolate? You always have tea at breakfast. You don't even like chocolate!
Dad: It's for Lena. She's working on her school project.
Mum: But it's nine o'clock. On a Sunday. Lena never gets up before eleven at the weekend. And then she spends all morning watching her favourite series online.
Dad: Well, she isn't watching anything now. She really is doing her homework.

In her room, Lena is talking to Mia.
Lena: Mia? I'm late with my History project and it's due tomorrow and I don't usually panic, but now I'm panicking! There's so much to do!
Mia: Poor you! Are you ready for the test, at least?
Lena: Wait. What test?
Mia: The Geography test? Tomorrow?
Lena: What? The test is tomorrow? No!

1 ▶ 19 🔊 4.9 Watch or listen. Why is Lena panicking?

2 Do you ever panic about schoolwork like Lena?

SET FOR LIFE

3 How do you plan your time when you work on a project? Discuss in pairs. Use the list below and add your own ideas.
- I make a note of the date when the project needs to be ready.
- I start working on the project immediately.
- I work a little every day.
- I plan for extra time to check my work.

4 Study the Grammar box. Find examples of the Present Simple and Present Continuous in the dialogue.

GRAMMAR | Present Simple and Present Continuous

We use the Present Simple for habits and routines.
Lena never *gets up* before eleven at the weekend.

We use the Present Continuous for something happening now/at the moment.
Lena*'s working* on her school project.

GRAMMAR TIME > PAGE 129

5 Choose the correct option.
1 *Does Luca run* / Is Luca running every day?
2 Susie *does / is doing* her homework right now.
3 Oliver *has / is having* pizza for lunch today.
4 Eva's brother *gets up / is getting up* at 9 a.m. at the weekend.
5 Who *do you text / are you texting* right now?
6 George *doesn't usually study / isn't studying* on Saturdays.

6 Complete questions 1–6 with *is*, *are*, *do* or *does*. Then, in pairs, ask and answer the questions.
1 *Are* you wearing jeans now?
2 _____ you wear jeans at school?
3 _____ you having lunch now?
4 _____ you always have lunch at school?
5 _____ your teacher talking to the class at the moment?
6 _____ your best friend often check his/her phone?

YOUR WORLD

7 In pairs, talk about what you usually do at the weekend and how it is different from what you are doing now. Think about:
- the clothes you wear.
- the activities you do.
- the people you spend time with.

At the moment, … At the weekend, I …

I can talk about what usually happens and what is happening now.

4.5 Listening and Vocabulary
Famous schools

1 Are there any famous schools in your town, region or country?

2 Read the definition. Are boarding schools popular in your country?

> **boarding school**
> a school where students live and study

3 🔊 4.10 Listen to the first part of a radio programme about a famous boarding school. Answer the questions.
1 In which city is it?
2 Is it a new school?
3 Do all the students live in the school?

4 🔊 4.10 Listen again and complete the information in the fact file.

Broadboard School
- private boarding school in the ¹_____ of London
- about ²_____ years old
- costs £35,000 for one ³_____
- has 750 students; about ⁴_____ live at school seven days a week

5 🔊 4.11 Listen to the second part of the programme. Choose the correct answer.
1 What time do most students get up?
   a at 8 a.m.   b at 6.30 a.m.   c at 7 a.m.
2 How long are the breaks?
   a fifty minutes
   b twenty minutes
   c fifteen minutes
3 What do the students do in the evening?
   a They study and then they relax.
   b They relax and then they study.
   c They relax and then they have dinner.

6 🔊 4.12 **WORD FRIENDS** Listen and complete the phrases.
1 *start* school
2 _____ classes
3 _____ to school
4 _____ for exams
5 _____ homework

7 Complete the questions with words from Exercise 6. Then, in pairs, ask and answer the questions.
1 Do you think it's a good idea to start *school* at ten o'clock every day?
2 What time do you usually _____ to school?
3 At your school, do you have _____ on Saturday mornings?
4 When do you usually do your _____?
5 Do you enjoy revising _____ exams?

YOUR WORLD

8 What are the good things about going to a boarding school? Tick (✓) the sentences you agree with. Then, in pairs, compare your ideas.
1 ☐ You live at school seven days a week.
2 ☐ You do lots of sport and activities.
3 ☐ It's very expensive.
4 ☐ You get to know your teachers and your classmates well.
5 ☐ There's a lot of time to study.
6 ☐ It isn't far to walk to school.
7 ☐ You spend the whole day with your school friends.
8 ☐ You don't often see your family.

A: It's good that you live at school seven days a week.
B: For me, it's a bad thing.

4.6 Speaking
Polite requests

VIDEO ▶ THE NEW VIDEO GAME

Mateo is working. Noah is on the phone to Lena.

Noah: Oh. Hi, Lena. No, we're still here. Mateo's doing his homework. I'm waiting for him. Who?
Mateo: Noah, I'm trying to work! Can you please be quiet?
Noah: Yes, of course. Sorry! OK, Lena. See you soon.
Mateo: Thanks, mate, and … sorry.
Noah: No worries. Can I play a game while you do your homework?
Mateo: Yes, no problem.
Noah: Erm … oh, you've got new wi-fi. Can you give me the code?
Mateo: Sure. Here it is.
Noah: Cheers! The screen's too small for this game. Can I use your laptop?
Mateo: Sorry, I'm using it.
Noah: Oh, OK. Yes! Awesome!
Mateo: What are you playing?
Noah: *Doughnut Race* – it's a new game.
Mateo: Can I see?
Noah: OK, just a second. New game … Start …
Mateo: It's really good. Come on, let's play a game. One game only.

One hour later, Noah's phone rings.

Noah: It's Lena! We're so late!
Mateo: My homework!

SOUNDS GOOD! Cheers! • No worries. • Awesome!

1 ▶ 20 ◉ 4.13 Watch or listen. Does Mateo finish his homework?

2 Study the Speaking box. Find examples of the phrases in the dialogue.

SPEAKING ▶ Polite requests

Request	☹	☺
Can I borrow/use your laptop?	Sorry, I'm using it. Sorry, I need it. Sorry, you can't.	Sure. Yes, OK. Yes, of course. Yes, no problem. OK, just a second.
Can I see it?		
Can I have the wi-fi code?		
Can you please be quiet?	Sorry, I can't.	
Can you tell me the answer?		
Can you help me with this exercise?		

3 ◉ 4.14 Complete the dialogues with one word in each gap. Listen and check. Then, in pairs, practise reading the dialogues.
1 A: *Can* you tell me the time, please?
   B: Yes, of _____ . It's twenty to eight.
2 A: Can you help me _____ my homework?
   B: _____ , I can't. I'm really busy.
3 A: Can _____ help me with this box?
   B: OK, _____ a second.

4 ◉ 4.15 Listen and choose the best response for each request. In pairs, compare your answers. Then listen again.
1 a Yes, OK.   b Sorry, I can't.
2 a Yes, of course.   b Sorry, you can't.
3 a Sorry, I can't.   b Sorry, I need it.
4 a Sorry, I can't.   b Sure.
5 a Sorry, you can't. b Sorry, I can't.

YOUR WORLD

5 In pairs, take it in turns to make and respond to requests. Use these ideas or your own. Don't be shy to say no!
Can I:
• borrow your phone/calculator?
• have your Chemistry notes/this poster?
• use your phone/tablet/pen?
Can you:
• answer the phone/the door?
• tell me your address/the wi-fi code?
• give me your notebook/a rubber?

A: *Can you answer the phone?*
B: *Sorry, I can't! My hands are wet!*

4.7 Writing
An announcement

1 Read the announcement and answer the questions.
1 What kind of club is it?
2 When and where do the students meet?
3 How can you join the club?

Park View School Film Club

Do you like watching films? We do! Come and join our school film club!

The club meets every Friday at four o'clock in room 306. We watch and talk about our favourite films. Every month we vote for the next four films we want to see. Members can also write film reviews for the school website. The best review wins two cinema tickets! To join, visit our website and complete the online form. The club is free and open to everyone.

We've got lots of free popcorn, but don't forget to bring your drinks.

Don't miss it! We'd love to see you!

2 Study the Writing box. Find examples of the phrases in the announcement in Exercise 1.

WRITING — An announcement

1 Invite people to join
Come and join our film/chess/photography club.

2 Give details: what, where and when, how to join
The club meets … at … in room …
We watch films/play chess/take photos/put on plays.
Members can also …
To join the club, complete the online form.
For more information, visit our website.
You can contact us at info@parkviewfilmclub.uk.

3 Dos and don'ts
Please book early.   Please bring/don't bring …
Don't forget to …   Don't be late.

4 Ending
Don't miss it!   We'd love to see you!
What are you waiting for?

3 Study the Language box. Find examples of time expressions in the announcement in Exercise 1.

LANGUAGE — Time expressions

at four o'clock   on Friday   every day/Friday
once a day/week/month/year   twice a day/week/month/year
four times a day/week/month/year

4 Complete the sentences with words from the Language box. Sometimes more than one answer is possible.

1 **Sat 6, Sat 20: go swimming**
I go swimming _twice a month_ .

2 **8 a.m., 8 p.m.: check emails**
They check their emails _____ .

3 **Mon 5, Mon 12, Mon 19, Mon 26: play tennis**
Jack plays tennis _____ .

4 **January, June: do a project**
We do a project _____ .

5 **9 a.m.: go running**
I go running _____ .

WRITING TIME

5 Write an announcement to invite people to join an after-school club.

1 Find ideas
Make notes for your announcement. Think about:
• what kind of club it is.
• where and how often it meets.
• who can join and how much it costs.
• things people need/don't need to bring.
• any other information.

2 Plan
Organise your ideas into paragraphs. Use the announcement in Exercise 1 to help you.

3 Write and share
• Write a draft announcement. Use the Language box and the Writing box to help you.
• Share your announcement with another student for feedback.
• Write the final version of your announcement.

4 Check
• Check language: are the time expressions correct? Is all the information clear?
• Check grammar: are the verb forms correct?

I can write an announcement.

Vocabulary Activator

WORDLIST 🔊 4.16

Classroom objects
calculator (n)
dictionary (n)
notebook (n)
pencil case (n)
poster (n)
rubber (n)
rubbish bin (n)
ruler (n)
sports bag (n)
textbook (n)
whiteboard (n)

Prepositions of place
behind (prep)
between (prep)
in (prep)
in front of (prep)
next to (prep)
on (prep)
under (prep)

School subjects
Art (n)
Biology (n)
Chemistry (n)
English (n)
Geography (n)
History (n)
Information Technology (IT) (n)
Maths (n)
Music (n)
PE (n)
Physics (n)

Word friends (making friends)
be there for someone
best friend
get to know someone
group of friends
make friends with someone
make new friends
meet someone for the first time

Word friends (learning)
do homework
go to school
have classes
revise for exams
start school

Extra words
activity (n)
after-school club (n)
awesome (adj)
be late with
boarding school (n)
book club (n)
borrow (v)
break (n)
chair (n)
Chemistry notes (n)
chess (n)
chocolate bar (n)
classmate (n)
classroom (n)
complete a form
desk (n)
drama/film club (n)
forget (v)
free (adj)
join a club
list (n)
lost property (n)
panic (v)
pen (n)
private school (n)
remember (v)
run (v)
shape (n)
school bag (n)
school hall (n)
school project (n)
snack bar (n)
spell (v)
teacher (n)
teachers' room (n)
tell a joke
test (n)
timetable (n)
type (v)
uniform (n)
wait (v)
waste your time
wi-fi (n)
wi-fi code (n)

---

1 Write the words for the definitions.
1 You write in this. n<u>o t e b o o k</u>
2 You use this in Maths lessons. c_____
3 You put your tracksuit in this. s_____ b__
4 You use a computer in this school subject. I_____ T_____
5 You do sport in this school subject. P_

2 Look at the picture. Find classroom objects from the wordlist and say where they are. Then, in pairs, describe your classroom or desks.
There's a notebook on the desk.

3 Complete the questions with words from the wordlist. Then, in pairs, ask and answer the questions.

> **YOU AND YOUR SCHOOL**
>
> 1 What time do you *start* school in the morning?
> 2 How many classes do you _____ every day?
> 3 What does the teacher write on the _____ in your classroom?
> 4 Who sits _____ front of you in class? Who sits behind you?
> 5 What do you and your _____ friend do at lunchtime?
> 6 Where do you _____ for exams – at home, with friends or at school?
> 7 When do you usually _____ your homework?

4 🔊 4.17 **PRONUNCIATION** Listen to how we pronounce the letter *u* in these words. Listen again and repeat.

> m<u>u</u>sic   st<u>u</u>dent   T<u>u</u>esday

5 🔊 4.18 **PRONUNCIATION** In pairs, say the sentences. Listen, check and repeat.
1 Exc<u>u</u>se me, can I <u>u</u>se your calc<u>u</u>lator?
2 St<u>u</u>dents <u>u</u>sually wear a <u>u</u>niform.

Revision

Vocabulary

1 Read the teachers' instructions and questions. Write the names of the school subjects.

1. Today we're learning a new song. Listen and sing with me.
   Music
2. What is 47 plus 36? Put your hand up if you know the answer.
   _____
3. What do we call animals that only eat meat?
   _____
4. Please look at the map of Europe and find Italy.
   _____
5. What is another name for H_2O?
   _____
6. Today's lesson is about America in 1492. Why is this date important?
   _____

2 Choose the correct option. Are the sentences true for you?
1. In Maths lessons, I always sit *between* / (*next to*) my best friend.
2. I always have a *rubber* / *poster* in my pencil case.
3. I usually *do* / *make* my homework before dinner.
4. I usually go *at* / *to* school by bike.
5. We sometimes play basketball in *PE* / *IT*.
6. There's a rubbish bin *under* / *between* my desk at home.

3 Complete the words in the sentences.
1. It's easy for Amy to m*ake* friends with people. She's got a lot of friends.
2. Max hasn't got a big g_____ of friends. He usually spends time with his b_____ friend.
3. Poppy is often nervous when she m_____ people for the f_____ time.
4. Sam loves getting to k_____ new people, and is friendly to everybody.
5. Emma is very kind and is always there f_____ her friends.

Grammar

4 Complete the text with the Present Continuous form of the verbs in brackets.

It's Sunday afternoon. Jack [1] *'s sitting* (sit) in his bedroom at home. He [2] _____ (not watch) a film and he [3] _____ (not play) games on his phone. He [4] _____ (revise) for an exam.

Jack's friends are at a different school. They [5] _____ (not revise) today and they [6] _____ (not do) homework. They [7] _____ (play) football in the park. They [8] _____ (laugh) and they [9] _____ (have) fun together. Poor Jack. Life isn't fair sometimes!

5 Make questions about the text in Exercise 4. Then, in pairs, ask and answer the questions.
1. where / Jack / sit / ?
2. he / watch / a film / ?
3. he / relax / ?
4. what / he / do / ?
5. his friends / revise / ?
6. what / they / do / ?
7. they / have / fun / ?
8. Jack / have / fun / ?

A: Where is Jack sitting?
B: He's sitting in his bedroom.

6 Choose the correct option.
1. Harry isn't watching TV. He *sleeps* / (*is sleeping*).
2. He usually *works* / *is working* on Sunday.
3. I can't talk right now. I *have* / *am having* dinner with my parents.
4. I always *wear* / *am wearing* a uniform to school – it's a rule!
5. *Do you do* / *Are you doing* homework now?
6. *Do you start* / *Are you starting* school at the same time every day?
7. Before I get up, I always *check* / *am checking* my phone!

Speaking

7 In pairs, make and respond to requests. Student A, use these ideas. Student B, go to page 136.

Can I:	Can you:
• borrow your textbook?	• give me some paper?
• copy your homework?	• open the window?

Dictation

8 🔊 4.19 Listen. Then listen again and write down what you hear during each pause.

SET FOR LIFE

My study routine

A Heeeelp!

B When you've got two hours to do your homework

C My Maths book? Yes, I've got it. At home!

D My friend: We've got a test tomorrow!
Me:

1 In pairs, discuss the questions.
1 Are you sometimes stressed about schoolwork?
2 What things make you feel stressed? Use the ideas below to help you.

> feeling tired   forgetting something   homework
> problems with other students   teachers   tests

2 Match the students in the photos above (A–D) with what they are saying (1–4).

1 I can't remember the dates of tests. I'm often late with homework too – I don't remember when the teachers need it.

2 I find it really difficult to study in the evening. I just want to read all of the messages from my friends … and play games … and watch videos!

3 I've got a lot of homework and I never know where to start! I also find it difficult to remember facts from lessons.

4 I never take the right things for the day. I do my homework on time, but then I forget to bring it to school! And I often forget my calculator for Maths or my trainers for PE.

3 Are you ever in situations like the ones in Exercise 2? When? Discuss in pairs.

4 Which tips are useful for the people in the photos? Match each person (A–D) with two tips. Can you add other useful tips to the list?

1 [B] [✓] Find a quiet place at home to do your homework.
2 [ ] [ ] Think of a big task as a lot of small tasks.
3 [ ] [ ] Write important dates in a diary or a phone calendar.
4 [ ] [ ] Pack your school bag every evening, ready for the next day.
5 [ ] [ ] Put your phone in a different room or don't look at your messages.
6 [ ] [ ] Write notes or draw pictures to help you remember what things you need for school.
7 [ ] [ ] Use notifications on your phone so you don't forget important dates.
8 [ ] [ ] Take notes in lessons and read them in the evenings.

Get organised

5 🔊 4.20 Listen to a podcast with smart study tips and tick (✓) the tips in Exercise 4 that you hear.

6 🔊 4.20 Listen again. What does Chloe say about smart students at the end of the podcast?

7 Do the quiz. Go to page 136 and check your result. Then, in pairs, compare your answers.

HOW SCHOOL-SMART ARE YOU?

How often do you:	often	sometimes	never
1 leave your homework to the last minute?	☐	☐	☐
2 study for a test at the last minute?	☐	☐	☐
3 forget about a homework task or a test?	☐	☐	☐
4 bring the wrong books to school?	☐	☐	☐
5 lose your lesson notes?	☐	☐	☐
6 play games when you are studying?	☐	☐	☐
7 finish your homework late?	☐	☐	☐
8 worry about schoolwork?	☐	☐	☐

8 Read the Useful Tips and think about your answers to the quiz in Exercise 7. Which tips are useful for you? Which things do you already do?

SET FOR LIFE

9 Try some of the study tips for a week, then report back to the class. Follow these steps.

1 Choose two of the study tips from this lesson that you think are useful for you.

2 Follow the tips for one week. Give each tip a score from 1 (= terrible) to 10 (= really useful).

3 Write a few sentences about your new study routine or take some photos (e.g. of the place where you study).

I write notes every evening and then …

4 Present your study routine to the class. Say which tips work for you and which don't.

Writing notes works for me because …

USEFUL TIPS

It's important to have a good study routine. It can help you do well at school and feel more relaxed.

AT SCHOOL
- Keep your school timetable in your bag or on your phone.
- Always take notes in class.
- Write important dates in a diary or calendar app.
- Don't be afraid to ask your teacher for help.

AT HOME
- Read your lesson notes at the end of each day.
- Plan a time and place for homework.
- Turn off your phone before you do your homework.
- Think of big homework tasks as a lot of small tasks.
- Prepare for school before you go to bed.

The sound of music

5

VOCABULARY
Musical instruments | Types of music | Opinion adjectives | Live music

GRAMMAR
Comparatives | Superlatives

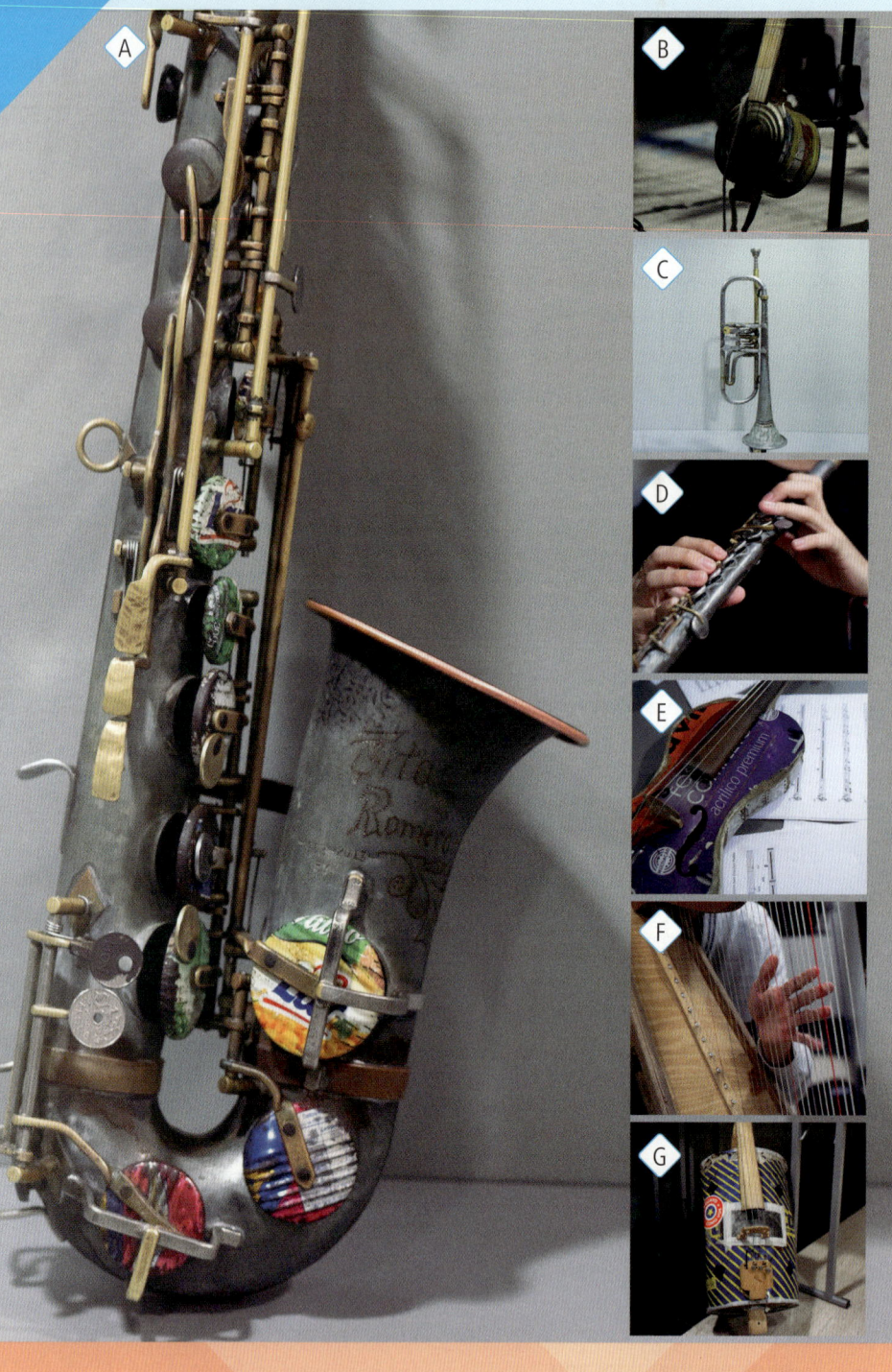

The Recycled Orchestra

People in the community of Cateura in Paraguay are poor. They don't have money to buy musical instruments. So they make their own instruments – from rubbish! They build violins from metal boxes, they make guitars from tins, and they use old spoons, coins and keys to make trumpets. Now the Recycled Orchestra plays all over the world!

5.1 Vocabulary

Music

1 Look at the photos and read the text above. What do the musicians use to make the instruments?

2 🔊 5.1 Study Vocabulary box A. Match instruments A–G in the photos above with seven of the words.

> **VOCABULARY A**   **Musical instruments**
>
> bass guitar ☐   cello ☐   drums ☐   flute ☐   guitar ☐
> harp ☐   keyboards ☐   piano ☐   saxophone [A]
> trumpet ☐   violin ☐

3 🔊 5.2 Listen and write the names of the instruments you hear. Then, in pairs, compare your answers.

Unit 5   62

4 🔊 **5.3** Study Vocabulary box B. What are your favourite types of music?

> **VOCABULARY B** ▸ **Types of music**
> classical   country   folk   hip-hop   jazz
> pop   R&B   rap   reggae   rock   techno

5 Complete the texts with words from Vocabulary boxes A and B.

Sheku Kanneh-Mason is a ¹c*lassical* musician. He plays the ²c_____ .

Lizzo is a pop and ³h_____-h_____ singer and songwriter. She plays the ⁴f_____ .

Daniel Platzman plays the ⁵d_____ in the American ⁶r_____ band Imagine Dragons.

6 🔊 **5.4** Listen and complete the dialogue with one word in each gap. Who is Mia thinking of? Go to page 136 and check.

Ali: Is it a man?
Mia: Yes, it is.
Ali: Does he play ¹*jazz*?
Mia: No, he doesn't.
Ali: Does he play ²_____ ?
Mia: Yes, he does.
Ali: Does he ³_____ ?
Mia: Yes, he does.
Ali: Can he play the ⁴_____ ?
Mia: Yes. He can also play the ⁵_____ .
Ali: Does he ⁶_____ in a group?
Mia: No, he doesn't. He's a solo artist.
Ali: Is he British?
Mia: Yes, he is.

7 Think of a famous musician. In pairs, ask and answer *yes/no* questions to find who your partner is thinking of. Use the dialogue in Exercise 6 to help you.

8 In pairs, do the quiz. Go to page 136 and check your answers.

The Big Music Quiz

1 What type of music is the boy in Photo A dancing to?
   a folk   **b** hip-hop   **c** jazz
2 How many strings has a bass guitar got?
   a four   **b** six   **c** eight
3 Who sings *No Time to Die*, the title song of the James Bond film?
   a Adele   **b** Billie Eilish   **c** Sam Smith
4 A ukulele is a type of small
   a flute.   **b** trumpet.   **c** guitar.
5 What type of music is Bob Marley famous for?
   a rock   **b** rap   **c** reggae
6 A group of three musicians or singers is called
   a a trio.   **b** a duo.   **c** a quartet.
7 *School of ____* is a film and musical about a teacher and a group of young musicians.
   a Rock   **b** Rap   **c** Jazz
8 What type of music are the people in Photo B dancing to?
   a techno   **b** R&B   **c** country

VIDEO ▶ **WIDER WORLD**

9 ▶ **21** Watch six people talking about music. Write down the instruments, types of music and musicians they mention.

10 In pairs, ask and answer the questions.
1 What instruments can you play?
2 What instrument do you want to learn to play?
3 Can any of your friends play an instrument?
4 What kind of music do you listen to?
5 Do you follow any singers, musicians or groups on social media?

I can talk about types of music and musical instruments.

5.2 Grammar
Comparatives

SEARCH FOR A STAR

Don't miss Saturday's final of the exciting TV talent show *Search for a Star*!

Our two finalists, Jaden and Louis, sing, dance and act for the last time. Then it's your turn to vote for the winner!

The prize: to star in the new theatre musical, *High School Rock*.

Who do you want to win? Write and tell us!

Jaden   **Louis**

Comments

Esme 12:57, 27 April
I want Jaden to win. He's got a stronger voice than Louis, and he's a more exciting dancer.

Max 17:34, 27 April
My vote is for Louis. He's a great actor. He's funnier and more confident than Jaden.

Ruby 21:16, 27 April
They're both amazing, but Louis is more relaxed in front of an audience.

Josh 18:25, 28 April
Jaden's shyer than Louis, but he's got a more interesting voice, and I think he's a better actor.

1 🔊 5.5 Read the online post and comments. What type of programme is *Search for a Star*? Who do Esme, Max, Ruby and Josh want to win?

2 Study the Grammar box. Find more examples of comparatives in the comments.

GRAMMAR ▸ Comparatives

Adjective	Comparative
shy	shy**er**
brave	brav**er**
sad	sad**der**
happy	happ**ier**
relaxed	**more** relaxed
difficult	**more** difficult
good	better
bad	worse

Jaden is **shyer than** Louis.

GRAMMAR TIME ▸ PAGE 130

3 Look at the judges' notes. Complete the sentences below with the comparative form of the adjectives in brackets.

	Jaden	Louis
Age	17	16
Height	1.73	1.81
Singing	10/10 Very nice voice!	9/10 A little quiet
Acting	9/10 Sometimes nervous!	10/10 Very confident!
Dancing	10/10 Amazing dancer!	9/10 Some good moves!

1 Jaden is *older* than Louis. (old)
2 Louis is _____ than Jaden. (young)
3 Louis is _____ than Jaden. (tall)
4 Jaden has got a _____ voice than Louis. (nice)
5 Jaden is _____ than Louis when he acts. (nervous)
6 Jaden is a _____ dancer than Louis. (good)

4 Make comparative sentences.
1 Shawn Mendes / young / Camila Cabello
   Shawn Mendes is younger than Camila Cabello.
2 Taylor Swift / tall / Selena Gomez
3 ballet / old / street dance
4 rock / popular / jazz
5 the harp / difficult to learn / the drums
6 a lot of pop songs / happy / rap songs

YOUR WORLD

5 In pairs, compare the things below. Use the adjectives to help you.

bad boring cheap cool exciting expensive
famous funny good modern nice old popular

Compare:
- two actors.
- two bands.
- two songs.
- two singers.
- two musical instruments.
- two TV shows.

Unit 5 64 I can compare two people or things.

5.3 Reading and Vocabulary
The Teenage Challenge

1 Do you sometimes go to music concerts? What type of concerts do you go to?

2 Read the title and introduction to the article. What do teenagers do in The Teenage Challenge? What is Hannah's challenge?

The Teenage Challenge

Do you like trying new things? Every week on The Teenage Challenge, a different teenager tries something new. This week, it's fifteen-year-old Hannah. Her challenge is to go to a classical music concert.

BEFORE THE CHALLENGE
What type of music do you like, Hannah?

R&B is cool, pop music is alright, but my favourite is rap. It's fast, fun and loud! I never listen to classical music, so I've got no idea what it's like. My friends think it's terrible. They say it's boring, and they think this challenge is hard!

THE DAY OF THE CHALLENGE
What's happening, Hannah?

I'm at the concert hall. It's a fantastic building. I'm really excited! There are people of all ages, but most of them are older. A lot of people are wearing smart clothes, but not me! The lights are going down and the musicians are getting ready to start. See you later!

AFTER THE CHALLENGE
What do you think of classical music now?

I quite like it! It's more interesting than pop music, and more relaxing than rap. It's quieter and you have time to think. Do I want to go again? Maybe, but I still prefer rap!

3 🔊 5.6 Read the whole article and choose the correct answer.
  1 Before the concert, Hannah
    a thinks classical music is boring.
    b only listens to rap music.
    c doesn't know much about classical music.
  2 At the concert, Hannah
    a doesn't like the building.
    b isn't the only young person.
    c is wearing elegant clothes.
  3 After the concert, Hannah
    a thinks classical music is OK.
    b likes classical music more than rap.
    c doesn't want to go to another classical concert.

4 🔊 5.7 Study the Vocabulary box. Which of the adjectives are not in the article? Write the adjectives in the correct column in the table below.

VOCABULARY — Opinion adjectives

alright   boring   brilliant   cool   fantastic   fun   great
hard   interesting   OK   terrible

+	+/–	–
brilliant	*alright*	

5 In pairs, compare these things. Use adjectives from the Vocabulary box.
  1 rock music – dance music
  2 pop music – jazz music
  3 action films – nature programmes
  4 the violin – the guitar
  5 watching TV – playing video games

A: *I think rock music is boring. Dance music is better.*
B: *I prefer rock music. I think dance music is terrible. You can't relax when you listen to it.*

YOUR WORLD

6 Choose one of the topics below and write about it. Use the adjectives in the Vocabulary box to help you.
  • my favourite singer/band
  • my favourite song
  • my favourite film
  • my favourite video game

My favourite singer is Bruno Mars. I think he's really cool. He's got a fantastic voice and he's never boring. His new songs are better than his old songs because the words are more interesting.

I can understand an article about a music challenge.

5.4 Grammar
Superlatives

VIDEO ▶ THE COOLEST GUITAR

Mateo: Thanks for your help, Lena. I really need a guitar – I've got my first lesson next week.
Lena: No problem.
Mateo: This is the cheapest guitar, but I think it's a child's guitar.
Lena: Yes, it is. You need something bigger.
Mateo: What about this?
Lena: That's the most expensive guitar in the shop!
Mateo: It's also the coolest! So, what's the best guitar for beginners?
Lena: Probably this one. It's easier to play than other guitars. It's £150.
Mateo: That's still expensive.

Lena: I've got an idea: borrow my guitar! The worst thing is to buy a guitar now. You aren't sure it's the instrument for you. When you're sure, you can look on the internet – the lowest prices are often online.
Mateo: Good advice. Thanks, Lena.
Lena: Right, let's go home!
Mateo: Before we go, can I play this guitar – the really cool one?
Lena: No, Mateo! Come on!

1 Look at the photo. What instrument does Mateo want to buy?

2 ▶ 22 🔊 5.8 Watch or listen and answer the questions.
  1 What's the problem with the first guitar?
  2 What's the problem with the other guitars?

3 Does Mateo make a good decision in the guitar shop? Why?/Why not?

SET FOR LIFE

4 Which sentences are true for you? Discuss in groups. What is the best thing to do?
When I go shopping,
 • I buy from the first shop I visit.
 • I compare prices at different shops/online.
 • I don't really look at prices.
 • I think before I buy something.

5 Study the Grammar box. Find more examples of superlatives in the dialogue.

GRAMMAR Superlatives

Adjective	Comparative	Superlative
cool	cooler	the coolest
nice	nicer	the nicest
big	bigger	the biggest
easy	easier	the easiest
famous	more famous	the most famous
good	better	the best
bad	worse	the worst

GRAMMAR TIME ▶ PAGE 130

6 Complete the sentences with the superlative form of the adjectives below.

| big expensive fast ~~long~~ old |

 1 The _longest_ opera is German. It's more than fifteen hours long!
 2 The world's _____ musical instrument is a violin. It's worth $16 million.
 3 The _____ instrument is a flute from Slovenia. It's more than 43,000 years old.
 4 The world's _____ drummer can hit the drums 1,208 times in one minute!
 5 The _____ violin in the world is more than four metres tall. You need three people to play it!

YOUR WORLD

7 In pairs, take it in turns to tell your partner about your family and friends. Use the ideas below.

| funny old tall fast runner good singer
long hair short hair unusual name |

Of my family and friends, my friend Ahmet is the funniest. My dad is the best singer in the family.

Unit 5 I can compare more than two people or things.

5.5 Listening and Vocabulary
Make Music Day

1 Look at the poster for Make Music Day. Where are the musicians? What instruments are they playing?

2 🔊 5.9 Study the Vocabulary box. Check you understand the words.

VOCABULARY — Live music

audience   band   concert   group   orchestra
singer   stage   street musician

3 🔊 5.10 Choose the correct option. Listen and check.

In a typical pop ¹audience / concert the singer and the band play on a ²concert / stage. They're higher up than the ³audience / group. It's different for the ⁴band / orchestra in a classical music concert, of course. And it's different for ⁵singers / street musicians too. They're right next to the audience.

4 🔊 5.11 Listen to a radio programme about Make Music Day. Which country is it from? What happens on Make Music Day?

5 🔊 5.11 Listen again and complete the notes with a word or a short phrase.

Make Music Day (MMD)

Date: ¹ 21 June
First MMD: Country: France
Year: ² _____
People play music: in streets, in ³ _____, at home
Takes place in: more than 1,000 cities in ⁴ _____ countries
More information: visit www.makemusicday.org or by ⁵ _____

6 In pairs, discuss the questions.
1 What do you like about Make Music Day?
2 Would you like to organise Make Music Day in your country? Why?/Why not?

7 🔊 5.12 **WORD FRIENDS** Complete the questions with the verbs below. Listen and check.

buy   ~~enjoy~~   go   play   see

1 What kind of live music do you *enjoy* the most?
2 How often do you _____ to concerts?
3 Do you ever _____ concert tickets online?
4 Which group or singer do you most want to _____ in a live concert?
5 Where do street musicians _____ music in your town?

VIDEO **WIDER WORLD**

8 ▶ 23 Watch seven people answering the questions in Exercise 7. Write down as many answers as you can.

9 In pairs, ask and answer the questions in Exercise 7.
A: What kind of live music do you enjoy the most?
B: I really enjoy classical music concerts and operas.

I can understand a radio programme about live music.

5.6 Speaking
Suggestions

VIDEO ▶ **WHAT DO YOU SUGGEST?**

Mia: Let's move this chair and film it here. There's lots of space.
Noah: Hmm, I'm not sure. It's a bit dark there.
Mia: What do you suggest?
Noah: Why don't we film it in the garden? The light's better.
Mia: OK, why not? What about clothes? How about this black top, Lena?
Noah: I'm not sure that's a good idea. Bright colours are better.
Mia: How about this red T-shirt?
Noah: Great idea! It's perfect! Now, for make-up …
Lena: Excuse me, guys. Can I make a suggestion?
Noah: Yes, of course.
Lena: Why don't you just point the camera and film? This isn't Hollywood!
Mia: Oh yes, Lena, you're right!
Lena: I really want to put my new song online tonight.
Mia: No problem.
Noah: Yes, sorry, Lena! … Perhaps just this hat?
Lena: No, Noah!

SOUNDS GOOD! • Excuse me! • You're right!

1 ▶ 24 🔊 5.13 Watch or listen and answer the questions.
   1 Why does Noah want to film the video in the garden?
   2 Why does Lena say, 'This isn't Hollywood!'?
   3 Why does Lena want to make a video?

2 Study the Speaking box. Find examples of the phrases in the dialogue.

SPEAKING Suggestions

Asking for suggestions
What do you suggest?
Have you got any (other) suggestions?

Making suggestions	Responding to suggestions
Can I make a suggestion?	Sure./Yes, of course.
Why don't you/we … ?	OK, why not?/Great idea!
How/What about … ?	Maybe./Perhaps./I'm not sure.
Let's …	I'm not sure that's a good idea.

3 🔊 5.14 Complete the dialogue with one word in each gap. Use the Speaking box to help you. Listen and check.

Liam: It's Make Music Day tomorrow. What can we do? Have you got any [1]*suggestions*?
Ada: Hmm … [2]_____ don't we have a party in your garden?
Liam: OK, why [3]_____ ? Emma can play her guitar, and we can all sing!
Ada: Great idea! [4]_____ invite Holly too.
Liam: Sure! What [5]_____ a barbecue? We can buy some food.
Ada: What do you [6]_____ ?
Liam: Chicken, baked potatoes, salad, …
Ada: Cool. Why [7]_____ you ask your parents tonight?
Liam: Oh, yes, of [8]_____ !

4 🔊 5.15 Listen to five suggestions. Respond with phrases from the Speaking box.

YOUR WORLD

5 Work in pairs. Student A, follow the instructions below. Student B, go to page 136.
   1 Read these situations to Student B. Respond to his/her suggestions.
      • I've got an English exam tomorrow.
      • I'm a little bit hungry.
   2 Listen to Student B's situations. Make suggestions. Use the ideas below or your own ideas.
      • listen to music/read a book
      • buy a ticket for a concert/get a book

I can ask for, make and respond to suggestions.

5.7 Writing
Text messages

1 Do you often message your friends or family? How often?

2 Read the messages and answer the questions.
   1 When is the Twenty One Pilots concert?
   2 How much are the tickets?
   3 How many tickets does Jake need to buy?

3 Study the Writing box. In pairs, find examples for each point in the messages.

WRITING Text messages

To make messages shorter, you can:
- leave out some words, e.g. *I, you, there's, there are, a/an, the, am/are, do, have.*
  Twenty One Pilots concert at Brighton Centre = There's a Twenty One Pilots concert at the Brighton Centre.
  Having a great time! = I'm having a great time!
- use symbols, letters and numbers to replace words.
  @ = at; 2 = to/too; 4 = for; b = be; c = see; u = you; r = are; y = why
- leave out some letters in words.
  plz = please; thx = thanks; sry = sorry; can't = cnt
- use acronyms for phrases:
  Kk = okay; idk = I don't know; gtg = I have to go

Jake 18.12
1 Great news! 😃 Twenty One Pilots concert @ Brighton Centre on Fri 3 April @ 7.30. Tickets r £25. U can buy them online. Want 2 go?

Martha 18.14
2 Yes! Can u get tickets 4 me and my sister, plz?

Jake 18.15
3 Kk, can get them today.

Martha 18.17
4 Thx. Cnt wait! Twenty One Pilots r best band ever! 🤗 Cu there!

4 Make the messages shorter. Use the Writing box to help you.
   1 I can't go out now.
      Cnt go out now.
   2 I've got the tickets for the concert.
   3 Are you at home?
   4 Do you want to meet later?
   5 Sorry, I have to go.
   6 I am waiting for you.

5 Study the Language box. Match emojis 1–6 with meanings a–f below. What other emojis do you use?

LANGUAGE Emojis

In text messages, we often use emojis instead of words.
1 😊 2 😭 3 🥰 4 😂 5 🙏 6 👍

a ☐ I love it/you!   d ☐ I'm happy.
b ☐ I'm sad.   e ☐ Very funny!/I'm laughing.
c ☐ Please./Thank you.   f ☐ Yes./OK./I like this.

6 Study the Language box. Then write out messages 1 and 4 in full.
Great news! There's a Twenty One Pilots concert …

WRITING TIME

7 Write a message to a friend. Suggest an event you can go to together. Then swap messages with a partner and reply.

1 Find ideas
Make notes for your message. Think about these questions.
- What is the event? (a sports event, a concert, a play, etc.)
- When and where is it?
- How much are the tickets?

2 Plan
Organise your ideas. Use Jake's first message to help you.

3 Write and share
- Write a draft message. Use the Language box and the Writing box to make it shorter.
- Share your message with another student for feedback.
- Write the final version of your message.

4 Check
- Check language: are the symbols and abbreviations correct? Is the message short?
- Check grammar: can you leave out some words and keep the message clear?

Vocabulary Activator

WORDLIST 5.16

Musical instruments
bass guitar (n)
cello (n)
drums (n)
flute (n)
guitar (n)
harp (n)
keyboards (n)
piano (n)
saxophone (n)
trumpet (n)
violin (n)

Types of music
classical music (n)
country music (n)
folk music (n)
hip-hop (n)
jazz (n)
pop (n)
R&B (n)
rap (n)
reggae (n)
rock (n)
techno (n)

Opinion adjectives
alright (adj)
boring (adj)
brilliant (adj)
cool (adj)
fantastic (adj)
fun (adj)
great (adj)
hard (adj)
interesting (adj)
OK (adj)
terrible (adj)

Live music
audience (n)
band (n)
concert (n)
group (n)
orchestra (n)
singer (n)
stage (n)
(street) musician (n)

Word friends
(enjoying live music)
buy (concert) tickets
enjoy music
go to a concert
play music
see a group/singer (in a live concert)

Extra words
act (v)
actor (n)
amazing (adj)
atmosphere (n)
beginner (n)
cheap (adj)
concert hall (n)
dance (v)
dancer (n)
difficult (adj)
expensive (adj)
famous (adj)
fast (adj)
funny (adj)
guitarist (n)
invite (v)
loud (adj)
make a video
modern (adj)
musical (n)
musical instrument (n)
popular (adj)
price (n)
prize (n)
professional (musician) (adj)
quiet (adj)
relaxing (adj)
sing (v)
song (n)
songwriter (n)
star (n)
string (n)
take a seat
take place in
(talent) show (n)
voice (n)
vote for something/
   someone
win (v)

1 Use the wordlist to find these things.
  1 a musical instrument you play with your mouth and hands *flute*
  2 a small instrument with four strings
  3 another word for *fantastic*
  4 a type of music that comes from Jamaica
  5 an adjective that means 'very bad'

2 Match the pictures with words from the wordlist.

1 *singer*
2 _____
3 _____
4 _____
5 _____
6 _____

3 In pairs, take it in turns to guess your partner's opinion about these things. Use opinion adjectives from the wordlist.
  1 R&B music   4 talent shows on TV
  2 classical music 5 musicals
  3 music lessons   6 ballet dancing

A: *You think R&B music is terrible.*
B: *False – I think it's great.*

4 In pairs, talk about these things. Use words from the wordlist.
  • types of music you like/don't like
  • instruments you would like to play

5 5.17 **PRONUNCIATION** Listen to how we pronounce the /æ/ and /ʌ/ sounds. Look at the underlined letters and decide which sound you hear. Write the words in the correct column.

b**a**nd cl**a**ssical c**o**untry dr**u**m
f**u**nny j**a**zz r**a**p tr**u**mpet

/æ/	/ʌ/
band	country

6 5.18 **PRONUNCIATION** Listen, check and repeat.

Revision

Vocabulary

1 Complete the text with the words below.

> band   brilliant   buy   concert
> enjoy   ~~play~~   rock   see

I love music, but I don't ¹*play* an instrument. My parents ² _____ music too and they often ³ _____ tickets for concerts. I like ⁴ _____ music. For my birthday, I want to go to a ⁵ _____ . I want to ⁶ _____ Metal Panda – they're the best rock ⁷ _____ in the world! The singer is ⁸ _____ .

2 Complete the words in the text. Use the photo to help you.

CLEAN BANDIT

In a typical pop ¹g*roup* there is a ²s _____ , a drummer, two ³g _____ players and a ⁴b _____ guitarist. But Clean Bandit are not a typical pop group! They mix pop music with classical music. They use guitars and ⁵d _____ , but they also play the ⁶k _____ , and the singer plays the cello. She's great! I love being in the ⁷a _____ at a Clean Bandit ⁸c _____ . It's a fantastic evening!

3 Complete the questionnaire with the words below. Then, in pairs, ask and answer the questions.

> go   orchestra   musicians   ~~play~~   see   singer

Music questionnaire

1 Who in your family can *play* music?
2 Do any of your friends play in a school _____ or group?
3 Who's your favourite _____ ? Does he or she sing in a band?
4 What do you think of street _____ ? Do you like the music they play?
5 Do you sometimes _____ to concerts? Who would you like to _____ in a concert?

Grammar

4 Complete the text with the comparative form of the adjectives in brackets.

Ask the music experts!

Have you got a question about music? Our experts are here to help you. This week's question is from thirteen-year-old Maisie Saunders from Edinburgh.

> Hi! I want to learn an instrument, but I can't decide between the trumpet and the saxophone. Which is better?

Good question, Maisie! A lot of people say that the saxophone is ¹*quicker* (quick) to learn than the trumpet, so it's ² _____ (good) for beginners. But a saxophone is ³ _____ (heavy) and usually ⁴ _____ (expensive) than a trumpet. The trumpet is ⁵ _____ (small), so it's ⁶ _____ (easy) to carry to lessons. They're both great instruments! Write and tell us what you decide and good luck!

5 Complete the questions with the superlative form of the adjectives in brackets. Then, in pairs, ask and answer the questions.
1 Who is *the worst* (bad) singer in your family?
2 Who is _____ (funny) person in your school?
3 What is _____ (interesting) programme on TV right now?
4 What is _____ (good) pop group in the world?
5 Who is _____ (successful) singer from your country?
6 Who is _____ (tall) person you know?

A: Who is the worst singer in your family?
B: My dad! No, my little sister – she's terrible!

Speaking

6 Work in pairs. There is a talent show at school next week, and you and your partner want to be in it. Role-play a dialogue. Make at least three suggestions. Use the ideas below or your own ideas.

> act a scene from a film   dance   play a musical instrument
> read a poem   sing a song   tell a funny story

A: What can we do at next week's talent show? Have you got any suggestions?
B: Let's …

Dictation

7 🔊 5.19 Listen. Then listen again and write down what you hear during each pause.

BBC CULTURE
Don't stop the music!

Why learn an instrument?

Many children learn to play an instrument when they are young. In the UK today, seventy-six percent of children do this. The most popular instrument to learn is the keyboard. And playing a musical instrument is good for us. Why?

A Scientists think that people who play an instrument become more intelligent. It changes their brain. They have a better memory and get better marks in tests.

B Playing an instrument also helps with physical things. When we learn to play an instrument, the brain sends quicker messages to our body, and our hearing can get better too.

C It's relaxing. When we play an instrument, we put our feelings into the music. And if we're worried, music helps us.

D We can play with other people. It's good to learn how to work together in a team. That's important for when we get a job.

E It's fun and exciting. People listen to music and they're happy. It's a great feeling – to make people happy with music.

So why are you waiting? Learn to play an instrument and change your life!

---

become (v) begin to be
brain (n) the part inside your head that makes you think and feel
hearing (n) the ability to hear
intelligent (adj) able to learn and understand easily
physical (adj) connected to the body

---

1 **VISIBLE THINKING** In pairs, look at the photos and discuss the questions.

THINK
1 What instruments are the people playing?
2 What instruments are popular with young people in your country?

PUZZLE
3 What would you like to know about musical instruments? Choose one of these questions or write your own question.
   a Which are the easiest/most difficult to learn?
   b Is playing an instrument good for you?

EXPLORE
4 Where do you think you can find answers to the questions in point 3?
- ask your music teacher
- learn to play music
- find a website
- talk to people

2 🔊 5.20 Read the article. Which question from Exercise 1 does it answer?

3 Read the article again and tick (✓) the sentences which are true.
People who can play an instrument:
1 ☐ can remember lots of things.
2 ☐ can move fast.
3 ☐ can hear well.
4 ☐ are never worried.
5 ☐ can work well with other people.

4 Can you play an instrument? If yes, how well? If not, what instrument would you like to play and why? Discuss in pairs.

BBC ▶ Feeling the music

5 In pairs, look at the photo and find these things.
- musicians
- the conductor
- a cello
- a baton
- a trumpet
- a drum

6 ▶ 25 Watch a TV programme about a musician and answer the questions.
1. Why is he sad?
2. Why can't he play in an orchestra?
3. What new thing can help him?
4. How many musicians are playing in the concert?

7 ▶ 25 Watch the video again. Choose the correct answer.
1. Vahakn and his father
   a. are disabled musicians.
   b. help disabled musicians.
2. The baton helps Kyungho because
   a. he can feel what the conductor is doing.
   b. it is easier to see.
3. The concert is the first time that Kyungho plays
   a. in front of an audience.
   b. with an orchestra and a conductor.

8 Would you like to hear this orchestra perform? Why?/Why not? Discuss in pairs.

PROJECT TIME

9 In groups of four, do a survey about music. Create a digital poster to present the results. Follow these steps.

1 In your group, read the survey questions and write the answer options (e.g. *a always b sometimes c once a week*).
- How often do you listen to music? How do you prefer to listen to music?
- What is your favourite type of music? What do you think of classical music?
- Can you play an instrument? If yes, what instrument?
- How often do you go to concerts? How well can you sing?

2 Complete your part of the survey.
- Ask 3–4 different people your questions (e.g. family/friends/class). They choose one of the options.
- Write down all the answers and write a few sentences about the results.

3 In your group, create your poster. You can use an online poster maker app or website.
- Collect your results and decide on a layout for your poster.
- Add pictures or other graphic elements to illustrate your results.
- Practise presenting your results to the class.

4 Share your poster with the class.
- Answer other students' questions.
- Ask questions and comment on the other posters.

Game on!

6

VOCABULARY
Sports | Sportspeople | Sports collocations | Places to play sport | Sports competitions

GRAMMAR
Was/Were | There was/There were | Past simple affirmative: regular and irregular verbs

SPORTS NEWS

A Di Angeli: 'It's great to be back!' ▶ 2:30

B Collins is closer to the Olympics ▶ 0:25

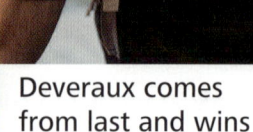

C Deveraux comes from last and wins the race! ▶ 1:32

D Lewis scores three points for New City ▶ 0:20

E Oliveira plays his last match ▶ 0:50

F Wallis wins a gold medal for England ▶ 1:25

6.1 Vocabulary

Sport

1 **I KNOW!** Close your books. How many sports do you know? In pairs, make a list.

2 🔊 6.1 Study Vocabulary box A. Which sports are on your list from Exercise 1? Which sports are in photos A–F above?

> **VOCABULARY A** ▶ **Sports**
>
> baseball   basketball   cycling   football   ice hockey
> ice-skating   judo   roller skating   running   skiing
> swimming   tennis   volleyball

3 Look at the sports website above. Which are your favourite sports to watch? To play?

My favourite sports to watch are …

4 🔊 6.2 Study Vocabulary box B. Match the sportspeople with the sports in Vocabulary box A. Which words can go with more than one sport?

> **VOCABULARY B** ▶ **Sportspeople**
>
> cyclist   player   runner   skater   skier   swimmer

Unit 6   74

5 Complete the questions in the quiz with the correct form of words from Vocabulary box B.

SPORTS QUIZ

1. To win this famous cycling race, *cyclists* do about 9,100 km in twenty-five days. What is the name of the race?
   a Tour de France
   b Trans-Siberian Extreme
   c Cycle UK

2. Michael Phelps is an American _____ . How many Olympic swimming gold medals has he got?
   a twenty-three   b eight   c eighteen

3. Usain Bolt is a very fast _____ . He's a world champion. Where does he come from?
   a USA   b Ethiopia   c Jamaica

4. When they race, ice _____ can go up to
   a fifty-three km/h.   b ten km/h.   c twenty-four km/h.

5. The first European _____ come from Norway. There are drawings of people skiing from
   a 40 BC.   b 400 BC.   c 4,000 BC.

6. Who is NOT one of the top 100 football _____ of all time?
   a Pelé   b Novak Djokovic   c David Beckham

6 In groups, do the quiz in Exercise 5. Go to page 137 and check your answers. What is your group's score? Which group has got the most points?

7 🔊 6.3 **WORD FRIENDS** Complete the phrases with verbs from the website on page 74. Listen and check.
1 *play* a match/a sport
2 _____ a (gold) medal/a race
3 _____ a goal/a point

8 🔊 6.4 Complete the texts with the correct form of words from Exercise 7. Listen and check.

VIDEO **WIDER WORLD**

9 ▶ 26 Watch seven people talking about sport. Write down as many sports as you can.

10 In groups, ask and answer the questions. Who is the most interested in sport?
1 How often do you play or do your favourite sport? How often do you win?
2 What other sports do you play?
3 Do you play any sports video games? Which ones and how often?
4 Do you ever watch sports live? Which ones?

What role does sport play in your life?

Chris | Erika | Beth | Kerry

Chris: Sport is in our family! I play basketball at school. I often ¹*score* points for my team. My brother is a professional footballer. He's brilliant! He usually scores one or two ² _____ in a match!

Erika: I'm an ice-skater. I train every day – early in the morning before school, and then again after school. My dream is to win a gold ³ _____ in the Olympics!

Beth: Cycling is my life! I really want to win a big ⁴ _____ one day, like UCI Women's World Tour.

Kerry: I'm new to sport. My cousin is teaching me how to ⁵ _____ tennis. It's quite hard, but I'm learning fast.

I can talk about sports and sportspeople.   **75** Unit 6

6.2 Grammar

Was/Were, There was/There were

1 🔊 **6.5** Read and listen to the interview. Find information about the things below.

> country   champions   crowd   final score
> number of teams   year

country: China

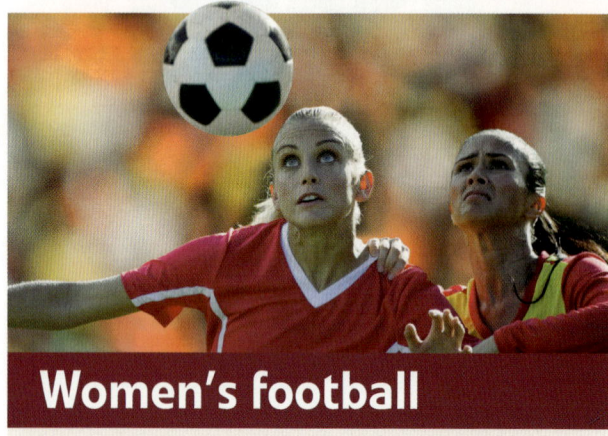

Women's football
An interview with PE teacher Ms Dilks
By Jo Bisset

Jo: When was the first Women's Football World Cup?
Ms D: It was in 1991.
Jo: Was it in Europe?
Ms D: No, it wasn't. It was in China.
Jo: How many teams were there?
Ms D: There were twelve teams.
Jo: Which teams were in the final?
Ms D: It was Norway vs. the USA.
Jo: Was there a big crowd?
Ms D: Yes, there was. There were 63,000 people in the stadium.
Jo: What was the final score?
Ms D: It was 2–1 to the USA.
Jo: Were you there?
Ms D: No, I wasn't! I was born in 1990. I was only one year old in 1991!

2 Study the Grammar box. Find examples of *was/were* and *there was/there were* in the interview.

GRAMMAR — Was/Were, There was/There were

+	–
I **was** in China. We **were** happy.	She **wasn't** in Brazil. They **weren't** sad.
?	
Were you there? Where **was** the match?	Yes, I **was**./No, I **wasn't**.

there is/isn't → there **was/wasn't**
there are/aren't → there **were/weren't**

GRAMMAR TIME > PAGE 131

3 🔊 **6.6** Complete the second part of the interview with the correct form of *was* or *were*. Listen and check.

Jo: Who's the best female footballer in the world?
Ms D: The American Megan Rapinoe, in my opinion. She ¹*was* the best player in the 2019 World Cup.
Jo: ² _____ the 2019 World Cup in the USA?
Ms D: No, it ³ _____ . It ⁴ _____ in France.
Jo: Which teams ⁵ _____ in the final?
Ms D: The USA vs. the Netherlands. The final score ⁶ _____ 2–0.

4 Complete the dialogue between Emily and her grandmother with the correct form of *there was* or *there were*.

Emily: ¹*Was there* a girls' football team at your school, Gran?
Gran: No, ² _____ . But ³ _____ a hockey team.
Emily: ⁴ _____ any boys in your hockey team?
Gran: No, ⁵ _____ , because ⁶ _____ a boys' hockey team and a girls' hockey team. Every year ⁷ _____ a hockey match – girls vs. boys. It was great fun!

5 🔊 **6.7** In pairs, choose the correct option to complete the questions about a sports match. Listen and check.
  1 What sport (*was*) / *were* it?
  2 *The match was / Was the match* in a stadium?
  3 When *was / were* the match?
  4 How many players *was / were* there?
  5 *There was / Was there* a big crowd?
  6 What *was / wasn't* the final score?
  7 *Was / Were* you the best player?
  8 *Was / Were* there a prize?

YOUR WORLD

6 In pairs, use the questions in Exercise 5 to talk about a time when you were a player in a sports match.

A: What sport was it?
B: It was volleyball.
A: Was the match in a stadium?
B: No, it wasn't. It was in a gym at school.

I can use was/were and there was/there were to talk about the past.

6.3 Reading and Vocabulary

Sports fun facts

1 What sports are popular in your country? Do you know any unusual sports?

2 🔊 6.8 Check you understand the words below. Then read texts 1–3. What sport is each text about?

> basket   cage   chase away   hole   pigeon

3 Read the texts again and answer the questions.
  1 Where does Rufus 'work'?
  2 Who was the first 'bird chaser'?
  3 How many players were there in early basketball teams?
  4 Who was inside the cage on basketball courts?
  5 What can't cycle ball players use?
  6 How old is cycle ball?

4 🔊 6.9 Study the Vocabulary box. Which places are mentioned in the texts?

VOCABULARY ▸ **Places to play sport**

> basketball court   football field/pitch   running track
> swimming pool   tennis court

5 In pairs, complete the text with words from the Vocabulary box in the correct form.

Did you know?

1 An Olympic swimming *pool* is 50 m x 25 m and it can hold 2,500,000 litres of water.
2 Most running _____ are 400 m long.
3 In NBA, the three-point line on a basketball _____ is 7.24 m away from the basket.
4 The oldest football _____ is Sandygate Stadium in England. It first opened in 1804.
5 The picture below shows the shape of the first tennis _____ .

SPORTS fun facts

Here are some interesting facts about sports.

1 Rufus the hawk has an important job: he keeps pigeons away from the tennis courts at Wimbledon. Before Rufus, birds were a big problem for tennis competitions because they were everywhere. Now Rufus chases them all away. Before him, there was Hamish, another hawk, but Rufus is a lot more famous. Check him out on social media!

2 In its early days, basketball was a very different sport from the one we play now:
- There were nine players in each team and the game was only thirty minutes long.
- The basketball court was about half the size of today's courts.
- The baskets were real baskets without a hole at the bottom.
- In the early 1900s there was a big cage around the players to stop the ball from hitting the fans.

3 Cycle ball, or radball, is like football, but the players can only move the ball with their bikes – no hands or feet! It isn't a new sport – it dates back to the year 1893. The countries with the most medals in cycle ball are Germany, the Czech Republic and Switzerland.

YOUR WORLD

6 In pairs, ask and answer the questions.
  1 Are there any places to play sport where you live?
  2 Do you ever play sport there?
  3 Which place is your favourite? Why?

There's a … in my town.
I (usually) play …
My favourite place is … I like it because …

I can understand short texts about sports facts.

6.4 Grammar

Past simple affirmative: regular and irregular verbs

VIDEO ▶ THE RUNNING COMPETITION

Mr H: Well done, Noah! You won the race!
Noah: What? No, Mr Harris, that's not right!
Mr H: Excuse me for a moment.
Noah: Wait, please. I wasn't …
Mia: I saw you, Noah! We all followed the signs and went round the park, but you ran through the park!
Noah: It was a mistake! I got lost! I saw a man running, so I followed him. I tried to tell Mr Harris.
Mia: Really?
Noah: Yes, but the man wasn't a runner. He wanted to take photos for the school website and he ran through the park to be at the finish line before anyone else. That's him, over there!
Mia: Oh, I see. Look, he's taking a photo of us now.
Noah: Come on, let's find Mr Harris and tell him.
Mia: Cheer up, Noah. At least you were a winner for … a minute?

1 ▶ 27 🔊 6.10 Watch or listen. Who is the real winner?

SET FOR LIFE

2 What do you usually do when you make a mistake? Discuss in pairs. What is the best thing to do?
 • tell people who should know and say sorry
 • wait until someone finds out and then say sorry
 • when someone finds out, say it wasn't your fault

3 Study Grammar box A. Write the Past Simple form of the verbs below. Then find the verbs in the dialogue and check.

follow   try   want

GRAMMAR A | **Past simple affirmative: regular verbs**

wait – wait**ed**   like – lik**ed**   jog – jog**ged**   carry – carr**ied**

Time expressions: this morning, yesterday, last night, last week, last month, last year

GRAMMAR TIME ➤ PAGE 131

4 6.11 Listen and repeat. Then write the verbs from Grammar box A in the correct column.

/d/	/t/	/ɪd/
call**ed**	watch**ed**	end**ed**
follow**ed**	danc**ed**	want**ed**

5 6.12 Find the Past Simple form of these verbs in the dialogue and complete Grammar box B. Listen and check.

GRAMMAR B | **Past simple affirmative: irregular verbs**

go – _went_   see – _____
get – _____   win – _____
run – _____

GRAMMAR TIME ➤ PAGE 131

6 6.13 Complete Lily's story with the Past Simple form of the verbs in brackets. Listen and check.

I ¹_went_ (go) for a run in the park yesterday. When I ²_____ (finish), I ³_____ (sit) on a bench. There was a book on it. Inside it, I ⁴_____ (find) two tickets for a tennis match. Then I ⁵_____ (see) a young man. 'That's my book!' he ⁶_____ (say). 'Were there any tickets inside it?' I ⁷_____ (smile) and I ⁸_____ (give) him the tickets. 'Do you like this book?' he ⁹_____ (ask). 'You can keep it!' I ¹⁰_____ (look) at the title of the book. It was Not Your Lucky Day!

YOUR WORLD

7 Go to page 137. In pairs, take it in turns to make a sentence in the Past Simple. Your partner must guess if your sentences are true or false.

A: I went jogging in the park last week.
B: False!
A: No, it's true. One point for me!

Unit 6   78   I can use the Past Simple to talk about past events.

6.5 Listening and Vocabulary
Sporting moments

1 Are you more often happy or sad when you watch your favourite sports player or team?

2 🔊 6.14 Study the Vocabulary box. Check you understand the words.

> **VOCABULARY** — **Sports competitions**
>
> cup   final   league   semi-final   tournament

3 🔊 6.15 Listen to a radio programme and match the sentence halves to make true sentences about the speakers.

1. ☐ Finn   a ran in a race.
2. ☐ Emma   b is a sports fanatic.
3. ☐ Sam   c talks about 2016.
4. ☐ Mason   d tells a sad story.

4 🔊 6.15 Listen again and choose the correct answer.

1. Where was Finn when Andy Murray won Wimbledon?
   A   B   C

2. What was Emma's best time for ten kilometres before last Sunday?
   A 32:40   B 39:14   C 40:30

3. How much were the train tickets that Sam bought?
   A £45   B £57   C £75

4. What does Mason do every day?
   A   B   C

5 🔊 6.16 **WORD FRIENDS** Complete the phrases with the verbs below.

do   go   lose   play (x2)   ~~win~~

1. *win* a game/a match/a tournament
2. _____ a game/a match/a tournament
3. _____ aerobics/exercise/judo
4. _____ cycling/jogging/running/swimming
5. _____ badminton/football/tennis
6. _____ for a team

6 Complete the sentences with the correct form of the verbs in Exercise 5.

1. Andy Murray *won* the Wimbledon tennis tournament in 2016.
2. Emma often _____ running.
3. Liverpool were in the cup final, but they _____ the game 2–1.
4. Jim _____ jogging every morning. At weekends he _____ badminton and he _____ judo. He _____ for the school football team.

7 🔊 6.17 Choose the correct option. Listen and check.

> I love sport. I often ¹*do /(go)*cycling and I ²*do / play* gymnastics after school, but my favourite sport is basketball. I ³*go / play* basketball a lot. I ⁴*play for / win* my school team. This year we ⁵*scored / won* our first three matches in the national tournament. In the final, I ⁶*lost / scored* twenty points! I was really happy.

VIDEO ▶ **WIDER WORLD**

8 ▶ 28 Watch six people talking about sporting moments. Tick (✓) the competitions they mention.

☐ European Championship   ☐ Global Cup
☐ Grand National   ☐ Olympic Games
☐ World Championship   ☐ World Cup

9 In groups, talk about a sporting moment when you were really happy or sad. Use the phrases in Exercise 5.

I play for my school team and last week we … I scored … I was really happy!

I can understand a radio programme about sports.

6.6 Speaking
Talking about hobbies and interests

VIDEO ▶ **WHAT ARE YOUR HOBBIES?**

Adam: Do you play basketball?
Mia: Yes, I do. I'm very keen on sports.
Adam: Me too. Lena isn't interested in sports at all. What other things do you do in your free time, Mia?
Mia: I love fashion. I made this T-shirt myself.
Adam: It looks really cool! You're not into fashion, Lena, are you?
Lena: Well, I've got other interests.
Adam: Like what?
Lena: You know – I play the guitar, I write songs, I'm a big fan of *Mrs Myers' Mysteries* …
Adam: Are you a fan of *Mrs Myers' Mysteries*, Mia?
Mia: The TV show? No, not really.
Adam: Do you play any musical instruments?
Mia: No.
Adam: Are you into shopping?
Mia: Oh yes, I love shopping!
Adam: But Lena hates shopping. How can you two be friends? You don't like the same things!
Mia: We just like … like hanging out together?
Lena: That's it!

SOUNDS GOOD! Me too. • Like what? • That's it!

1 ▶ 29 🔊 6.18 Watch or listen. What do both Mia and Adam like doing?

2 Study the Speaking box. Find examples of the phrases in the dialogue.

SPEAKING — Talking about hobbies and interests

What are your hobbies/interests?
What do you do in your free time?
Are you into sports?

I go running/swimming.
I do a lot of sport/dancing.
I play video games/football.
I hang out with my friends.
I (don't) like running.   I love shopping.

I'm (very) keen on sports.
I'm a big fan of skateboarding/this TV show.
I'm interested in sport.   I'm (really) into fashion.
Not really.   I'm not (really) into sport.

3 Complete the text with one word in each gap.

My whole family are ¹*into* sports. My dad ²_____ running every morning. My sister's ³_____ on ice-skating – she wants to be in a TV ice-skating competition. Mum's a big ⁴_____ of exercise too. She ⁵_____ a lot of dancing and swimming. I'm interested ⁶_____ water sports.

4 🔊 6.19 Complete the dialogue with sentences a–f. Listen and check.

Kate: Are you into sports?
Jack: ¹*Yes, I am. I'm very keen on football.*
Kate: Do you play any other sports?
Jack: ²_____
Kate: What are your other hobbies and interests?
Jack: ³_____
Kate: Do you watch TV?
Jack: ⁴_____
Kate: Really? I love TV! What's your favourite game?
Jack: ⁵_____
Kate: What else do you do in your free time?
Jack: ⁶_____
Kate: Me too!

a I'm not very keen on it. I prefer video games.
b I'm really into music. I listen to it all the time.
c I do a lot of cycling and I play table tennis.
d I like hanging out with my friends.
e *Doughnut Race*! I play it every day.
f Yes, I am. I'm very keen on football.

YOUR WORLD

5 In pairs, ask and answer about your hobbies and interests. Use the Speaking box and the dialogue in Exercise 4 to help you. Tell the class about your partner.

I can talk about hobbies and interests.

6.7 Writing

A report

1 Look at the photo. What is a tug of war? Do you think it is fun? Why?/Why not?

2 Read the report and answer the questions.
1. Who wrote the report?
2. What is it about?
3. Is it a positive report in general?
4. What is the negative comment?
5. What was the best part of the day?

3 Study the Writing box. Find examples of the phrases in the report.

> **WRITING** — A report about a sports event
>
> **What, when, where**
> Last weekend/Saturday I went to a charity sports day/a football match.
> Two days ago I took part in a charity walk/run/race.
> It was/It took place in Hamilton Park.
>
> **1 Details and opinions**
> There were about/over 200 people at the event.
> There were lots of fun things to do.
> Our team won the match 3–2.
> The event/match was exciting/boring.
> The food was excellent/disappointing.
>
> **2 Best/Worst part**
> The best/worst part of the event/match was …
>
> **3 General opinion**
> In general, it was a fun/boring event.
> Overall, it was a good/terrible experience.

4 Study the Language box. Find examples of adverbs of degree in the report in Exercise 1.

> **LANGUAGE** — Adverbs of degree
>
> Use **quite**, (**not**) **very** and **really** before adjectives to comment on how good or bad something is.
> The food was **quite expensive**.
> The singing was**n't very good**.
> The match was **really exciting**.

5 Think of a sports event you went to. Write sentences about the event using adverbs from the Language box.

I went to a tennis match last June. The game was really exciting. The food wasn't very good.

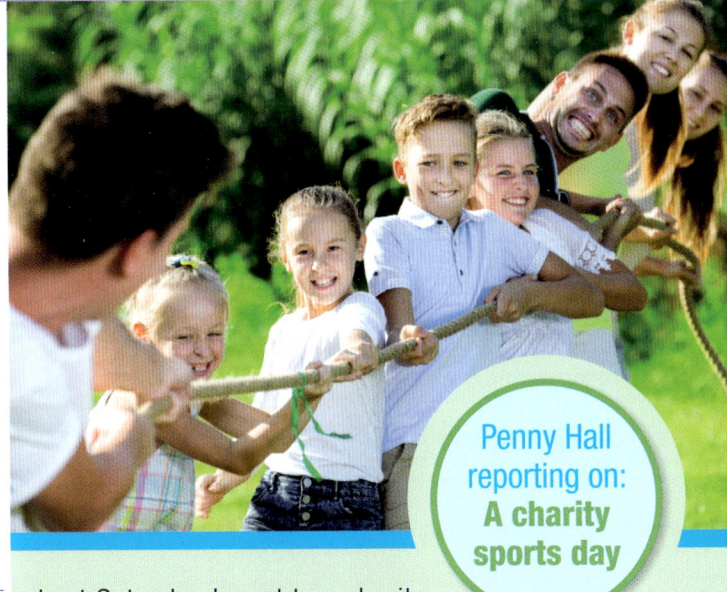

Penny Hall reporting on: A charity sports day

1. Last Saturday I went to a charity sports day. It was for the Selsby Animal Shelter and it took place in Hamilton Park. There were over 200 people at the event and lots of fun things to do. My favourite things were the tug of war and the skateboarding competition. There was also food and a local band. The band was very good, but the food was quite disappointing.

2. The best part of the day was a football match between children and parents. The children won the match 2–1. It was really exciting.

3. In general, it was a fun event and everybody enjoyed it.

WRITING TIME

6 Write a report about a sports event you attended.

1 Find ideas
Make notes for your report. Think about:
- the type of event, time and place.
- the best/worst parts of the event.
- the important details.
- your general opinion of the event.

2 Plan
Organise your ideas into paragraphs. Use Penny's report to help you.

3 Write and share
- Write a draft report. Use the Language box and the Writing box to help you.
- Share your report with another student for feedback.
- Write the final version of your report.

4 Check
- Check language: did you use the correct adjectives and adverbs of degree?
- Check grammar: are the verbs in the correct form of the Past Simple?

I can write a report.

Vocabulary Activator

WORDLIST 6.20

Sports
baseball (n)
basketball (n)
cycling (n)
football (n)
ice hockey (n)
ice-skating (n)
judo (n)
roller skating (n)
running (n)
skiing (n)
swimming (n)
tennis (n)
volleyball (n)

Sportspeople
cyclist (n)
player (n)
runner (n)
skater (n)
skier (n)
swimmer (n)

Word friends
(sports)
play a match/a sport
score a goal/a point
win a (gold) medal
win a race

Places to play sport
basketball court
football field/pitch
running track
swimming pool
tennis court

Sports competitions
cup (n)
final (n)
league (n)
semi-final (n)
tournament (n)

Word friends
(sports)
do aerobics
do exercise
do judo
go cycling
go jogging/running
go swimming
lose a game/a match
lose a tournament
play badminton
play football
play for a team
play tennis
win a game/a match
win a tournament

Extra words
ball (n)
basket (n)
be a fan of
be interested in
be into
be keen on
bike (n)
champion (n)
championship (n)
charity walk/run (n)
competition (n)
crowd (n)
disappointing (adj)
do gymnastics
event (n)
fan (n)
finish line (n)
hang out with friends
hobby (n)
hold (v)
interest (n)
jog (v)
sports day (n)
sports fanatic (n)
sportsperson (n)
stadium (n)
surf (v)
team (n)
(the) Olympics (n)
(the) World Cup (n)
train (v)
winner (n)
yoga (n)

1 Use the wordlist to find these things.
1 two sports places with the word *court*
  basketball court, …
2 three winter sports
3 five ball sports
4 five sports with races

2 Match pictures 1–9 with words from the wordlist.

1 *judo*   2 _____   3 _____
4 _____ 5 _____   6 _____
7 _____ 8 _____   9 _____

3 Choose two correct options in each item. Use the wordlist to check your answers.
1 win *a race / a medal / a goal*
2 do *judo / baseball / exercise*
3 go *cycling / running / tennis*
4 a *swimming / tennis / basketball* court

4 Complete the sentences with words from the wordlist. Then, in pairs, say if the sentences are true for you.
1 I sometimes *win* races on school sports days.
2 I often _____ cycling with my friends at the weekend.
3 My dad doesn't _____ much exercise.
4 My friend plays _____ a basketball team.
5 I hate it when my team _____ a game.

5 6.21 **PRONUNCIATION** In pairs, listen and find one word in each group with a different pronunciation from the others. Look at the underlined letters to help you.
1 f<u>i</u>nal   t<u>i</u>me   l<u>i</u>fe   t<u>i</u>cket
2 tenn<u>i</u>s   c<u>y</u>cling   sw<u>i</u>mming   p<u>i</u>tch
3 tr<u>y</u>   m<u>i</u>ss   f<u>i</u>nish   w<u>i</u>n

6 6.22 **PRONUNCIATION** Listen, check and repeat.

Unit 6 82

Revision

Vocabulary

1 Complete the sentences with one word in each gap.

1. It was a fantastic football match. The team played really well, and I scored two *goals*.

2. Before a tournament, I train for an hour a day in the gym and two hours on the tennis _____.

3. We cycle 150 kilometres a day for five days. I want to come first and _____ the race!

4. In a typical week, I go to the _____ pool twice a day, six days a week.

5. I took my shoes off at the end of the race, and I think I left them next to the running _____ !

2 Who is speaking in Exercise 1? Write the names of the sportspeople.
   1 *football player*

3 Complete the questionnaire with the words below. Then, in pairs, ask and answer the questions.

final   go   loses   matches   medals   ~~play~~   pool   team

Sports questionnaire

Sport and you
1. Do you *play* any sports? Do you play for a _____ ?
2. Do you sometimes _____ running in the park?
3. Do you live near a swimming _____ ? How often do you go swimming?

Your favourite team
4. Which is your favourite sports team? Do they usually win their _____ ?
5. How do you feel when your team _____ ?

Sport on TV
6. Did you watch the _____ of the last football World Cup?
7. Did your country win any gold _____ in the last Olympics?

Grammar

4 Choose the correct option.

The strangest race ever

The men's marathon at the 1904 Olympics ¹*was* / *were* one of the strangest races ever. ² *They / There* were thirty-two runners in the race, but only fourteen finished.

It was a very hot day and there ³ *wasn't / weren't* any water for 17 km. The roads ⁴ *was / were* full of cars and people, so it was very dangerous.

The first runner to finish ⁵ *was / were* an American, Fred Lorz. But for 18 km of the race, he ⁶ *was / were* in a car! So the winner of the gold medal ⁷ *was / were* the man in second place, Thomas Hicks. He was very ill during the race, and his team carried him over the finish line! It ⁸ *wasn't / weren't* a fast race. In fact, it was the slowest marathon in Olympic history!

5 Make sentences in the Past Simple.
1. we / walk / to school / this morning
   We walked to school this morning.
2. Sam / have / toast for breakfast
3. I / run / five kilometres / last weekend
4. Josh / text / a friend / last night
5. we / see / a good film / last week
6. they / go / to France / last summer

Speaking

6 Order the words to make questions about free time. Then, in pairs, ask and answer the questions.
1. you / into / fashion / are / ?
2. keen on / video games / are / you / ?
3. you / skateboarding / are / a fan of / ?
4. sport / you / interested in / are / ?
5. your / other hobbies / what / are / ?

A: *Are you into fashion?*
B: *Yes, I am. I love clothes!*

Dictation

7 🔊 6.23 Listen. Then listen again and write down what you hear during each pause.

Unit 6

SET FOR LIFE

Don't give up!

1 Look at the photos. How are the people feeling? Can you guess what the situation is in each photo?

2 Read the online posts. Do not read the replies yet. What problems do Sara and Matt have?

3 Read the replies to the posts. Which suggestion do you think is better? Can you think of any other suggestions?

4 🔊 6.24 Listen to Sara and Matt explaining what they did next. Complete the sentences with *Sara* or *Matt*.
1 _____ tried to solve the problem.
2 _____ walked away from the problem.
3 _____ is happy with his/her decision.
4 _____ is sorry about his/her decision.

1 SaraJane
I'm the captain of the school football team and we are TERRIBLE! We played a match at the weekend, and we lost 6–0! It's really disappointing. 😞 I don't know what to do.

Gracie909
Why don't you speak to your team? Discuss what's wrong and ask them to try harder.

JJtheGreat
That's easy – just tell them that you don't want to be captain any more. Then leave!

2 Matt07
Three of my friends are in a band. They're really good! I love playing the guitar too, but they never ask me to be in the band. 😞 I guess they need someone who can play really well – and that just isn't me at the moment. What can I do?

Simone33
Just forget about the guitar and find a new hobby!

DazB
What about looking for some guitar lessons? You can learn online for free.

Units 5–6 I can be strong when things are difficult.

Be strong in difficult situations

5 Think about a time when you had a problem like Sara's or Matt's. Complete the notes.

1 What was the problem?
_____

2 Tick (✓) the emotion(s) you felt. Were you:
☐ sad? ☐ upset? ☐ disappointed?
☐ angry? ☐ worried? ☐ calm?

3 Tick (✓) the things you did.
☐ I tried to relax.
☐ I tried to forget about the problem.
☐ I talked to someone about the problem.
☐ I tried to solve the problem on my own.
☐ I ate junk food.
☐ I did some exercise.

4 Do you think you solved the problem?
☐ Yes ☐ No

6 Which of the things you ticked in Exercise 5 helped you in your difficult situation?

7 Read the Useful Tips. In pairs, discuss the questions.
1 Think about your answers in Exercise 6. Are you strong in difficult situations?
2 Which tips can help you be stronger next time you have a problem?

SET FOR LIFE

8 In pairs, create some 'positivity cards'. Follow these steps.

1 Think of short, positive messages or instructions to help you when you meet a problem in the future.

2 Write them on small cards or design some cards digitally.

3 Add pictures or decoration if you want.

4 Present your cards to the class.

USEFUL TIPS

Problems are a normal part of life. It's important to stay positive and learn how to stay strong in difficult times.

- Find someone to talk to about your problems.
- Think about all the positive things in your life.
- Remember other problems that you solved.
- Think about the things you can change.
- Take care of yourself. Sleep, exercise and eat well.
- Find ways to relax.
- Don't give up! Stay positive!

Don't give up! You can do this!

Feeling down? Go for a walk!

LIFE IS SOMETIMES HARD. ALWAYS BE KIND TO YOURSELF!

Progress Check Units 1-6

Vocabulary and Grammar

1 Choose the correct answer.
1. Two cute baby cats with ___ eyes need a home.
   a green   b slim   c blonde
2. This ___ serves mushrooms with pasta. It's my favourite!
   a burger bar   b sandwich bar   c vegetarian café
3. I always ___ my emails before I go to bed.
   a message   b meet   c check
4. I've got a ___ to help me do my Maths homework.
   a calculator   b notebook   c poster
5. Do you ___ music? Can you play an instrument? Then why not come to music club on Wednesdays?
   a see   b enjoy   c buy
6. There are no ___ classes at the moment because there's no snow on the mountain.
   a swimming   b ice-skating   c skiing

2 Complete the text with one word in each gap.

It isn't easy to ¹*make* new friends if you are shy. I ²_____ a very quiet person at the beginning of the school year. And then I joined the basketball team. Now I'm not ³_____ shyest student in my class because I have lots of friends on the team. I really enjoy spending time ⁴_____ them. For me, a team sport is the best way to ⁵_____ to know other people. Now we're in the semi-finals and we're so busy! I'm working hard but I'm happier ⁶_____ I was before.

3 Complete the sentences with the correct form of the words in brackets.
1. This Geography textbook is very *interesting* (INTEREST). Do you want to read it?
2. Beyoncé is my favourite _____ (SING).
3. There's a great _____ (ITALY) pizzeria near here. Are you hungry?
4. Anita is a very good _____ (RUN). She always wins all her races.
5. Gerry is my cat. He's very _____ (FRIEND).
6. I was _____ (RELAX) last week because I was on holiday.

Speaking

4 Match questions 1–5 with responses a–f. There is one extra response.
1. ☐ Are you into water sports?
2. ☐ What would you like?
3. ☐ What kind of sports do you like?
4. ☐ Can I borrow your ruler?
5. ☐ What do you do in your free time?

a I really like team sports.
b I play the trumpet.
c Sorry, I'm using it.
d No, not really.
e Great idea.
f I'd like a strawberry smoothie, please.

5 In pairs, do the speaking task.
Student A: Go to page 137.
Student B: Go to page 138.

Listening

6 In pairs, answer the questions.
1. What time do you start and finish school every day?
2. How many students are there in your school?
3. Do you have a break for lunch? How long is it?

7 🔊 PC1–6.1 Listen and complete the notes with a word or a short phrase.

Kent Secondary School News
Number of students in Year 8: ¹*113*
Lunchtime: ²_____
Price of school lunches: ³_____
Sports in the new gym building: ⁴_____
When courses start: ⁵_____

Reading

And the winner is …

What do you do in your free time? I sing in a group. In the past I preferred swimming, but my best friend Millie joined the group two years ago and she liked it a lot, so I decided to try. Now I would like to become a singer in the future!

There were only eight people in the group when I started, but now there are thirty singers. We sing pop and rock songs. We learn new songs every month, but there are popular songs that we sing at every concert. We meet twice a week and sing for an hour. I'd like to sing for two or three hours – I'm never tired!

Singing in a group is amazing. You can learn how to sing and make some good friends. But what I really enjoy is taking part in competitions. It's so exciting to travel to new places and spend time with people who have the same passion!

Last month we were in the final of the *Let's Sing!* music competition. On the day of the final, I was relaxed, but Millie was really nervous. She likes singing on stage for an audience, so that wasn't the problem, but she gets stressed before competitions because she doesn't enjoy them. Our music teacher always helps us when we feel stressed. She told Millie, 'It's OK. You can do it!' And can you guess? We were the best group there!

8 Read the article and choose the correct answer.
1. The author joined the singing group because
   a she wanted to become a singer.
   b she wanted to try a different hobby.
   c her best friend joined.
2. The author says that
   a the group never sings popular songs.
   b the meetings are too long.
   c the number of people in the group changed.
3. For the author, the best thing about singing in a group is
   a learning how to sing.
   b singing in competitions.
   c meeting new people.
4. Millie was nervous on the day of the final because
   a she isn't very good at singing.
   b she doesn't like being on stage.
   c she doesn't like competitions.

Writing

9 In pairs, look at the photos. Which musical event do you prefer? Why?

A

B

10 Write a report about a musical event. Write about these things.
- what kind of event it was and where it took place
- how many people there were and what you did
- what you liked or did not like about the event

The digital age

7

VOCABULARY
Computers and technology | Dates in history | Everyday technology | Using a smartphone

GRAMMAR
Past Simple: negative | Past Simple: questions and short answers

7.1 Vocabulary
History and technology

THE HISTORY OF COMPUTERS

How much do you know about the history of computers? Try our quiz to find out!

1 In the nineteenth century, an English engineer designed a machine that could do maths. People call him 'the father of the computer'. His name was Charles _____ .

a Chaplin   b Darwin   c Babbage

2 Today's computers are small enough to fit in our hands, but the first computer in 1945 was as big as _____ .

a a car
b a large room
c a football stadium

3 In 1992, IBM invented Simon – the world's first _____ . It had a screen, a keyboard and an address book, but the battery life was only one hour!

a smartphone
b tablet
c printer

4 In 1964, Doug Engelbart made the first computer mouse. He made it out of _____ .

a wood
b metal
c glass

5 Fifty years ago, Steve Jobs built the first Apple computer in _____ . Now, Apple is one of the biggest companies in the world!

a his parents' garage
b his bedroom
c his science class at school

6 In 1993, Aleksandr Serebrov became the first person to play on a games console _____ .

a on Mount Kilimanjaro
b underwater
c in space

7 The first laptop, the Osborne 1, appeared in the _____ . It had a very small screen (just 12 cm) and it was very heavy (11 kg), but a lot of people bought it!

a 1960s   b 1980s   c 1990s

8 In 1969, the astronauts on Apollo 11 used a computer to land on the moon. Today's smartphones are _____ times faster than that computer.

a a hundred   b a thousand   c a million

Unit 7

1 **I KNOW!** What technology do you use at home and at school? In two minutes, write down as many items as you can.

2 🔊 7.1 Study Vocabulary box A. Which items can you see in the photos below?

VOCABULARY A ▸ **Computers and technology**

computer   games console   headphones   keyboard
laptop   mouse   printer   screen   smartphone   tablet

1
2
3
4
5
6

3 Complete the definitions with words from Vocabulary box A.
1 A *laptop* is a small computer. The screen closes over the keyboard.
2 You wear _____ on your ears to listen to music.
3 You use a _____ to write words on a computer.
4 You use a _____ to print information from a computer.
5 You use a _____ to move around a computer screen.
6 A _____ is smaller than a laptop. You don't use a mouse – you use your fingers on the screen.

4 In pairs, do the quiz on page 88. Then go to page 137 and check your answers.

5 In pairs, find the Past Simple forms of the verbs below in the quiz. Then complete the table.

~~appear~~   ~~become~~   build   buy   design
invent   make   use

Regular verbs	Irregular verbs
appear – appeared	*become – became*
_____	_____
_____	_____
_____	_____

6 🔊 7.2 Study Vocabulary box B. Order the phrases from the oldest to the most recent. Listen and check.

VOCABULARY B ▸ **Dates in history**

☐ in 2004   ☐ in 1993   ☐ in the 1960s
☐ in the nineteenth century   ☐ fifty years ago

7 Read the article. Complete the time expressions and write the Past Simple form of the verbs in brackets.

THE HISTORY OF VIDEO GAMES

- In ^{1}*the* 1970s, computer programmers ^{2}*invented* (invent) the first electronic games. People played on special machines in shopping centres and restaurants.

- ^{3}_____ 1975, an American company ^{4}_____ (make) the first games console for the home. There was only one game!

- About forty years ^{5}_____, Nintendo® ^{6}_____ (build) *Super Mario Bros*. Millions of people bought the games.

- At the end of the twentieth ^{7}_____, more people ^{8}_____ (have) computers at home. Games were more exciting and realistic.

- The first smartphones with an internet connection ^{9}_____ (appear) about twenty ^{10}_____ ago. Mobile games became very popular.

Today, people play games on consoles, tablets and smartphones, at home, outside – everywhere! What's the future of games? Who knows?

YOUR WORLD

8 In pairs, talk about:
- the items of technology you use a lot.
- when you got them.
- what you like about them.

I use my games console a lot, especially at the weekend. I got it two years ago. I like it because …

I can talk about computers and technology and dates in history.

7.2 Grammar

Past Simple: negative

NOTTINGHAM IN THE FOURTEENTH CENTURY

POSTS

Carlos: Wow! Guys, look at this picture from a website about the history of Nottingham! Nottingham had a castle in the Middle Ages, but it didn't have a station! 😯

Olivia: Also, people wore shoes or boots in the Middle Ages, but they didn't wear trainers. And people didn't say 'cool' in the Middle Ages! 😃

Paul: Children ate cakes in the fourteenth century, but they didn't drink orange juice!

Lottie: LOL! You saw dogs and pigs in towns in the fourteenth century, but you didn't see chihuahuas.

1 In pairs, talk about the oldest buildings in your town. What are they? When do they date from?

The Old Town dates from the Middle Ages.
I think the castle dates from the 1800s.

2 🔊 7.3 In pairs, look at the picture above. What is strange about it? Read the comments and check.

3 Study the Grammar box. Find more examples of Past Simple negatives in the comments.

> **GRAMMAR** **Past Simple: negative**
>
> It **didn't have** a station.
> People **wore** boots, but they **didn't wear** trainers.
> Children **played** games, but they **didn't play** on smartphones.
>
> GRAMMAR TIME > PAGE 132

4 In pairs, make more sentences about the mistakes in the picture. Use the ideas below to help you.

> bananas   buses   cameras   helicopters
> plastic bottles   smartphones   sunglasses   tractors
> trainers   T-shirts   TVs   video games

People didn't wear/eat/use/play/drive … in the Middle Ages.
They didn't have … in the fourteenth century.
You didn't see … in the Middle Ages.

5 Complete the sentences with the Past Simple form of the verbs in brackets.
1. I <u>walked</u> (walk) to the shops, but I _____ (not buy) anything.
2. Lily _____ (have) a shower this morning, but she _____ (not wash) her hair.
3. Last night Oliver _____ (go) to bed early, but he _____ (not sleep) well.
4. We _____ (work) hard yesterday, but we _____ (not feel) tired.
5. They _____ (come) to the party on Saturday, but they _____ (not stay) long.
6. Chloe _____ (tell) me what to do, but I _____ (not understand).

VIDEO — WIDER WORLD

6 ▶ 30 Watch five people talking about what they did last night. Write down the places and activities they mention.

7 In pairs, talk about what you did/didn't do last night. Use the ideas below or your own.

> do homework   go to bed early   have a shower
> listen to music   see a film   stay at home
> talk to friends   watch TV

Last night I did homework. I didn't see a film. …

I can use the Past Simple to talk about what did and didn't happen in the past.

7.3 Reading and Vocabulary
Everyday technology

1 Do you save energy at home? How? Discuss in pairs.

2 🔊 7.4 Study the Vocabulary box. Match the items in the box with the rooms where you usually find them. Sometimes more than one answer is possible.

bathroom   bedroom   kitchen   living room   study

> **VOCABULARY** → Everyday technology
>
> charger   cooker   electric toothbrush   fridge   hairdryer
> speaker   toaster   washing machine

3 In pairs, say which of the things in the Vocabulary box you often/never use.

4 🔊 7.5 **WORD FRIENDS** Write the words below in the correct group. Some words can go in both groups.

cooker   electric toothbrush   hairdryer
phone   speaker

1 turn on/turn off: _cooker,_ _____
_____

2 charge: _____
_____

5 🔊 7.6 Read the article and choose the best title.
a Is technology bad for you?
b What can you do to help the planet?
c Can new technology save the planet?

6 Read the article again. Choose the correct answer.
1 What is the author's opinion of technology?
  a Our lives are worse because of technology.
  b There are good and bad things about technology.
  c We need to stop using all technology to save the planet.
2 What did Lottie do last week?
  a She didn't use any electricity at home for an hour.
  b She didn't use any electricity at school all week.
  c She used less electricity at school than usual.
3 What does Sam think?
  a People buy more things than they need.
  b All of the Earth's pollution comes from factories.
  c It's better to buy new things than second-hand things.

YOUR WORLD

7 Imagine you can only charge or turn on one thing in your home. What do you choose? Why? In pairs, compare your answers.

☐ fridge ☐ light
☐ washing machine ☐ cooker
☐ computer ☐ electric toothbrush
☐ smartphone ☐ games console

Simple ideas can make a big difference! So, what are YOU doing?

150 years ago people didn't have fridges, washing machines or smartphones. We didn't drive cars or fly in aeroplanes. Now the world is full of technology. It makes our lives easier, but it creates a lot of problems for our planet and its climate. What can we do? The good news is you don't need to completely stop using your fridge or smartphone to help the planet! We spoke to two teenagers with some great ideas.

Lottie
Last week, my school had a Zero Power Hour. We turned off everything that uses electricity – computers, lights, printers – for an hour every day. At home, I turned off the lights every time I left a room. And I didn't turn on the heater in my bedroom – I just wore a sweater!

Sam
My friends and I organised a second-hand sale. We spend billions of pounds on clothes, electronics and games, then we throw them away. Factories create a lot of pollution when they make new things. We don't need more, we just need to repair and share the things that we already have.

I can understand an article about everyday technology.

7.4 Grammar

Past Simple: questions and short answers

VIDEO ▶ HOW STRANGE!

Lena: Dad, I can't find my hairdryer.
Dad: Well, don't look at me. I haven't got it.
Lena: Can you help me find it? I'm late for school!
Dad: OK. When did you last use it?
Lena: Yesterday morning. It was next to my bed.
Dad: Did you look under the bed?
Lena: Yes, I did. I searched my whole room. It's not there.
Dad: Did Mum take it?
Lena: I don't know. She's in the shower.
Mum: No, I'm here now. What is it?
Lena: Did you take my hairdryer?
Mum: No, I didn't. But that's funny. I can't find my hairdryer either. Did you put it somewhere, Alex?
Dad: Your hairdryer? No, I didn't. How strange! Who's taking all the hairdryers?
All: Adam!
Lena: Adam, did you take our hairdryers?
Adam: Er, yes, I did. I'm using them.
Lena: But why, Adam? What did you do?
Adam: I dropped a cup of tea on my trousers, so I'm drying them! Here you are – all finished! Right, time for school. Don't be late, Lena!
Lena: Aargh!

1 ▶ 31 🔊 7.7 Watch or listen. What is Lena looking for? Who has got it and why?

2 Study the Grammar box. Find more examples of Past Simple questions and short answers in the dialogue.

GRAMMAR — Past Simple: questions and short answers

Did you look under the bed?   Yes, I did./No, I didn't.
Did Adam take Lena's hairdryer? Yes, he did./No, he didn't.
When did you last use it?

GRAMMAR TIME > PAGE 132

3 In pairs, order the words to make questions about your morning. Then ask and answer the questions.
1 get up early / you / did / ?
2 you / have / a shower / did / ?
3 your hair / wash / you / did / ?
4 did / you / for breakfast / have / what / ?
5 walk / you / did / to school / ?
6 arrive / what time / you / at school / did / ?

A: *Did you get up early?*
B: *Yes, I did! I got up at half past six.*

4 Complete the questions with the Past Simple form of the verbs below.

go   have   ~~learn~~   live   see   start

1 *Did you learn* (you) English at primary school?
2 Which primary school _____ (you) to?
3 _____ (you) nice teachers there?
4 When _____ (you) secondary school?
5 _____ (your family) in a different house/flat when you were little?
6 _____ (you/often) your grandparents when you were little?

5 Match questions 1–6 in Exercise 4 with answers a–f below.
a ☐ I went to Aston Primary School.
b ☐ No, we didn't. We learned Spanish.
c ☐ No, I didn't. They lived a long way from our house.
d ☐ I started a year and a half ago.
e ☐ Yes, we did. We lived in London.
f ☐ Yes, I did. They were very friendly.

YOUR WORLD

6 In pairs, ask and answer the questions in Exercise 4. Tell the class about your partner.

Jacob went to Manor Primary School. …

Unit 7 92 I can use the Past Simple to ask and answer questions about the past.

7.5 Listening and Vocabulary
When I was younger

The terrific 2010s

Did you enjoy being a child in the 2010s? Share your memories here! Here are some of mine.

I loved *The Penguins of Madagascar*!

My first ever mobile phone!

Games and more on my smart watch!

Usain Bolt – the fastest man on Earth!

High-tops – comfortable and cool!

Camila Cabello was the sound of the summer!

1 In pairs, look at the webpage. How many of the things/people in the photos do you know?

2 🔊 7.8 Listen and match the speakers (1–3) with the questions they answer (a–f). There are two questions for each speaker.
- a ☐ Who was your idol when you were seven or eight?
- b ☐ Did you have a favourite singer or group when you were little?
- c ☐ Which cartoons did you like?
- d ☐ What was your first phone like? What did you do with it?
- e ☐ What toys did you like best?
- f ☐ Do you remember any fashion from when you were younger?

3 🔊 7.8 Listen again and write down the speakers' answers to the questions in Exercise 2.

4 🔊 7.9 **WORD FRIENDS** Complete the phrases with the verbs below. Listen and check. What other things can you do with a smartphone?

| count | download | get | ~~look up~~ |
| make | take | text | use |

1 *look up* information
2 _____ directions
3 _____ a friend
4 _____ steps
5 _____ a call
6 _____ games
7 _____ the internet
8 _____ a selfie/ a photo

5 Complete the questions with words from Exercise 4. Then, in pairs, ask and answer the questions.

What do you use your phone for?
1 How often do you *take* photos on your phone? What of?
2 What kind of games do you _____ on your phone? What's your favourite game?
3 Do you often _____ up information online? Which websites do you use?
4 How often do you _____ your friends?
5 Do you _____ your steps? How many steps do you take a day?
6 Do you sometimes _____ directions with your phone? Where to?

VIDEO **WIDER WORLD**

6 ▶ 32 Watch five people answering the questions in Exercise 2. Write down the things and people they mention.

7 In pairs, talk about when you were younger. Ask and answer the questions in Exercise 2.

Barack Obama was my idol when I was younger.

I can understand an interview about childhood.

7.6 Speaking

Agreeing and disagreeing

VIDEO ▶ I DON'T AGREE

Mateo: Hi, Noah. Are you OK?
Noah: Not really. I had an argument with Mia this morning and I'm texting her to say 'sorry'.
Mateo: That's probably a good idea, but don't text her, call her. It's friendlier.
Noah: I'm not sure. I want to think about what to say. It's easier to write it in a text.
Mateo: Perhaps that's true, but you can call her and still think about what you want to say first.
Noah: Maybe you're right, but I'm shy, so I think a text is better.
Mateo: Sorry, but I don't agree. I think texts are good for making plans or for funny messages …
Noah: That's true.
Mateo: … but for more serious things, it's better to talk.
Noah: OK, I agree.
Mateo: Look, here's Mia. Just say 'sorry' to her. Don't think about it so much.
Mia: Hi, guys. How are things?
Noah: Hi, Mia. I'm really sorry about this morning. I was wrong.
Mia: Oh, don't worry about it!
Mateo: There, that was easy!
Noah: You're right!

SOUNDS GOOD! Are you OK? • Hi, guys. • Don't worry about it!

1 Do you often text your friends? When and why do you text them?

2 ▶ 33 🔊 7.10 Watch or listen and answer the questions.
1 Who is Noah texting? Why?
2 What is Mateo's suggestion?
3 Is Mia angry at the end of the story?

3 Do you think Mateo's suggestion is good? Is it better to text or talk after an argument? Why?

SET FOR LIFE

4 What do you do after an argument with someone? Discuss in pairs. Use the ideas below. What is the best thing to do?
- I always say 'sorry'.
- I wait for the other person to say 'sorry'.
- I don't say anything.
- I do something nice for the other person.

5 Study the Speaking box. Find examples of the phrases in the dialogue.

SPEAKING Agreeing and disagreeing

Agreeing
I agree.
I think so too.
That's true.
You're right.

Maybe
Maybe you're right, but …
Perhaps that's true, but …
I'm not sure.

Disagreeing
(Sorry, but) I don't agree/I disagree.

6 🔊 7.11 Complete the dialogue with one word in each gap. Use the Speaking box to help you.

Mum: Teenagers spend too much time on their smartphones these days.
Dad: I think [1] _so_ too. They don't hang out with friends anymore!
Girl: Sorry, but I [2] _____ agree. Smartphones are really useful.
Mum: Maybe you're [3] _____ , but people don't go out. They prefer to stay inside and look at their phones.
Girl: Perhaps that's [4] _____ . Come on then, let's go for a walk.
Mum: OK. I just need to check my phone first!

YOUR WORLD

7 In pairs, take it in turns to read these statements to your partner. Does he/she agree? Use the Speaking box and Exercise 6 to help you.
- We can't live without computers.
- Social media is bad for young people.
- Homework is a bad idea.

Unit 7 94 I can agree and disagree with someone.

7.7 Writing

An email

1. Read Matt's email and tick (✓) the things he writes about.
   1. ☐ what he did yesterday/today
   2. ☐ plans for the future
   3. ☐ funny or surprising news

---

① Hi Sarah,

② How are you? I tried to call but there was no answer. Did your exam go OK?

③ Grandma came to stay yesterday. This morning we went to the Science Museum. We saw Sir Tim Berners-Lee's computer. He used it to invent the World Wide Web! Then we took a virtual reality trip through space – it was really exciting! After that, we went to a pizzeria for lunch, before going home.

④ Guess what! I've got a new phone. Well, it isn't new – it's my dad's old phone, but it's much better than my old one. The camera is amazing!

⑤ Call me!

⑥ Take care,
Matt

---

2. Study the Writing box. Find examples of the phrases in Matt's email.

WRITING — An email with personal news

① Greetings
Hi Sarah,/Hi Auntie Lynne,

② Ask for news
How are you?   Did your exam go OK?
Did you have a nice birthday?

③ Give your news from the last few days
Grandma came to stay yesterday.
I saw a film with some friends last night.
Next/Then/After that …

④ Add some funny/surprising news
Guess what! I've got a new phone.
A funny thing happened yesterday. I …

⑤ Closing sentence
See you soon.   Write soon.   Call me.

⑥ Ending
Lots of love,   Take care,   Best wishes,

3. In pairs, find examples of the Past Simple in Matt's email.

4. Study the Language box. Then complete the sentences below with one missing word and the Past Simple form of the verbs in brackets.

LANGUAGE — Past time expressions

We often use these time expressions with the Past Simple.
Yesterday …   At the weekend …
On Saturday/Monday night/Friday morning …
Last Tuesday/weekend/week …
Two days/A month ago …

1. What _did you do_ (you/do) _yesterday_ ?
2. _____ Saturday afternoon I _____ (see) my cousins.
3. I _____ (have) a party a week _____ .
4. _____ the weekend, we _____ (go) for a walk.
5. _____ (you/have) a good time on your holiday _____ week?

WRITING TIME

5. Write an informal email to a friend with your news from last week.

1 Find ideas
Make notes for your email. Think about:
- what you did last week.
- something funny or surprising that happened to you.

2 Plan
Organise your ideas into paragraphs. Use Matt's email to help you.

3 Write and share
- Write a draft email. Use the Language box and the Writing box to help you.
- Share your email with another student for feedback.
- Write the final version of your email.

4 Check
- Check language: are the past time expressions correct?
- Check grammar: are most verbs in the Past Simple?

I can write an email.

Vocabulary Activator

WORDLIST 🔊 7.12

Computers and technology
computer (n)
games console (n)
headphones (n)
keyboard (n)
laptop (n)
mouse (n)
printer (n)
screen (n)
smartphone (n)
tablet (n)

Dates in history
fifty years ago
in 1993
in 2004
in the 1960s
in the nineteenth century

Everyday technology
charger (n)
cooker (n)
electric toothbrush (n)
fridge (n)
hairdryer (n)
speaker (n)
toaster (n)
washing machine (n)

Word friends (using technology)
charge a phone/an electric toothbrush
turn off a toaster/speaker
turn on a hairdryer/charger

Word friends (using a smartphone)
count steps
download games
get directions
look up information
make a call
take a selfie
take a photo
text a friend
use the internet

Extra words
appear (v)
astronaut (n)

battery (life) (n)
become popular
build (v)
camera (n)
company (n)
computer programmer (n)
create problems
dangerous (adj)
design (v)
electricity (n)
electronic game (n)
engineer (n)
factory (n)
go out (v)
heater (n)
heavy (adj)
invent (v)
land on the moon
light (n)
machine (n)
make a (big) difference
make life easier
message (n)
Middle Ages (n)

scientist (n)
social media network (n)
planet (n)
plastic (n)
pollution (n)
print (v)
repair (v)
science museum (n)
share (v)
smart watch (n)
social media (n)
take care
text (n)
throw away (v)
toy (n)
use (v)
useful (adj)
virtual reality (n)
webpage (n)
website (n)

---

1 Use the wordlist to find these things.
1 five items of technology you can play games on *computer, …*
2 three items of technology you usually find in a kitchen
3 two things you can use with a smartphone to listen to music
4 one item of technology you usually find in a bathroom

2 What can you do with these smartphone apps? Match them with phrases from the wordlist.
1 *use the internet*

3 Match 1–6 with a–f to make words. Check your answers in the wordlist. Then choose three words and write true sentences about you.
1 [c] head   a top
2 [ ] key   b brush
3 [ ] lap   c phones
4 [ ] smart   d dryer
5 [ ] tooth   e board
6 [ ] hair   f phone

I often use headphones to listen to music.

4 In pairs, discuss the questions. Use the wordlist to help you.
1 Which electronic devices do you find the most useful in your home?
2 What can you do to save energy at home?
3 What was your first smartphone/computer like? What did you use it for?

5 🔊 7.13 **PRONUNCIATION** Listen to the words below and write them in the correct column according to the word stress.

| become   cartoon   cooker   headphones |
| invent   laptop   machine   printer |

1 Oo	2 oO
cooker	become

6 🔊 7.14 **PRONUNCIATION** Listen, check and repeat.

Revision

Vocabulary

1 Choose the correct answer.

NEWS   **ARTICLES**   HOME

The history of the smartphone

The first smartphone appeared many years ¹____ , near the end of the ² ____ century. You could use it to ³ ____ a call or send an email, but you couldn't look ⁴ ____ information on the internet. ⁵ ____ 2007, Apple designed the iPhone. Suddenly, people could use their phone to play music, ⁶ ____ photos, watch movies, ⁷ ____ directions, and much more. And to do all of these things, you simply touched the ⁸ ____ with your finger! It was amazing!

1	a ago	b past	c before
2	a twenty	b twenties	c twentieth
3	a make	b do	c go
4	a in	b up	c on
5	a In	b At	c On
6	a do	b make	c take
7	a make	b get	c do
8	a mouse	b printer	c screen

2 Complete the sentences with the correct technology words.
1. You wash your clothes in a *washing machine*.
2. You use an _____ to clean your teeth.
3. You put food in a _____ to keep it cold.
4. You use a _____ to make dinner.
5. To play loud music at a party, you need a _____ .
6. You can make toast in a _____ .
7. You dry your hair with a _____ .
8. You use a _____ when the battery on your phone is low.

3 Choose the correct option. Then choose two time expressions and write true sentences about you.
1. I got my first smartphone *six months ago* / *last six months*.
2. Emma started primary school *in* / *at* 2014.
3. I'm not sure, but I think we moved to our house *in 2010s* / *in the 2010s*.
4. A Scottish scientist, Alan MacMasters, invented the electric toaster in the *nineteen* / *nineteenth* century.

Grammar

4 Complete the sentences with the Past Simple form of the verbs in brackets.
When I was eight years old:
1. I *had* (have) a tablet, but I _____ (not have) a phone.
2. I _____ (listen) to a lot of music, but I _____ (not listen) to rap.
3. I _____ (not go) to school by bus. My mum _____ (take) me in her car.
4. I _____ (eat) most food, but I _____ (not like) green vegetables.
5. I _____ (play) video games, but I _____ (not play) online with friends.

5 Complete the questions. Then, in pairs, ask and answer the questions.
1. *Did you have* (you / have) a good night's sleep?
2. What time _____ (you / get up) this morning?
3. What _____ (you / have) for breakfast?
4. _____ (you / leave) home before your parents?
5. How _____ (you / come) to school?
6. Where _____ (you / go) after school yesterday?

A: Did you have a good night's sleep?
B: No, I didn't. I had a terrible night's sleep!

Speaking

6 In pairs, follow the instructions below. Then swap roles.
- Student A: make a sentence that is true for you using the ideas below.
- Student B: agree or disagree with Student A's opinion.

cartoons		useful
social media		dangerous
History lessons		brilliant
electric toothbrushes	is	fun
the 2010s	are	cool
games consoles	were	expensive
smartphones		boring
the twenty-first century		exciting

A: I think cartoons are cool.
B: I don't agree. I think they're boring.

Dictation

7 🔊 7.15 Listen. Then listen again and write down what you hear during each pause.

BBC CULTURE

Museums of the future

The living past

When you think of museums, what image do you see? Lots of old things behind glass? Well, maybe it's time to look again!

1 In the past, people went to museums just to look at exhibits and to read information. It was quite serious – and maybe a little boring too! But museums in the twenty-first century are changing. People still want to learn about the past, but now they want to really experience it too!

2 Some museums are 'living museums'. When you go there, you can walk down streets from the past, visit old shops and have conversations with people from history (well, actors in costumes!). Sleepovers are popular at museums too – bring a sleeping bag, listen to stories of the past, then sleep among the dinosaurs!

3 Other museums have the latest technology. In the past, museums only used 'audio guides', but now some of them can offer their visitors a special app. When you look through your phone or tablet at an exhibit, you can see what it looked like when it was new. You can also find games and quizzes on museum apps.

---

exhibit (n) an object that people go to see in a museum
experience (v) when you experience something, it happens to you
sleeping bag (n) a long, soft bag you can sleep in
sleepover (n) when a group of young people stay all night and sleep at someone's house

---

1 In pairs, discuss the questions.
1 What are some famous museums in your country?
2 Can you name any other museums in the world?
3 When was the last time you went to a museum? Where was it? What did you see?

2 Look at the photo. What do you think is special or different about this museum?

3 🔊 7.16 Read the article and match headings a–d with paragraphs 1–3. There is one extra heading.
a ☐ Going digital
b ☐ Museums then and now
c ☐ Museums in crisis
d ☐ Getting close to history

4 **VISIBLE THINKING** Follow these steps.
THINK
1 Think about museums in general and make notes. What is your opinion? Why? Use the adjectives below to help you. Then do the same for a museum you know.

> amazing   boring   exciting
> fun   interesting   unusual

I think most museums are boring because you can't touch anything.

PAIR
2 In pairs, tell each other what you think and why.
SHARE
3 Share your opinions with the class and listen to other students' ideas. Are they similar to yours?

BBC ▶ Museums in the UK

5 Look at the photo from a video about museums in the UK. In pairs, discuss the questions.
1 What sort of museum do you think this is?
2 When did people live in houses like this?
3 What do you think is inside?

6 ▶ 34 Watch the video and check your answers to Exercise 5.

7 ▶ 34 Watch the video again. Match the museums below with descriptions 1–4.

☐ HMS Caroline
☐ The London Motorcycle Museum
☐ The Pitt Rivers Museum   ☐ St Fagans

1 a traditional museum in Oxford
2 a museum in London that closed
3 a ship from the First World War
4 an outdoor museum in Wales

8 Which of the museums from the video would you like to visit? Why?

PROJECT TIME

9 In groups of three, create a digital presentation about an interesting museum. Follow these steps.

1 In your group, choose a museum. Decide who can find the answers to these questions.
- Where is the museum? How old is it? Is it traditional or modern?
- What type of exhibits does it have? Which are its most famous exhibits?
- How many people visit it every year? Why is it popular?

2 Individually, create your part of the presentation.
- Find information and photos for your slides.
- Decide on the titles of the slides.
- For each slide, write a short text and add the photos.

3 In your group, create your presentation. You can use a presentation program.
- Put the slides together and think of a title.
- Check and edit your presentation.
- Practise giving the presentation as a group.

4 Share your presentation with the class.
- Answer other students' questions.
- Ask questions and comment on the other presentations.

Our world

8

VOCABULARY
Geography | Learning languages | Communicating | Verb + preposition collocations

GRAMMAR
Modal verbs: *have to/don't have to, mustn't* | Articles: first and second mention

8.1 Vocabulary
Geography

Teen travel guide

COUNTRIES | CONTINENTS | GAMES AND COMPETITIONS | FUN FACTS

Join our competition!
Tell us about an unusual place you know.

Crater Lake is one of the most beautiful lakes in North America and the deepest lake in the United States (around 350 m). It sits at the top of a mountain, Mount Mazama, which is also a volcano. The lake formed 7,770 years ago, when the top of the volcano fell in and the hole filled with water. Because it is so deep and its waters are so clear, the lake is an amazing dark blue colour. I really want to go there one day!

Angie, 14

I'm from Büsingen, a German village. What is unusual about it? Büsingen is not in Germany. It's in Switzerland! So, although our village belongs to one country (Germany), it is geographically inside another country (Switzerland). In Büsingen, we have two postcodes (Swiss and German), we use both German and Swiss money (euros and Swiss francs) and our phone numbers are German or Swiss. There's even a street where one side is in Germany and the other is in Switzerland!

Elias, 13

Tashirojima is an unusual island in Japan because its cat population is about six times bigger than the human population! People believe that cats bring good luck, so they feed them and look after them. My family and I went there two years ago. We stayed in a place in the south – it has holiday houses in the shape of a cat!

Izumi, 15

1 Look at the photos on page 100. Which place looks most interesting to you? Why?

2 Read the texts on page 100 and answer the questions.
  1 Who lives in the place he/she writes about?
  2 Who visited the place in the past?
  3 Who would like to visit the place in the future?

3 🔊 8.1 Study the Vocabulary box. Which of the words can you find in the texts?

VOCABULARY — Geography

Compass points
east north south west

Continents
Africa Antarctica Asia Australia Europe
North America South America

Countries
capital city flag language money population village

Nature
island lake mountain ocean river sea volcano

4 In groups, decide if the sentences are true (T) or false (F). Go to page 137 and check. Which group has the highest score?

FAST GEOGRAPHY FACTS
True or false?

1 ___ The capital of Brazil is Rio de Janeiro.
2 ___ The word for Mexican money is *real*.
3 ___ The Japanese flag is red with a white circle.
4 ___ Switzerland has four official languages.
5 ___ Australia is both a country and a continent.
6 ___ Antarctica is north of Australia.
7 ___ The Niger River is in South America.
8 ___ There are no mountains in Denmark.
9 ___ The Atlantic is the biggest ocean on Earth.
10 ___ Vesuvius is a volcano in Italy.

5 Complete the online post with the correct form of words from the Vocabulary box.

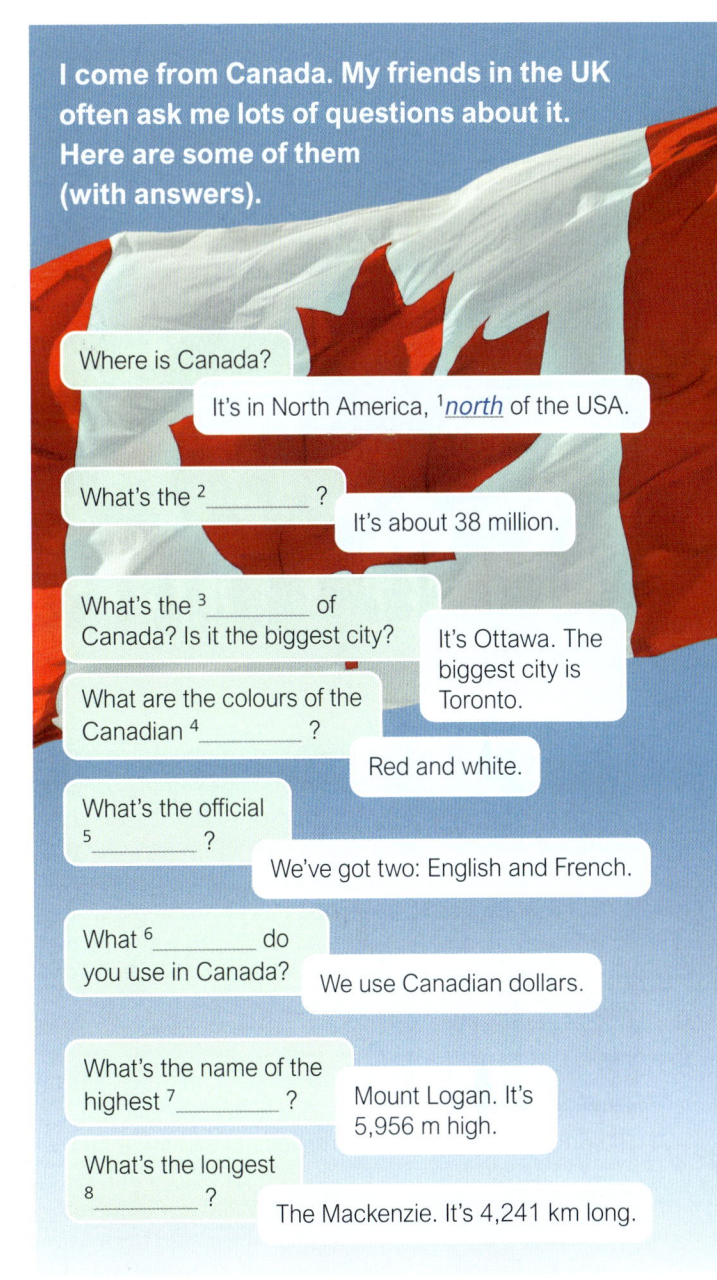

I come from Canada. My friends in the UK often ask me lots of questions about it. Here are some of them (with answers).

Where is Canada?
It's in North America, ¹*north* of the USA.

What's the ² _____ ?
It's about 38 million.

What's the ³ _____ of Canada? Is it the biggest city?
It's Ottawa. The biggest city is Toronto.

What are the colours of the Canadian ⁴ _____ ?
Red and white.

What's the official ⁵ _____ ?
We've got two: English and French.

What ⁶ _____ do you use in Canada?
We use Canadian dollars.

What's the name of the highest ⁷ _____ ?
Mount Logan. It's 5,956 m high.

What's the longest ⁸ _____ ?
The Mackenzie. It's 4,241 km long.

VIDEO — **WIDER WORLD**

6 ▶ 35 Watch five people talking about their countries. Match names 1–5 with flags a–e.
1 ☐ Lara   3 ☐ Akwasi   5 ☐ Renae
2 ☐ Matt   4 ☐ Junko

a b c d e

7 In pairs, ask and answer the questions in Exercise 5 about your country or another country you know well.

I can talk about different places.

8.2 Grammar

Modal verbs: *have to/don't have to, mustn't*

1 🔊 8.2 Read paragraph A of the article. Which country has the most surprising rule?

Cultural dos and don'ts

A

When you travel, you have to know about the cultural rules in the countries you visit. For example, in China you have to take a present with two hands, but in the USA you don't have to use two hands to accept a present – one is fine. In Spain, in the summer, many people have a siesta after lunch. You don't have to sleep, but you have to be quiet. And in Britain you have to wait in a queue for everything and you mustn't go in front of other people.

B

In Japan you ¹*have to / mustn't* take off your shoes when you visit someone's home. But in France you ²*have to / don't have to* take off your shoes – you can keep them on. Austrians are very punctual, so you ³*don't have to / mustn't* be late for a meeting in Vienna. In Germany you ⁴*have to / don't have to* wait for the green light to walk across the street, but in Egypt you ⁵*have to / don't have to* wait – you can cross any time! And in Singapore you ⁶*have to / mustn't* chew gum in public.

2 Study the Grammar box. Find more examples of *have to, don't have to* and *mustn't* in paragraph A of the article.

GRAMMAR — Modal verbs: *have to/don't have to, mustn't*

You **have to** be quiet. = It's necessary.
You **don't have to** sleep. = It isn't necessary.
You **mustn't** be late. = Don't do it!

GRAMMAR TIME ▶ PAGE 133

3 🔊 8.3 Read paragraph B of the article and choose the correct option. Listen and check.

4 🔊 8.4 Listen and complete the sentences with *have to, don't have to* or *mustn't*.
1 In Italy you _____ leave food on your plate.
2 In China you _____ leave food on your plate.
3 In Italy you _____ be on time for parties.
4 In Germany you _____ arrive on time.
5 In the UK you _____ put your phone on silent mode on the train.

5 Match sentences 1–5 with notices A–E.
1 ☐ You have to walk here.
2 ☐ You don't have to eat here, but you can if you want.
3 ☐ You mustn't use your phones in class.
4 ☐ You have to talk in English all the time.
5 ☐ You mustn't say anything at this time.

A Don't use Spanish in the English class!

B NO RUNNING IN THE CORRIDORS!

C Why not try the school cafeteria today?

D Turn off your mobiles!

E DO NOT TALK DURING THE EXAM.

YOUR WORLD

6 Write sentences about the rules at your school and at home. Use these ideas to help you. Then, in pairs, compare your answers.
- get up at 6 a.m. every day
- use my smartphone in class
- do homework before I go to bed
- do housework every day

I don't have to get up at 6 a.m. every day. What about you?

I can use *have to/don't have to* and *mustn't* to talk about cultural rules.

8.3 Reading and Vocabulary

Languages

1 🔊 **8.5** Listen to people saying, 'Hello, how are you?' in different languages. What languages are they? Choose the correct option.
   1 *Turkish / Portuguese*
   2 *Swahili / Chinese*
   3 *Spanish / Italian*
   4 *Korean / Dutch*

2 🔊 **8.6** Read the article quickly. Which languages from Exercise 1 does it mention?

3 Read the article again and complete the information with a number or short phrase.
   1 total number of languages in 2021: *7,139*
   2 how many languages disappeared between 1900 and 1999: _____
   3 where Tehuelche came from: _____
   4 number of people who speak Chinese as their first language: _____
   5 total number of English speakers in the world: _____

4 🔊 **8.7** Study the Vocabulary box. Which words/phrases can you find in the text?

> **VOCABULARY** Learning languages
>
> bilingual   foreign language   grammar
> native language   native speaker   speak fluently
> understand   vocabulary

5 Complete the sentences with the correct form of words and phrases from the Vocabulary box.
   1 The *native language* in the Netherlands is Dutch, but most people can speak English too.
   2 My friend Agnes is from Sweden and she is _____ – she speaks Swedish and English.
   3 Be careful with your _____ . You can't say, 'I working at the moment.' It's 'I'm working at the moment.'
   4 Mark speaks Italian _____ because he spends all his holidays there.
   5 I can _____ Spanish people when they speak slowly.
   6 We have to learn two _____ languages at school: English and German.
   7 My English _____ is getting better – I learn new words every day.

Talking about world languages

How many languages are there in the world?

The correct answer is: fewer than there were last year. A study shows that in 2021 there were 7,139 languages, but the number changes every year. That's because languages are a living thing; when people stop using them, they die. In the twentieth century alone, we lost 110 languages. One example is Tehuelche, a South American language. It disappeared when its last speaker died in 2019.

Which language has the largest number of speakers in the world?

That is a difficult question to answer. If we think of countries and populations, surely, the country with the largest number of people has the most speakers. Well, not exactly. If we count native speakers only, the four top languages are: Mandarin Chinese (921 million), Spanish (471 million), English (370 million) and Hindi (342 million). But if we count native speakers together with people who speak the language fluently as a foreign language, the numbers change. English becomes the top language (1.348 billion speakers), and Mandarin Chinese comes second (1.120 billion speakers). For Mandarin Chinese, that's around eighty-two percent native speakers. But for English, the native speakers are only around eighteen percent!

VIDEO ▶   **WIDER WORLD**

6 ▶ **36** Watch eight people talking about languages. Write down the languages they mention.

7 In pairs, ask and answer the questions.
   1 What's your native language?
   2 Are you bilingual? Do you know any bilingual people?
   3 How many native speakers of your language are there?
   4 What are the two most popular foreign languages in your country?
   5 Do you think English is an easy language? Is it easier to speak or to understand?

I can understand an article about world languages.

8.4 Grammar

Articles: first and second mention

VIDEO ▶ THE CULTURE VLOG

Noah: Action!

Lena: Welcome to the International Schools Culture vlog. Today we're playing a memory game. The topic is British culture. Mateo, to win the game, you have thirty seconds to remember the objects in detail.

Mateo: OK, I'm ready.

Lena: Let's start! A cup of tea. A London bus. A black cab. A plate of fish and chips. A bag with the UK flag. A British bulldog. An umbrella. A five-pound note. Your time begins now!

Mateo: Uh, there was a black cab, **a cup** of tea …

Lena: What colour was the cup?

Mateo: White, gold and pink?

Lena: Correct!

Mateo: There was **a** blue **bag** …

Lena: What was on the bag?

Mateo: The UK flag?

Lena: Correct!

Mateo: A British bulldog, **a plate** of fish and chips …

Lena: Was there anything else on the plate?

Mateo: Ketchup?

Lena: Correct!

Mateo: An umbrella and **a five-pound note**.

Lena: Cor … What? This is not the five-pound note! That's Mia and Noah!

Mia: Oops! Sorry! My mistake!

Noah: Mia!

Mateo: Noah is a very cute dog!

Noah: Cut!

1 ▶ 37 🔊 8.8 Watch or listen. What mistake did Mia make at the end?

2 ▶ 37 🔊 8.8 Watch or listen again. Answer the questions.
1. What is the game about?
2. Who is the presenter of the game?
3. How long has Mateo got?
4. Does he remember all the photos?

3 Study the Grammar box. Look at the words in bold in the dialogue. Find the second time these things are mentioned in the dialogue.

> **GRAMMAR** | **Articles: first and second mention**
>
> The first time we mention something, we use *a* or *an*. There was *a* photo. | The second time we mention something, we use *the*. Who was in *the* photo?

GRAMMAR TIME > PAGE 133

4 Complete the sentences with *a/an* or *the*.
1. We made *a* video about British culture and wrote _____ article about British food. 326 people watched _____ video last week and seventy-eight people read _____ article.
2. I've got _____ camera and _____ smartphone. I don't use _____ camera very often, but I use _____ smartphone every day.
3. Johan made _____ joke, but no one laughed. _____ joke wasn't funny.
4. I ordered _____ omelette and _____ cookie for lunch. _____ omelette was good but _____ cookie was awful.

YOUR WORLD

5 Complete the questions with *a/an* or *the*. Then, in pairs, ask and answer the questions.
1. Do you have *a* favourite book by _____ author from your country? What is the title of _____ book? Who is _____ author?
2. When was the last time you watched _____ exciting film? Did you talk about _____ film with your friends?
3. Is there _____ famous museum in your city? What is the name of _____ museum?
4. I'm thinking of _____ famous actor. Ask me some questions. Can you guess _____ actor?

I can use *a/an* and *the* to refer to things.

8.5 Listening and Vocabulary
Communication

1 🔊 8.9 Study the Vocabulary box. What types of communication can you see in the photos above? Write the words from the Vocabulary box in the correct column in the table below.

VOCABULARY > **Communicating**

conversation   email   letter   phone call
(social media) post   text message   Tweet   video call

Speaking	Writing
conversation	email

2 Which three types of communication do you use the most with your friends?

3 🔊 8.10 Listen to a class of English language students in the UK. What is the class about?
  a how to write emails and messages
  b communication problems
  c foreign languages

4 🔊 8.10 Listen again and choose the correct answer.
  1 The teacher tells a story about
    a a phone call.   b a text message.
    c a social media post.
  2 The teacher's surname is
    a What.   b Watt.
    c Wott.
  3 Sonia wanted to eat
    a a ham sandwich.   b some strawberries.
    c a jam sandwich.
  4 Mario
    a lives in the US.   b made a mistake.
    c did something brave.
  5 Himari's
    a dog is noisy.   b father is noisy.
    c father sleeps in the garden.

5 🔊 8.11 **WORD FRIENDS** Complete the phrases with the verbs below. Listen and check.

ask   call   chat   ~~have~~   make   post   send

1 *have* a conversation
2 _____ a phone call
3 _____ someone
4 _____ someone a question
5 _____ online
6 _____ a message on social media
7 _____ a text

6 Complete the sentences with the correct form of words from Exercise 5.
  1 My dad and I *had* a good conversation at breakfast this morning.
  2 My mum asks me a lot of _____ about school.
  3 My best friend lives in New Zealand. We often _____ online.
  4 I _____ a message on Facebook yesterday and I got thirty-six likes!
  5 I _____ a friend on the phone last night. We talked for hours.
  6 I don't like making phone _____ . It's quicker and cheaper to send a _____ .

YOUR WORLD

7 In pairs, say if the sentences in Exercise 6 are true for you.
  A: I had a good conversation with my dad at breakfast this morning. We talked about music. What about you?
  B: No, I didn't have a good conversation. I never talk to anyone at breakfast!

I can understand a conversation about communication problems.

8.6 Speaking
Checking understanding and clarifying

VIDEO ▶ DO YOU UNDERSTAND?

Noah: Look, this is a game I designed. Would you like to play?
Mateo: Uh huh.
Mia: OK.
Mateo: What's the name of the game?
Noah: *Dragons and Volcanoes.*
Mia: Cool!
Noah: We have two dice – one green, one red. The green one is for moving your dragon forward; the red one is for moving another dragon back.
Mateo: Do you mean moving another player's pawn back?
Noah: That's right.
Mia: I'm not sure I get it.
Noah: Look. For example, green is four, so I move my dragon forward four squares: one, two, three, four, right? Red is five, so I choose, let's say, Mateo's dragon and move it back five squares. Do you get it now?
Mia: Oh, right! Can you do the opposite if it's a better move for you? Like this. Do you understand what I mean?
Noah: Oh, I see. Yes, we can do that. That's a very good idea, Mia. Now, are we ready to play?
Later …
Mia: Yes!
Noah: What's the score?
Mateo: Mia four, Mateo two, Noah zero!
Noah: I don't believe it! I designed this game!

SOUNDS GOOD! Let's say … • What's the score? • I don't believe it!

1 ▶ 38 🔊 8.12 Watch or listen. Who won the game?

2 What does Mia do when she does not understand the rules of the game?

SET FOR LIFE

3 What do you do when you do not understand something? Discuss in pairs. Use the ideas below. What is the best thing to do?
- I ask for an explanation.
- I take a break and then try again.
- I try to find the answer online.

4 Study the Speaking box. Find examples of the phrases in the dialogue.

SPEAKING | **Checking understanding and clarifying**

Check people understand
Do you know/understand what I mean?   (Do) you see?
Do you get it/understand?   … , right?

Say you don't understand
I'm sorry, I don't get it/understand.
I'm not sure I get it/understand.

Ask for clarification
What do you mean?   Do you mean … ?

Say you understand
Now I get it/understand.   I see.   Oh, right!

5 🔊 8.13 Complete the dialogue with one word in each gap. Listen and check.

Grandpa: Can you help me order this game online?
Chris: OK, first put the game in your basket.
Grandpa: I'm not ¹*sure* I understand.
Chris: See this? It says 'Add to basket'. Just click on it.
Grandpa: I'm ² _____ , I don't ³ _____ .
Chris: Let me show you. You do this … and then this. Do you get ⁴ _____ now?
Grandpa: I ⁵ _____ ! So it's like putting your shopping in a basket at the supermarket!
Chris: That's right.

YOUR WORLD

6 In pairs, tell your partner how to play your favourite video or board game. Use the Speaking box to help you.
Student A: Explain the rules. Check Student B understands what you're saying.
Student B: Say you understand/don't understand. Ask for clarification.

I can check people understand me and say if I understand.

8.7 Writing
'How to' tips

1 Do you follow any vloggers? Who are they? What do you like about their vlogs?

2 Read Tod's 'how to' tips. Are they good tips? Discuss in pairs.

Tod's top tips: how to make a vlog

1 Prepare well.
You don't have to be original, but you have to talk about something interesting. Learn about your subject. Look for fascinating facts. And find a good name for your vlog.

2 Look good.
Think about your clothes and your hair. You don't have to wear anything special, but you mustn't look untidy. Check the room and the lighting. Ask your friends and family for help. And don't forget to edit your videos.

3 Be happy.
Look at the camera and smile at your audience. You mustn't shout at your viewers – talk to them.

4 Don't worry.
Not an instant internet success? Don't worry about it. Try again next time.

3 Study the Writing box. Find more examples of imperatives and modal verbs in Tod's tips.

WRITING 'How to' tips

Number your tips and give them short headings
1 Prepare well.   4 Don't worry.

Use imperatives to give advice
Learn about your subject.   Don't worry about it.

Use the modal verbs *have to*, *don't have to* and *mustn't* to show what is or isn't necessary
You have to talk about something interesting.
You don't have to be original.
You mustn't shout at your viewers.

4 Study the Language box. Find examples of verbs and prepositions in Tod's tips.

LANGUAGE Verbs and prepositions

- learn about
- talk about
- think about
- worry about
- look at
- shout at
- smile at
- believe in
- ask for
- look for
- talk to

5 Complete the sentences with the correct prepositions. Then match them with 'how to' topics a–e below.
1 [e] Never worry *about* exams.
2 ☐ Smile _____ people and introduce yourself.
3 ☐ Learn _____ recording and editing.
4 ☐ Talk _____ a parent before you give information online.
5 ☐ Think _____ your characters. Who are they? What do they do?

a how to write a short story
b how to make an online video
c how to be safe on the internet
d how to make new friends
e how to enjoy school

WRITING TIME

6 Write four 'how to' tips.

1 Find ideas
Choose a topic from Exercise 5 or use your own ideas. Make notes for your tips. Think about:
- what tips you want to give.
- what equipment you need.
- what you have to/don't have to/mustn't do.

2 Plan
Organise your tips into numbered paragraphs. Use Tod's tips to help you.

3 Write and share
- Write a draft of your tips. Use the Language box and the Writing box to help you.
- Share your tips with another student for feedback.
- Write the final version of your tips.

4 Check
- Check language: are the prepositions after verbs correct?
- Check grammar: are the imperatives and modal verbs correct?

I can write 'how to' tips.

Vocabulary Activator

WORDLIST 🔊 8.14

Geography
Africa (n)
Antarctica (n)
Asia (n)
Australia (n)
capital city (n)
east (n)
Europe (n)
flag (n)
island (n)
lake (n)
language (n)
money (n)
mountain (n)
north (n)
North America (n)
ocean (n)
population (n)
river (n)
sea (n)
south (n)
South America (n)
village (n)
volcano (n)
west (n)

Learning languages
bilingual (adj)
foreign language (n)
grammar (n)
native language (n)
native speaker (n)
speak fluently
understand (v)
vocabulary (n)

Communicating
conversation (n)
email (n)
letter (n)
phone call (n)
(social media) post (n)
text message (n)
Tweet (n)
video call (n)

Word friends (communicating)
ask someone a question
call someone
chat online
have a conversation
make a phone call
post a message on social media
send a text

Extra words
accept a present
arrive on time
author (n)
believe in (v)
black cab (n)
border (n)
bring good luck
chew gum
clear (adj)
complain (v)
continent (n)
count (v)
cross the street
cultural rules
deep (adj)
die (v)
disappear (v)
in public
learn about (v)
look at (v)
look for (v)
make a joke
make a mistake
official language (n)
original (adj)
phone number (n)
place (n)
postcode (n)
punctual (adj)
second language (n)
shout at (v)
side (n)
smile at (v)
take off (your shoes)
talk about (v)
talk to (v)
top (of a mountain) (n)
untidy (adj)
unusual (adj)
vlog (n)
wait in a queue
worry about (v)
wrong (adj)

1 Complete the sentences with the correct form of words from the wordlist.
1 The opposite of 'south' is <u>north</u>.
2 You need _____ to buy things.
3 A _____ can explode with hot lava.
4 The UK _____ is red, white and blue.
5 I send lots of text _____ to my friends every day.

2 In pairs, do the quiz. Complete the sentences with words from the wordlist. Then go to page 138 and check your answers.

WORLD QUIZ

1 The Amazon is a <u>river</u> in South America.
2 Iceland is an _____ in the Atlantic Ocean.
3 The Pacific is the world's largest _____ .
4 The _____ of Wales is white and green with a red dragon.
5 Nine of the ten highest _____ s in the world are in the Himalayas.
6 Canberra is the _____ city of Australia.
7 The continent of Asia is to the _____ of Europe.
8 Loch Ness is a cold water _____ in Scotland.

3 Make a quiz for a partner. Write five 'True or false' sentences about places in the world. Use the sentences in Exercise 2 and the wordlist to help you. Then swap with your partner and do his/her quiz.

4 Complete the questions with words from the wordlist. Then, in pairs, ask and answer the questions.
1 When did you last _____ online with a friend?
2 How often do you make _____ calls? Who do you call?
3 Do you post _____ on Twitter?
4 What foreign _____ would you like to learn?

5 🔊 8.15 **PRONUNCIATION** Listen to how we pronounce the /ʃ/ and /tʃ/ sounds. Then, in pairs, practise saying the words.

/ʃ/: <u>sh</u>oe, conver<u>s</u>ation, o<u>c</u>ean, _____ , _____ , _____ , _____

/tʃ/: <u>ch</u>at, na<u>t</u>ure, ques<u>t</u>ion, _____ , _____ , _____ , _____

6 🔊 8.16 **PRONUNCIATION** Write the words below in the correct group in Exercise 5. Use the underlined letters to help you. Listen, check and repeat.

<u>ch</u>ew   offi<u>c</u>ial   fu<u>t</u>ure   ki<u>tch</u>en   popula<u>t</u>ion   wa<u>tch</u>
<u>sh</u>op   <u>s</u>ugar

Revision

Vocabulary

1 Look at the map. Complete the text about Ghana with one word in each gap.

Ghana is a country in West Africa. It has three neighbours: Burkina Faso to the ¹*north*, Ivory Coast to the ²_____ and Togo to the ³_____. To the ⁴_____ is the Atlantic ⁵_____. Ghana has a ⁶_____ of 30 million people. The ⁷_____ city is Accra. The official ⁸_____ is English.

2 Complete the sentences with the words below.

> bilingual   fluently   foreign   grammar   ~~native~~

1 It's impossible for me to pronounce English words like a *native* speaker.
2 To get a good job, you have to speak a _____ language.
3 You can learn to speak a language _____ in two years.
4 I'd like to be _____ and speak English and my own language fluently.
5 English _____ is easy – except for irregular verbs.

3 Complete the sentences with the words below.

> ask   conversation   letter   ~~make~~   post   questions

1 I need to *make* a phone call.
2 Do you and your friends _____ funny messages on Facebook?
3 My grandparents always _____ me a lot of _____ about school.
4 We had an interesting _____ about all the places we'd like to visit.
5 My cousin in Australia always sends me a _____ on my birthday.

Grammar

4 Complete the rules with *have to*, *don't have to* or *mustn't*. Then write about your school rules.

School rules around the world

- In Brazil, students ¹*have to* get up very early because school starts at 7.00 a.m.
- In France, some schoolchildren only ²_____ go to school for four days a week. They ³_____ go to school on Wednesdays.
- In Thailand, children ⁴_____ wear shoes in the classroom. They ⁵_____ take their shoes off before they enter school.
- In the USA, most students ⁶_____ wear a uniform. They can wear their own clothes.

5 Complete the questions with *a*, *an* or *the*. Then, in pairs, ask and answer the questions.

1 Is there *a* park near your house? What's _____ park called? Is there _____ café there?
2 Did you have _____ holiday last summer? Did you stay in _____ nice place? Did it have _____ swimming pool? Did you use _____ pool a lot?
3 Is there _____ shopping centre in your town? Has it got _____ sports shop? How often do you go to _____ shopping centre?
4 Did you get _____ text from _____ friend yesterday? What did _____ text say?

Speaking

6 Work in pairs. Student A, follow the instructions below. Student B, go to page 138.

- Student A, explain to Student B how to take a video with your phone. Use the phrases below to make sure he/she understands you.

> Do you get it?   Do you see?   … , right?

- Swap roles. Student B is explaining something to you. Use at least three of the phrases below to say you understand/don't understand.

> I'm sorry, I don't get it.   I'm not sure I understand.
> What do you mean?   Now I get it.   I see.   Oh, right!

Dictation

7 🔊 8.17 Listen. Then listen again and write down what you hear during each pause.

109   Unit 8

SET FOR LIFE

Doing things differently

1 Match the activities below with photos A–F.

☐ bow ☐ eat with your hands ☐ give presents
☐ point ☐ shake hands ☐ wave

2 Look at the photos. In which photo(s) are the people:
1 saying hello?
2 saying goodbye?
3 giving or receiving gifts?
4 eating food?
5 showing something to another person?

3 In pairs, discuss the questions.
1 Do you usually do the things in the photos?
2 Look at the situations in Exercise 2 again. What do you do in these situations?

4 Read the forum posts and answer the questions.
1 What problems do Leila and Greg have?
2 Why do you think they have these problems?

STUDENT EXCHANGE FORUM
Hosting a foreign student?
Share your cultural experiences!

Leila At the moment a group of students from Greece are visiting my school in the UK. They're really nice and friendly, but they often arrive late. For example, yesterday we arranged to meet at two o'clock. They all arrived at about half past two, but they didn't explain why.

Greg I'm American and I'm staying with an Egyptian family at the moment. We had dinner together last night and the food was really nice. But there was one problem. Every time my plate was empty, they offered me more food. I didn't want to be rude, so I said yes. This happened again and again!

I can understand different cultures.

Understand people from different cultures

5 🔊 8.18 Listen to Leila and Greg talking about their problems. Check your answers to Exercise 4.

6 🔊 8.18 Listen again. What did Leila and Greg learn about other cultures? Choose the correct option.
1 In Greece it's usually *rude / OK* to be late.
2 Leila decides to be more *careful / relaxed* about time.
3 Egyptian people *sometimes / never* offer guests food when they say 'No'.
4 In the future, Greg *must / mustn't* take a little more food and then leave it on his plate.

7 In pairs, complete the questionnaire about your culture. Then compare your answers with another pair. Use expressions from the Useful Phrases box.

In my country, people usually shake hands when they meet someone new.

Tell us about your culture!

1. What do you do when you meet someone new?
   a shake hands   **b** kiss   **c** bow
2. What do you do when you say goodbye to somebody?
   a shake hands   **b** kiss   **c** wave
3. When you meet someone, do you arrive
   a a little late?   **b** at exactly the right time?
   c a little early?
4. How do you eat your main meal?
   a with our hands   **b** with knives and forks   **c** a different way
5. What do you do when you visit someone in their house for the first time?
   a bring a small gift   **b** bring nothing
   c bring large gifts for everyone
6. Tell us something you do in your culture that maybe people from other cultures don't do.

8 Read the Useful Tips. Which tip do you think is the most important? Why?

SET FOR LIFE

9 In pairs, prepare a cultural guide for visitors to your country. Follow these steps.

1. Think of five or six tips for visitors. Use your answers in Exercise 7 and your own ideas.
2. Write the tips. Use expressions from the Useful Phrases box.
3. Check your tips. Are some cultural rules similar in other countries?
4. Present your guide to the class.

USEFUL TIPS

People from different cultures can sometimes behave differently. They can find different things rude or polite. It's important to try to understand their way of looking at the world.

- Remember that people can have different ideas about the world.
- Be open to other people's ideas.
- Ask questions if you want to know more about a culture.
- Remember that we share a lot of things too.

USEFUL PHRASES

In my culture/country:
- people always/usually/often/never …
- it's normal to …
- it's rude/polite to …
- you have to/must …
- you don't have to/mustn't …

On the go

9

VOCABULARY
Means of transport | Getting around | Travel collocations | Holiday activities | Weather

GRAMMAR
Present Continuous for future arrangements | *Be going to* for future plans

CITY LIFE

How we choose to travel around the city is important. When there are fewer cars in the streets, there is less traffic and the air is cleaner. In some cities, it is easy to get around without a car. Let's have a look.

The Australian city of Melbourne has the largest tram network in the world. What makes this even more attractive is the Free Tram Zone. If you travel only in this part of the city, you don't have to buy a ticket!

One of the cities with the best public transport in the world is Berlin. Its underground (U-Bahn) and train network (S-Bahn) take you anywhere around the German capital. At busy times, there's a train every five minutes.

Copenhagen is one of the top cities for bikes. Cycling is easy, fast and safe, so more than sixty percent of its people choose it as their main form of transport.

9.1 Vocabulary

Transport and travel

1 **I KNOW!** What means of transport do you often use? In pairs, make a list.

2 🔊 9.1 Study Vocabulary box A. Which means of transport are public and which are private? Which can you see in photos A–C above?

VOCABULARY A **Means of transport**

aeroplane/plane   bicycle/bike   boat   bus   car   coach
motorbike   taxi   train   tram   underground/metro

3 Read the article above and choose the best summary.
 a Fast public transport
 b Good for you, good for the planet
 c The cheapest way to travel

4 🔊 9.2 Study Vocabulary box B. Which word is not a place?

> **VOCABULARY B** ▸ **Getting around**
>
> bus station   bus stop   car park   cycle lane
> train/metro/underground station   traffic

5 🔊 9.3 Listen to two friends talking about transport in their town. Complete the sentences with the correct form of words from Vocabulary box B.
1. Paul is annoyed with the _____ .
2. There's a _____ next to them.
3. Paul's idea is to have a few big _____ around the town.
4. He thinks that there has to be a _____ or a _____ next to the car parks.
5. Beth often has to wait at the _____ for twenty minutes or more.

6 🔊 9.4 **WORD FRIENDS** Complete the phrases with the verbs below. Listen and check.

> drive   ~~get~~   get   go (x2)   park   ride   take   wait (x2)

1. _get_ into/out of a car/a taxi
2. _____ a car
3. _____ on foot
4. _____ by bike/bus/car/motorbike
5. _____ a bike/a motorbike
6. _____ a car/a motorbike (in a car park)
7. _____ a bus/a train/your car
8. _____ at the bus stop
9. _____ on/off a bus/train/bike
10. _____ for a bus

7 Choose the correct option.

FACTS FOR TRAVELLERS

London
1. When you get *into* / *on* or *off* / *out of* the train in the London Underground, or Tube, you often hear the message 'Mind the gap'. It tells you to be careful because there's a gap between the train and the platform.
2. You can't *wait* / *park* your car on double yellow lines.
3. If you *drive* / *ride* your car into the city centre, you have to pay £15 or more.

Amsterdam
4. There are 513 km of cycle *lanes* / *streets* in the city.

New York
5. If you only want to travel one or two stops on the underground, or subway, as they call it in the US, think again: it is usually faster to go *by* / *on* foot.

Prague
6. You can *travel* / *take* the bus, tram and metro using the same ticket.
7. You can see some of the city's most beautiful sights *by* / *with* boat.

8 🔊 9.5 Complete the comments with one word in each gap. Listen and check.

How do you get to school?

Jude: My friend's mum ¹_drives_ us to school. He's got two sisters so there are four of us. I get ²_____ the car last, so there's never enough room! And Dan's sisters fight all the time! I can't wait to get out ³_____ the car when we get to school!

Cara: I ⁴_____ the 8.15 bus. Sometimes I'm late and I have to wait ⁵_____ the 8.30 bus. I try to be on time because I hate waiting ⁶_____ the bus stop!

VIDEO ▶   **WIDER WORLD**

9 ▶ 39 Watch seven people talking about how they get to school or work. Write down the means of transport they mention.

10 In groups, talk about which means of transport you use:
- to get to school.
- to go to the city centre.
- to visit friends or relatives in another town.
- to go on holiday.

A: *How do you get to school?*
B: *I usually go on foot. My dad sometimes drives me if the weather isn't good.*

I can talk about means of transport and travel.

9.2 Grammar

Present Continuous for future arrangements

1 🔊 9.6 Do you know the person in the photo? Read the posts and check.

Harry Styles fan page

HARRY STYLES AT THE O2 ARENA!

1derboy: Wow! Harry Styles is playing at The O2 in London on 22 June! Are you guys going?

Ron08: I'm not going. We're going on holiday that day.

AnnaBL: Yes, I am! 😃 I'm going with Andy. His mum is giving us a lift from Southend. What about you, 1derboy?

1derboy: Yes, I'm going too. I live in London, so I'm taking the bus. You're lucky you're going with a friend – I'm going on my own. 😢

Andy: Why don't we meet before the concert? We're going to Perfect Pizza on Berner Street first – my mum got us a table for seven o'clock. You're welcome to join us.

1derboy: Great, thanks, Andy! BTW, what are you guys wearing to the concert?

Andy: We're wearing our Harry Styles T-shirts, of course! 😉

2 Read the posts again. In pairs, answer the questions.
1. When is the London O2 concert?
2. Who plans to go to the concert by car?
3. Where do they agree to meet? What time?

3 Study the Grammar box. Find examples of the Present Continuous in the posts.

> **GRAMMAR** — **Present Continuous for future arrangements**
>
> We're going to the concert on 22 June.
> He isn't going. He's going on holiday.
> Are you coming with us tomorrow?   Yes, we are.

GRAMMAR TIME ▶ PAGE 134

4 Complete the posts with the Present Continuous form of the verbs in brackets.

HARRY STYLES – December concerts

1derboy: Harry Styles ¹*is giving* (give) a concert in Birmingham on Thursday. I ² _____ (go) – I've got a ticket already.

MeGirl: I can't go. My sister and I ³ _____ (sing) in the school concert that evening. 🙁 What about you, Andy?

Andy: I ⁴ _____ (not go), but my mum is. She ⁵ _____ (see) Harry in Birmingham on Thursday. And she ⁶ _____ (go) to his Sheffield concert on Saturday. On the twenty-eighth, he ⁷ _____ (play) in Manchester – she's got a ticket for that too!

5 In pairs, plan an afternoon in town. Follow the instructions below.

Student A
- Start the conversation. Ask Student B if he/she is doing anything on Friday.
- On Saturday you are travelling to the city to see a musical. Ask Student B if he/she is doing anything on Sunday evening.
- Suggest going to the cinema at 6 p.m. on Sunday.

Student B
- You are visiting a friend on Friday. Ask Student A if he/she is doing anything on Saturday.
- You don't have any plans for Sunday.
- You think Student A's suggestion is a good idea.

6 **YOUR WORLD** In pairs, talk about what is in your diary for the next few weeks. Use the ideas below or your own.

I	meet
My family and I	visit
My friend(s) and I	watch
	have lunch with

A: Adrian and I are meeting next week.
B: Where are you meeting?

Unit 9 — I can use the Present Continuous to talk about future arrangements.

9.3 Reading and Vocabulary
Holidays

1. Work in pairs. Where do you usually spend your holidays?
   - in a quiet village
   - visiting a city
   - on a beach
   - by a lake
   - at home
   - in the mountains

2. 🔊 9.7 Read the article below. In pairs, say which holiday sounds the most interesting.

3. Read the article again. Match people A–C with questions 1–7.
   1. ☐ Who doesn't like being active on holiday?
   2. ☐ Who is going to two different places this summer?
   3. ☐ Who wants to return to a place he/she went to before?
   4. ☐ Who had a bad shock on holiday?
   5. ☐ Who remembers a great holiday when he/she was young?
   6. ☐ Who is very excited about his/her next holiday?
   7. ☐ Who became ill on his/her holiday?

4. 🔊 9.8 Study the Vocabulary box. Which activities do the people in the article mention?

VOCABULARY | Holiday activities

- ☐ hiking
- ☐ sailing
- ☐ shopping
- ☐ sightseeing
- ☐ skiing
- ☐ sunbathing
- ☐ surfing
- ☐ swimming
- ☐ walking

5. Where in your country can you do the activities in Exercise 4? In pairs, make a list and share it with the class.

6. **YOUR WORLD** In pairs, imagine you are going on a short holiday together. Discuss the points below to plan your holiday. Then present your plan to the class.
   - Where are you going?
   - How are you getting there?
   - What activities are you doing each day?

IT'S ALMOST HOLIDAY TIME!

Green Lanes School Magazine

We asked, 'What is the best holiday you ever had? What is your worst holiday ever? What are your plans for this summer?' Here's what you said.

A Anna
Last year we went to a Greek island and I spent two weeks on the beach swimming, sunbathing and – the best part: doing absolutely nothing! We all loved it, so we're going to another Greek island this summer. My worst holiday? Camping in Scotland when I was nine. I found a snake in my tent! I was so scared that I slept in the car for the rest of the holiday!

B Oliver
We travel a lot in the summer. This year we're visiting family in Sweden and then we're going hiking in the Peak District in the north of England. I can't wait! My best holiday was in London. I was five and my parents took me to a huge toy shop. I was so excited! When it was time to leave, I didn't want to go, so I hid inside a play tent. My parents and the shop manager looked for me everywhere. When they found me, the manager was so happy that she gave me the play tent as a present!

C Claire
I love activity holidays, so I'm going sailing in Croatia for two weeks. I'd like to go on a city holiday too because I love sightseeing and shopping. My last holiday in Paris, however, was a disaster. We only went for the weekend, but I got a really bad cold on the first day. I spent the biggest part of the holiday in my hotel room, in bed. I'd like to go back one day and do all the fun things I missed.

I can understand an article about holidays.

9.4 Grammar

Be going to for future plans

VIDEO ▶ SUMMER PLANS

Noah: It's the last week of school! Can you believe it?
Mia: I can't wait for the summer break! I want to save money for a new bike, so I'm going to get a job.
Noah: What kind of job?
Mia: I'm going to work for my aunt. She's got an ice cream shop in Cornwall.
Noah: Are you going to spend the whole summer there?
Mia: No, only four weeks. How about you?
Noah: I'm going to do some art workshops.
Mia: That sounds like fun too.

Noah: What about Lena? Do you know what she's going to do?
Mia: She's going to do a Spanish course. She's packing her bags now, I think. What are you going to do, Mateo?
Mateo: Well, we aren't going to go on a family holiday because Dad's on tour in South Europe with his jazz band, but I'm going to join him for a month.
Noah: Poor Mateo! He's going to have such a horrible time: sun, sea and music. All the things he hates!
Mateo: Well, it's not a free holiday! I'm going to help the band. You know, pack and carry stuff. I'm also going to …

1 ▶ 40 🔊 9.9 Watch or listen. In your opinion, which of the friends is going to have the best holiday? Why?

2 What plans do the friends have? Why do you think these plans are important to them? Discuss in pairs.

SET FOR LIFE

3 What personal goals and plans have you got? Do you think these ideas can help you achieve a goal? Why?/Why not? Discuss in pairs.
- Choose a realistic goal.
- Plan what you need to do to meet your goal.
- Take small steps.
- Set a timetable and follow it.

4 Study the Grammar box. Find more examples of *be going to* in the dialogue.

GRAMMAR ▶ Be going to for future plans

I'**m going to get** a job.
We **aren't going to go** on a family holiday.
What **are** you **going to do**?
Are you **going to spend** the whole summer there?
Yes, I **am**./No, I'**m not**.

GRAMMAR TIME ▶ PAGE 134

5 Complete the sentences with the correct form of *be going to* and the verbs in brackets.
1. I 'm going to stay (stay) with my family in the USA.
2. You _____ (finish) this project next week.
3. Tim _____ (not come) on holiday with us.
4. When _____ (we/meet) again?
5. They _____ (have) a video call to talk about their school project.
6. Next summer I _____ (get) a job too.

6 Look at the table and make sentences about the people's plans for next weekend. Use *be going to*.

	Eva	Jo and Leo	Adam
get up early	✓	✗	✓
go shopping	✓	✗	✗
watch TV	✗	✓	✓

Ann is going to get up early. She …

YOUR WORLD

7 In pairs, ask and answer questions about your plans for this summer. Use these ideas or your own.
- paint my room
- play (a sport)
- get a job
- learn (a language/a musical instrument)

A: *What are you going to do this summer?*
B: *I'm going to paint my room.*

Unit 9 | 116 | I can use *be going to* to talk about future plans.

9.5 Listening and Vocabulary
World weather

1 In pairs, look at the photos. What do they show? Where in the world do you think these places are?

2 🔊 9.10 Study the Vocabulary box. Use the words to describe the weather in photos A–F.

VOCABULARY Weather

cloudy   cold   foggy   hot   rainy   snowy
sunny   warm   windy

3 🔊 9.11 Listen to three people talking about today's weather in their city. Write the names of the cities and match them with photos A–F.

Speaker	Name of city	Photo
1		
2		
3		

4 🔊 9.12 Listen and choose the correct answer.
1 The weather in London is
   a cloudy.
   b warm.
   c windy.
2 The weather in Athens at the moment is
   a great.
   b foggy.
   c cold.
3 Ian's grandfather says that in Scotland
   a it often rains.
   b the weather never changes.
   c it's never warm.

5 🔊 9.12 Listen again and answer the questions.
1 How high are the passengers flying at the moment?
2 What is Lisa doing after lunch?
3 Where is Ian going with his grandfather?

VIDEO **WIDER WORLD**

6 ▶ 41 Watch six people talking about the weather and answer the questions.
1 Is it warm at the moment?
2 Did it rain yesterday?
3 Which month is the most popular?

7 In pairs, ask and answer the questions.
1 What's the weather like today?
2 What was the weather like yesterday?
3 What's your favourite month for the weather?

I can understand conversations about the weather.

9.6 Speaking
Asking for and giving directions

VIDEO ▶ LOST IN THE CITY

Noah: Excuse me, how do I get to Bank Sports Centre?
Girl: Oh, erm, let me think … Go straight on and then turn left at the traffic lights. Go past the Tube station and then take the second turning on the right. It's at the end of the street, on the right. You can't miss it.
Noah: Thanks.

Later, at the sports centre …

Noah: Sorry I'm late!
Mateo: Finally! Why didn't you answer my texts?
Noah: My phone's dead! Where's Mia?
Mateo: Good question. Oh, that's her. Hello? Where are you?
Mia: I'm in Berner Street but I can't find the sports centre.
Mateo: That's because it's in Barker Street, Mia!
Mia: Oh! And how do I get to Barker Street?
Mateo: It's not far. Go to the end of Berner Street, then turn right at the crossroads.
Mia: Mateo, listen, I haven't got much bat– …
Mateo: Hello? Mia?
Noah: What happened?
Mateo: I think her battery's dead too! What a day!

SOUNDS GOOD! Sorry I'm late! • Finally! • My phone's dead!

1 Look at the photo. What is Noah doing?

2 ▶ 42 🔊 9.13 Watch or listen. Why is Mia late?

3 Study the Speaking box. Find examples of the phrases in the dialogue.

SPEAKING — Asking for and giving directions

Excuse me, where's the … ?
How do I get to … ?
Is there a … near here?

There's a … in Barker Street.
Go to the end of the road/Berner Street.
Go straight on.
Go past the Tube station/cinema.
Turn left/right (into Barker Street).
Turn left at the crossroads/traffic lights.
Take the first/second turning on the left.
It's next to/opposite the …
It's on the left/right.
It's not far. You can't miss it.

4 🔊 9.14 Complete the dialogue with words from the Speaking box. Listen and check.

Girl: Excuse me, where's Bank Sports Centre?
Woman: Go to the ¹*end* of the road. Turn right ²_____ Maple Street. Go ³_____ the Odeon Cinema. Then ⁴_____ the second turning on the left. The sports centre is ⁵_____ the right. You can't ⁶_____ it.

5 🔊 9.15 You are outside the Tube station. Listen and follow the directions on the map. Where do they take you?

6 **YOUR WORLD** In pairs, look at the map in Exercise 5. You are at the Plaza Cinema. Ask for and give directions.
Student A, ask for directions to the Curry Palace and then to Young's Theatre.
Student B, ask for directions to the A–Z Bookshop and then to the library.

Go out of the cinema and … Then …

Unit 9 — I can ask for and give directions.

9.7 Writing
An invitation email

To: Dylan   **From:** Nick

1. Hi Dylan,
2. How are things? Anna, my cousin from Canada, is coming to stay with us for the summer. I'm planning a welcome party for her on Saturday and I'd like to invite you. 🙂 I'm going to invite Josh and Maisie too.
3. The party is at my house and it starts at 7 p.m.
   I hope you can come.
4. Take care,
   Nick

To: Nick   **From:** Dylan

Hi Nick,
Thank you for inviting me.
5. I'd love to come! I'm really looking forward to it.
   See you soon,
   Dylan

To: Nick   **From:** Maisie

Hi Nick,
Thanks for the invitation. I'm
5. sorry, but I can't come. I'm going away on holiday next Friday.
   I hope you have a lovely time!
   Take care,
   Maisie

1 In pairs, read the emails quickly and answer the questions.
  1. Who is the welcome party for?
  2. Who else is Nick going to invite?
  3. What time and where is everyone meeting?
  4. Can Dylan and Maisie go to the party?

2 Study the Writing box. Find examples of the phrases in the emails.

WRITING ▸ An invitation email

Greetings
1. Hi Dylan,
   How are you?   How are things?

Invitation
2. I'm celebrating (my birthday on) …
   We're going to the cinema.
   I'm having a party.
   I'm planning a surprise/welcome party for …
   … and I'd like to invite you.

Meeting arrangements
3. Let's meet …   The train leaves at …
   We're all meeting at …   The party starts at …

Ending
4. I hope you can come.
   See you soon,   Take care,   Lots of love,

Responding to an invitation
Thanks for the invitation.
5. (+) I'd love to come! I'm really looking forward to it.
   (−) I'm sorry, but I can't come. I hope you have fun!

3 Study the Language box. Find examples of future time expressions in the emails.

LANGUAGE ▸ Future time expressions

today   tonight   tomorrow   on Saturday   in June
this evening/week/month/year   next week/month/year

WRITING TIME

4 You are celebrating your birthday next Saturday. Write an email inviting a friend to come. Swap invitations with a partner and write a reply.

1 Find ideas
Make notes for your invitation email. Think about:
- what type of celebration it is.
- the time and place.
- special instructions.

2 Plan
Organise your ideas into paragraphs. Use Nick's email to help you.

3 Write and share
- Write a draft email. Use the Language box and the Writing box to help you.
- Share your email with another student for feedback.
- Write the final version of your email.

4 Check
- Check language: are future time expressions correct?
- Check grammar: did you use the Present Continuous for arrangements and *be going to* for plans?

I can write and respond to an invitation email.

Vocabulary Activator

WORDLIST 🔊 9.16

Means of transport
aeroplane/plane (n)
bicycle/bike (n)
boat (n)
bus (n)
car (n)
coach (n)
motorbike (n)
taxi (n)
train (n)
tram (n)
underground/metro (n)

Getting around
bus station (n)
bus stop (n)
car park (n)
cycle lane (n)
metro station (n)
traffic (n)
train station (n)
underground station (n)

Word friends
(travel)
drive a car
get into a car/taxi
get off a bike

get off a bus/train
get on a bike
get on a bus/train
get out of a car/taxi
go by bike/motorbike
go by bus/car
go on foot
park a car (in a car park)
park a motorbike (in a car park)
ride a bike/motorbike
take a bus/train
take your car
wait at the bus stop
wait for a bus

Holiday activities
hiking (n)
sailing (n)
shopping (n)
sightseeing (n)
skiing (n)
sunbathing (n)
surfing (n)
swimming (n)
walking (n)

Weather
cloudy (adj)
cold (adj)
foggy (adj)
hot (adj)
rainy (adj)
snowy (adj)
sunny (adj)
warm (adj)
windy (adj)

Extra words
activity holiday (n)
be late
by a lake
camp (v)
camping (n)
city centre (n)
city holiday (n)
clean air (n)
cloud (n)
crossroads (n)
destination (n)
do a course
drive (v)
get a cold
get a job

give someone a lift
go on holiday
go straight on
go past
in the mountains
invitation (n)
invite (v)
on a beach
on tour
pack (v)
platform (n)
public transport (n)
safe (adj)
sky (n)
snow (n)
subway (n)
summer break (n)
tent (n)
ticket (n)
traffic lights (n)
train network (n)
travel (v)
turn left/right
Tube station (n)
umbrella (n)
visit a city
visit family

---

1 Use the wordlist to find these things.
  1 four words to describe winter weather *cold, …*
  2 two holiday activities you can do in the mountains
  3 six means of road transport

2 Look at the chart. Write sentences about the weather. Then, in pairs, say what the weather is like where you are today.

Today's weather in Europe

¹Athens ²Berlin ³Dublin
⁴London ⁵Madrid ⁶Moscow
⁷Paris ⁸Rome ⁹Warsaw

1 It's hot in Athens.

3 In pairs, take it in turns to tell your partner about your best holiday ever. Use words from the wordlist and these ideas.
• Where did you go?
• How did you travel there?
• What activities did you do?
• What was the weather like?

4 🔊 9.17 **PRONUNCIATION** Listen to how we pronounce the /eɪ/ and /ɑː/ sounds. Write the words in the correct column. Look at the underlined letters to help you.

c<u>a</u>r   f<u>a</u>r   p<u>a</u>rk   p<u>a</u>st   pl<u>a</u>ne   r<u>a</u>iny   s<u>a</u>iling   st<u>a</u>tion

1 /eɪ/	2 /ɑː/
plane	car

5 🔊 9.18 **PRONUNCIATION** In pairs, say the sentences. Listen, check and repeat.
  1 We st<u>a</u>rted walking to the c<u>a</u>r p<u>a</u>rk.
  2 We're w<u>a</u>iting for a tr<u>a</u>in.
  3 Is it f<u>a</u>r to the c<u>a</u>r?
  4 What's the n<u>a</u>me of this pl<u>a</u>ce?
  5 Where did Gr<u>a</u>ndma p<u>a</u>rk the c<u>a</u>r?
  6 On r<u>a</u>iny d<u>a</u>ys, my tr<u>a</u>in is alw<u>a</u>ys l<u>a</u>te.

Revision

Vocabulary

1 Write the words for the definitions.
1 People wait here for a bus. *bus stop*
2 People use this to travel fast under a city.
3 People leave their cars here – for example, when they go shopping.
4 It's a good idea to use this when you ride your bike in a city.
5 It's a type of bus that people use for long journeys.
6 It's got two wheels like a bicycle, but it's much faster.

2 Complete the text with one word in each gap. Then, in pairs, talk about how you get to school.

I sometimes go to school on ¹*foot*, but usually I go ² _____ bus. I'm lucky because there's a bus ³ _____ in front of my house. The eight o'clock bus is often busy and I can't get ⁴ _____ it, so I have to wait ⁵ _____ the next bus. I ⁶ _____ off the bus at the park – it's next to my school. Some of my friends ⁷ _____ their bikes to school. There are cycle ⁸ _____ everywhere, so it's very safe.

3 Look at Abby's holiday diary. What did she do last week?
On Monday she went sightseeing and shopping.

MON
TUES
WED
THUR

Grammar

4 What is Bella doing this weekend? Write sentences using the Present Continuous.
She's playing tennis on Saturday morning.

Saturday	morning	play tennis
	afternoon	go shopping
	evening	go to Katie's party
Sunday	morning	make a cake
	afternoon	visit Grandpa
	evening	do homework

5 Make questions with *be going to*. Then match questions 1–5 with answers a–e.
1 where / you / go / in the summer / ?
   Where are you going to go in the summer?
2 how / you / get / there / ?
3 what / you / do / ?
4 where / you / stay / ?
5 what / you / buy / ?

a ☐ With an English family.
b ☒ I'm going to go to London.
c ☐ A Chelsea football shirt!
d ☐ By train.
e ☐ I'm going to do an English course and go sightseeing.

6 In pairs, ask and answer about your holiday plans. Use the questions from Exercise 5 to help you and add your own ideas.
A: *Where are you going to go in the summer?*
B: *I'm going to go to the beach.*
A: *Are you going to go surfing?*

Speaking

7 In pairs, take it in turns to ask for and give directions:
1 from your school to the town centre.
2 from the bus/train station to your school.

Dictation

8 🔊 9.19 Listen. Then listen again and write down what you hear during each pause.

Unit 9

BBC CULTURE

Who needs planes?

Around the world

These days there are many different ways to travel around the world. The record for the fastest journey around the world by plane is just forty-seven hours.

In the nineteenth century planes didn't exist, but the idea of travelling around the world was still exciting. The French writer Jules Verne published *Around the World in 80 Days* in 1872. In the book, Phileas Fogg has to travel from London through Egypt, India, Japan and the USA, and be back in London eighty days later. Travelling by steam trains and boats, he wins the challenge!

Sadly, it's very difficult to make Fogg's journey today. For example, if you want to go from Japan to the USA by sea, you have to go on a cruise ship. The cruise can take twenty days! And passenger ships from New York to England only sail about twelve times a year.

One part of the journey is still the same. Fogg travelled on the Indian railway from Mumbai to Kolkata – a journey of 2,000 kilometres and three days. These days it only takes thirty hours!

So, to explore the world and find adventure, who needs planes?

challenge (n) a difficult situation that tests you
cruise (n) a holiday on a ship, visiting different places
steam (n) the gas that water changes into when it is hot

---

1 Look at the map and the photo. In pairs, discuss the questions.
  1 When in history do you think the train is from?
     a the 1700s
     b the 1800s
     c the 1900s
  2 The map shows a journey from a famous book. How long was the journey?
     a eighty days
     b eight weeks
     c eight months

2 🔊 9.20 Read the article and check your answers to Exercise 1.

3 Read the article again and answer the questions. Find the correct numbers and dates.
  1 How long was the fastest journey around the world by plane?
  2 When did Jules Verne publish *Around the World in 80 Days*?
  3 How long can it take to travel from Japan to the USA on a cruise ship?
  4 How many ships are there between New York and England every year?
  5 How far is Mumbai from Kolkata?
  6 How long does the train journey from Mumbai to Kolkata take today?

4 Would you like to travel around the world? What countries would you like to see? How would you travel? Discuss in pairs.

BBC ▶ Get on board

5 In pairs, look at the photo and discuss the questions.
1. What is happening in the photo?
2. How often do you travel by train?
3. When was the last time you travelled by train?

6 ▶ 43 Watch the video about two different train journeys. Which cities do the two journeys start from?

7 ▶ 43 Watch the video again. Find out:
1. the three cities you can travel to from the UK on the Eurostar.
2. three countries the Trans Siberian Express travels through.
3. the length of the journey from Moscow to Beijing on the Trans Siberian Express.

8 (VISIBLE THINKING) Follow these steps.
WHY DO YOU SAY THAT?
1. Study the discussion question and choose your answer.
   Question: Which means of transport do you think is the best?
   Answer: *planes / trains / cars*
2. Tick (✓) the reason(s) you can use to support your opinion. Can you add two more reasons?
   ☐ They're the fastest.
   ☐ They're very exciting.
   ☐ They're quite cheap.
3. In pairs, discuss the question. Give your opinion and all your reasons.
   A: *I think cars are the best.*
   B: *Why do you say that?*
   A: *Because they're quite cheap and …*

PROJECT TIME

9 In groups of four, create a travel plan for a school trip of a few days. Follow these steps.

1 In your group, talk about your school trip.
- Decide where you can go.
- Decide who can create the travel plan for each day. Each member of the group plans one day.

2 Individually, create your part of the travel plan.
- Find information about means of transport and interesting things to do and see.
- Complete the travel plan.
- Find photos of the things you want to see on the day.

3 In your group, complete your travel plan and prepare a map. You can also create a digital map of the trip.
- Put the information and photos together.
- Add the places you're going to visit to the map.
- Practise presenting the plan and the map as a group.

4 Share your travel plan with the class.
- Answer other students' questions.
- Ask questions and comment on the other travel plans.

Progress Check Units 1–9

Vocabulary and Grammar

1 Choose the correct answer.

When my grandparents were children

The world ¹___ very different when my grandparents were children. My gran was a teenager ²___ the 1970s. Back then, families ³___ have smartphones. Gran's family only had one phone and it was in the hall next ⁴___ the living room. Everybody listened to her phone conversations! I'm happy that I have my own smartphone and nobody knows what I'm saying to my friends! With a smartphone my life is ⁵___ . For example, this weekend I'm going to go ⁶___ in the forest with my friends. I bought train tickets and I invited my friends – all on my phone!

1	a is	b were	c was
2	a in	b at	c to
3	a mustn't	b don't	c didn't
4	a in	b of	c to
5	a more easy	b easier	c easiest
6	a hiking	b surfing	c sightseeing

2 Complete the text with one word in each gap.

What transport ¹*do* you like in general? I enjoy cycling. I ²_____ ride a bike well because I learned when I was young. There are lots of cycle paths in my town, and I go cycling every weekend. When it's cold or rainy, I usually go ³_____ school by bus or train. There's a bus stop near my house, so it's a very short walk. There's also a train station, but ⁴_____ bus stop is closer.

A lot of people prefer travelling by car, but I think it's boring because you can't see lots of things. Last week we ⁵_____ shopping in Cardiff by train with our friend Amelia. Next weekend we ⁶_____ going to the beach – by train, of course!

3 Complete the second sentence with the word in bold so that it means the same as the first one. Use no more than four words.

1 The film was boring. **WAS**
  I *was bored* during the film.
2 We often swim at the weekend. **SWIMMING**
  We often _____ at the weekend.
3 You can find a new word in the dictionary. **UP**
  You can _____ a new word in the dictionary.
4 Can I use your phone to call my mum? **MAKE**
  Can I _____ to my mum from your phone?
5 My pet cat is bigger than all the other cats in our street. **THE**
  My pet cat is _____ in our street.
6 It always rains here in February. **IS**
  The weather _____ here in February.

Speaking

4 Choose the correct response.
1 Do you know what I mean?
  a No, I'm not sure I get it.   b OK. Why not?
  c I think so too.
2 How do I get to the post office?
  a I don't think that's a good idea.
  b You can't miss it.
  c Take the first turning on the left.
3 Can I make a suggestion?
  a Here you are.   b Sure!
  c It's not far.
4 Can you tell me the time?
  a OK, just a second.   b Sorry, I'm using it.
  c Sorry, we haven't got any time.
5 I think that film was great.
  a I don't mind.   b Now I get it.
  c I agree.

5 In pairs, do the speaking task. Go to page 139.

Listening

6 Do you agree with the statements? Why?/Why not? In pairs, compare your ideas.
1 I don't like school trips. I prefer holidays with my family.
2 I don't want to learn any new things during my holidays – I just want to do nothing.
3 The best holiday is at home – you save money on hotels and travel!

7 🔊 PC1–9.1 Listen and choose the correct answer.
1 Who is Ryan going to go on holiday with?
   a his friends   b his parents
   c his cousins
2 Which sport is Ryan going to learn?
   a sailing   b swimming
   c surfing
3 How long is Hannah's holiday in France?
   a a weekend   b a week
   c a month
4 How do they prefer to get around Paris?
   a on the metro   b by bus
   c on foot

Reading

8 Describe the photos. What are the people doing? Read the posts quickly and match paragraphs 1–3 with people A–C.

Amazing people

There are lots of famous people who do amazing things. But what about people we know? Who do you think is great?

1 ☐ I admire my teacher Mr Kelly. He loves travelling. He went to India last year, and he spent a month in Kenya two years ago. Next year he's going to China! He plays the guitar, the violin and the drums. Last month he took part in the London Marathon for the first time. He ran all the way!

2 ☐ My grandma Rose is amazing. She's ninety, but she can use the computer and mobile phone – I showed her how to do it. She takes great photos and then posts them on her Facebook page. She also loves video chats and she's going to start a vlog about being a ninety-year-old grandma! I think she's wonderful.

3 ☐ My friend Matt is a great person. Last year he decided to travel around Spain and Portugal on his bike during the holidays. He isn't rich. He works in a sports centre in the evenings, but he spends all the money on his studies. To save money for his trip, he worked all year at a fast food restaurant at weekends. He wrote a blog about his cycling trip. I read it from time to time and I really liked it.

9 Read the posts again and match people A–C with questions 1–5.
Who:
1 ☐ learned to use technology?
2 ☐ wrote about their travels online?
3 ☐ is good at both sports and music?
4 ☐ travelled in Europe?
5 ☐ tried a new activity recently?

10 Read the posts again and answer the questions.
1 What countries did Mr Kelly go to?
2 What is Rose very good at doing?
3 What new thing does Rose want to do?
4 Where did Matt work to get money for the holiday?
5 How often did he write the blog about his trip?

Writing

11 Make a list of five things that you enjoy doing with friends. In pairs, compare your lists. Do you enjoy the same things?

12 You are going to spend Saturday with a friend. Write an email to him/her about your plans. Write about these things.
• where you're going to meet
• how your friend can get there
• what you're going to do

Grammar Time

1.2

Can

+	I/You/He/She/It/We/They can speak English.
−	I/You/He/She/It/We/They can't (cannot) sing.
?	Can I/you/he/she/it/we/they dance? Yes, I/you/he/she/it/we/they can. No, I/you/he/she/it/we/they can't.

1 Complete the sentences with *can* or *can't*.
1. Our dog Toby <u>can</u> swim – he's really good!
2. A: _____ your parents speak English?
 B: Yes, they _____ .
3. My sister can speak Italian, but she _____ speak Spanish.
4. A: _____ you drive?
 B: No, we _____ .
5. My best friend _____ dance – she's fantastic – but I _____ .
6. A: _____ your brother use a phone?
 B: No, he _____ . He's two!

2 Look at the table and make sentences about what the people can/can't do.

	Billy	Aga and Suri
spell	✗	✓
read music	✓	✗
count to ten in a foreign language	✓	✓
use a computer	✓	✓

Billy can't spell. He can …

3 Complete the sentences with names of famous people in your country.
1. _____ can speak English very well.
2. _____ can't speak English.
3. _____ can play football very well.
4. _____ can dance, but he/she can't sing.
5. _____ can play the guitar well.
6. _____ can swim really fast.

4 Look at Exercise 3. Make four similar sentences about your friends and family.
1. _____
2. _____
3. _____
4. _____

1.4

Have got

+	I/You/We/They've got (have got) blue eyes. He/She/It's got (has got) blue eyes.
−	I/You/We/They haven't got (have not got) blue eyes. He/She/It hasn't got (has not got) blue eyes.
?	Have I/you/we/they got blue eyes? Yes, I/you/we/they have. No, I/you/we/they haven't. Has he/she/it got blue eyes? Yes, he/she/it has. No, he/she/it hasn't.

1 Order the words to make sentences.
1. A: a pen / got / she / has / ?
 Has she got a pen?
 B: hasn't / no / she
 No, she hasn't.
2. got / any pets / haven't / they
3. have / new / got / books / we
4. any cousins / hasn't / he / got
5. A: they / got / have / red hair / ?
 B: yes / have / they
6. got / have / lots of friends / I

2 Make questions with *have got*. Then, in pairs, ask and answer the questions.
1. you / a bike / ?
 Have you got a bike?
2. your parents / brown eyes / ?
3. your best friend / blonde hair / ?
4. you / a TV in your bedroom / ?
5. your friends / skateboards / ?
6. your mum / a mobile phone / ?
7. your neighbour / a small family / ?
8. you / a watch / ?

A: *Have you got a bike?*
B: *No, I haven't. Have you got … ?*

3 Write a short description of a friend. Use *have got*.

Amy is tall. She's got long hair and green eyes.

2.2

There is/There are + some/any

With *there is/there are*, before plural countable nouns, we use:
- *some* in affirmative sentences.
- *any* in negative sentences and questions.

	Singular	Plural
+	There's (is) an apple. There's (is) a banana.	There are four carrots. There are some drinks.
−	There isn't (is not) a pizza.	There aren't (are not) any chips.
?	Is there a plate? Yes, there is./ No, there isn't.	Are there any forks? Yes, there are./ No, there aren't.

1 Look at the notes and make sentences about Layla's menu for her mum's birthday meal. Use *there is/there are*.

A special menu for Mum's birthday

1 a cheese sandwich ✓
2 muffins ✗
3 boiled eggs ✓
4 a glass of cola ✓
5 a hot dog ✓
6 crisps ✗
7 a banana ✓
8 biscuits ✓
9 an apple ✗
10 grapes ✓

1 There's a cheese sandwich on the menu.

2 Make questions with *there is/there are*. Then, in pairs, ask and answer the questions.
1 a table / your kitchen / ?
2 fish fingers / your fridge / ?
3 a café / your school / ?
4 vegetarian meals / your school café / ?
5 a fridge / your bedroom / ?
6 a pizzeria / your street / ?
7 tomatoes / a pizza / ?
8 eggs / an omelette / ?

A: Is there a table in your kitchen?
B: Yes, there is.

2.4

Countable and uncountable nouns | Quantifiers

Some nouns are countable (e.g. *bananas*) but other nouns are uncountable (e.g. *cheese*).
Countable nouns can be singular (e.g. *a/one banana*) or plural (e.g. *bananas*). Uncountable nouns have no plural form.
I've got three bananas. NOT ~~I've got three breads~~.

Countable nouns		Uncountable nouns
Singular	**Plural**	bread, butter, cheese, cola, ketchup, soup
a banana	bananas	
a burger	burgers	
an egg	eggs	

With uncountable nouns and plural countable nouns, we use *some/any* instead of *a/an*.
I've got some bread. NOT ~~I've got a bread~~.

	Countable nouns	Uncountable nouns
+	There's a burger. There's an egg. There are some chips. There are a lot/lots of chips.	There's some cheese. There's a lot/lots of soup.
−	There aren't any cookies. There aren't many beans.	There isn't any bread. There isn't much butter.
?	Are there any forks? How many forks are there?	Is there any cola? How much cola is there?

1 Write the words below in the correct place in the table.

~~apple~~ biscuits burger chips crisps knife
mayonnaise salt spaghetti tomato water

	Countable	Uncountable
Singular	apple	
Plural		

2 Write sentences with the words in Exercise 1. Use *there is/there are* and *a/an* or *some*.
There's an apple.
There are some biscuits.

3 Choose eight words from Exercise 1 and make a shopping list. Write the quantities. Then, in pairs, ask questions to find out what is on your partner's list.

A: Are there any apples on your shopping list?
B: Yes, there are.
A: How many apples are there?

Grammar Time **127**

Grammar Time

3.2

Present Simple: affirmative and negative

We use the Present Simple to talk about routines and habits.

+	I/You/We/They get up late. He/She/It studies hard.
–	I/You/We/They don't (do not) eat breakfast. He/She/It doesn't (does not) tidy up every day.

Spelling rules: *he/she/it*
Most verbs add *-s*: *eat – eats*
Verbs ending in *-ch, -o, -sh, -ss* and *-x* add *-es*:
wash – washes
Verbs ending in consonant + *-y* cut the *-y* and add *-ies*:
study – studies

Time expressions
always, usually, often, sometimes, never, once a week, every three weeks
Adverbs of frequency (*never, often,* etc.) usually go before the main verb, but after the verb *to be*.
They sometimes complain.
They don't often go to the cinema.
She is often tired.
Longer phrases usually come at the end.
I go to the cinema once a week.
We don't use *not* with *never* because *never* already has a negative meaning.
She never eats meat. NOT ~~She doesn't never eat meat.~~

1 In pairs, say how often you do these things. Use a time expression from the box above.
- go to the cinema
- tidy your room
- have breakfast
- check social media
- help in the kitchen
- write long letters

2 Complete the text with the Present Simple form of the verbs in brackets.

Every morning my budgie Cody ¹*tells* (tell) us he's happy to see the sun and ² _____ (wake) us up! We ³ _____ (not have) a problem with this in the winter. But in the summer he ⁴ _____ (start) at 4 a.m. and he ⁵ _____ (not stop) – we ⁶ _____ (not like) it at all! Cody ⁷ _____ (know) many words. He often ⁸ _____ (say) 'Pretty boy!' and 'Lovely apple!', but his favourite words are 'Be quiet, Cody!'.

3 Think of a person you know well. Write eight sentences about what he he/she does or doesn't do on a typical day.

3.4

Present Simple: questions and short answers

Yes/No questions and short answers

Do	I/you/ we/they	go to school?	Yes, I/you/we/they do. No, I/you/we/they don't.
Does	he/she/it	get up early?	Yes, he/she/it does. No, he/she/it doesn't.

Wh- questions
What time does he get up?
Where does she come from?
How often do you visit your grandparents?
Which languages do they speak?

1 Complete the questions with *do* or *does*. Then, in pairs, ask and answer the questions.
1 *Does* your best friend live near you?
2 _____ your grandparents often visit you?
3 _____ your dad like sport?
4 _____ you like Mondays?
5 _____ your mum work in a bank?

2 Complete the questions with the question words below. Then, in pairs, ask and answer the questions.

~~how often~~   what   what time   when   where

1 *How often* do you text your friends?
2 _____ do your cousins live?
3 _____ do you usually do on Sundays?
4 _____ do you go to bed on Fridays?
5 _____ do you visit your grandparents?

3 In pairs, write questions for these answers. Sometimes more than one answer is possible.
1 I usually watch TV in the evening.
  When do you usually watch TV?
  What do you usually do in the evening?
2 My mum works in an office.
3 My brothers go to bed at ten.
4 I see my grandparents once a month.
5 No, we don't. We hate rock music!

4 Choose a favourite musician or sports star. Write six questions you would like to ask him/her about his/her life.
How often do you go to parties?

4.2

Present Continuous

We use the Present Continuous to talk about what is happening now.

+	−
I'm (am) working. You/We/They're (are) working. He/She/It's (is) working.	I'm not (am not) sleeping. You/We/They aren't (are not) sleeping. He/She/It isn't (is not) sleeping.
?	
Am I reading? Are you/we/they reading? Is he/she/it reading?	Yes, I am./No, I'm not. Yes, you/we/they are./ No, you/we/they aren't. Yes, he/she/it is./ No, he/she/it isn't.
What are you doing? Why are they smiling?	

Spelling rules: -ing
Most verbs add -ing: eat – eating
Verbs ending in -e cut the -e and add -ing: make – making
One-syllable verbs ending in vowel + consonant double the final consonant: sit – sitting

Time expressions
now, at the moment, today

1 Complete the sentences with the Present Continuous form of the verbs in brackets.
1 Dana *isn't studying* (not study) – she _____ (use) the internet.
2 Two men _____ (run) out of that shop!
3 _____ (they/study) for their English test?
4 I can't speak to you now. I _____ (read).
5 A: _____ (you/have) a good time?
   B: Yes, we _____ . It's a great concert.

2 In pairs, take it in turns to mime one of the actions below for your partner to guess.

> check your email   drive a tractor   eat spaghetti
> feel bored   have a shower   make a pizza
> play a video game   play with a cat   walk in the rain

A: Are you making a pizza?
B: No, I'm not. I'm playing a video game!

3 Think about a famous person in your country. What do you think they are doing at the moment? Write five sentences.

The President is having an English lesson.

4.4

Present Simple and Present Continuous

We use the Present Simple to talk about habits and routines.
I usually go to bed after midnight.
Jack never watches TV in the morning.

We use the Present Continuous to talk about something happening now/at the moment.
I'm playing a video game at the moment.
Noah can't come to the phone right now – he's having a shower.

1 Look at the table and make sentences about the people. Use the Present Simple and the Present Continuous.

	Usually	At the moment
Jim	not eat meat	eat a burger
Maria	not watch TV	watch a film
Jack	not work hard at school	do his homework
Luke and Seb	wear tracksuits	wear white shirts
Cara and I	not enjoy classes	have fun

Jim doesn't usually eat meat, but he's eating a burger at the moment.

2 Make questions in the Present Simple or the Present Continuous. Then, in pairs, ask and answer the questions.
1 you / wear / trainers / at the moment / ?
2 your friends / usually / wear / trainers to parties / ?
3 when / you / usually / do / your homework / ?
4 your classmates / have / fun / now / ?
5 your parents / often / listen / to music / ?
6 how often / you / speak / English / after school / ?

A: Are you wearing trainers at the moment?
B: Yes, I am.

3 Choose three classmates you know well. Write sentences about what they often/usually do in English classes. Use the Present Simple.

Tiago usually sits next to the window.
Lena always works hard.

4 Write sentences about what the people from Exercise 3 are doing now. Use the Present Continuous.

Tiago is looking out the window.
Lena is doing an exercise.

Grammar Time

5.2

Comparatives

We use the comparative to compare people, things or places. To form it, we use adjective + -er + than or more + adjective + than.
I'm taller than my sister.
English is more interesting than Maths.

Adjective	Comparative
Short adjectives: + -er	
strong	stronger
Short adjectives ending in -e: + -r	
cute	cuter
Short adjectives ending in vowel + consonant: double the final consonant + -er	
big	bigger
Adjectives ending in -y: cut the -y + -ier	
friendly	friendlier
Long adjectives: more	
intelligent	more intelligent
Irregular adjectives	
good	better
bad	worse

1 Write the comparative form of the adjectives.

bad – worse	happy –	sad –
brave –	lazy –	good –
cool –	nice –	successful –
fit –	old –	talented –
funny –	original –	thin –

2 In pairs, compare these people, places and things. Use the adjectives in brackets.
  1. Canada / Ireland (small, big)
     Ireland is smaller than Canada.
     Canada is bigger than Ireland.
  2. Harry Styles / Brad Pitt (young, old)
  3. rap / reggae (good, bad)
  4. Beyoncé / Billie Eilish (successful)
  5. science fiction films / horror films (interesting)

3 Write ten sentences about you and a friend. Use comparative adjectives.

I'm older than my friend Sarah.
She's got longer hair than me.

5.4

Superlatives

We use the superlative to compare one thing, person or place to a bigger group of things, people or places. To form it, we use the + adjective + -est or the most + adjective.
I'm the tallest person in my family.
English is the most interesting subject at school.

Adjective	Superlative
Short adjectives: + -est	
strong	the strongest
Short adjectives ending in -e: + -st	
cute	the cutest
Short adjectives ending in vowel + consonant: double the final consonant + -est	
big	the biggest
Adjectives ending in -y: cut the -y + -iest	
friendly	the friendliest
Long adjectives: most	
intelligent	the most intelligent
Irregular adjectives	
good	the best
bad	the worst

1 Write the superlative form of the adjectives.

bad – the worst	happy –	sad –
brave –	lazy –	good –
cool –	nice –	successful –
fit –	old –	talented –
funny –	original –	thin –

2 Make sentences with superlative adjectives. Then, in pairs, compare your sentences.
  1. big / city in our country
     The biggest city in our country is …
  2. interesting / film this year
  3. happy / person I know
  4. bad / pop group in the world
  5. brave / person in history

3 Write six sentences about your family. Use superlative adjectives.

The oldest person in my family is my great grandfather – he's eighty-five.
The person with the longest hair in my family is …

6.2

Was/Were, There was/There were

The past form of the verb *to be* is *was* or *were*.

+	I/He/She/It	was	in China.
	You/We/They	were	at the match.
	There	was	a girls' team.
	There	were	two teams.
−	I/He/She/It	wasn't (was not)	in the team.
	You/We/They	weren't (were not)	happy.
	There	wasn't (was not)	a big crowd.
	There	weren't (were not)	any goals.
?	Was he at the match? Yes, he was./No, he wasn't.		
	Were they good? Yes, they were./No, they weren't.		
	Was there a winner? Yes, there was./No, there wasn't.		
	Were there many goals? Yes, there were./No, there weren't.		

Time expressions
in 1991 (nineteen ninety-one), in 2020 (twenty twenty)

1 Complete the dialogue with the correct form of *was* or *were*. Then, in pairs, practise the dialogue.
   A: Where ¹*were* the Olympic Games in 2012?
   ² _____ they in Rio, in Brazil?
   B: No, the 2012 Olympics ³ _____ in Rio. They ⁴ _____ in London.
   A: So, when ⁵ _____ the Games in Brazil?
   B: I think it ⁶ _____ in 2016.
   A: ⁷ _____ you there?
   B: No, I ⁸ _____ .

2 Complete the dialogue with the correct form of *there was* or *there were*. Then, in pairs, practise the dialogue.
   A: ¹*There were* three goals in the first half – two for France!
   B: How many goals ² _____ in the second half?
   A: Also three – the final score was France 4 Croatia 2.
   B: ³ _____ a big crowd?
   A: Yes, ⁴ _____ . ⁵ _____ exactly 78,011 people in the stadium.
   B: That's a lot! And ⁶ _____ any red cards?
   A: No, ⁷ _____ .

6.4

Past Simple affirmative: regular and irregular verbs

Regular verbs
To form the Past Simple of regular verbs, we usually add *-ed* to the verb.
I/You/He/She/It/We/They walked home.

Spelling rules
Most verbs add *-ed*: *play – played*
Verbs ending in *-e* add *-d*: *move – moved*
Verbs ending in vowel + consonant double the consonant and add *-ed*: *stop – stopped*
Verbs ending in consonant + *-y* cut the *-y* and add *-ied*: *carry – carried*

Irregular verbs
Many verbs are irregular in the Past Simple.
come – came   do – did   win – won (See page 135.)

Time expressions
this morning, yesterday, last night, last week, last month, last summer, last year, an hour ago, in 2010, when I was six

1 Write the Past Simple form of the verbs.

ask – *asked*	try –	dance –
do –	go –	win –
see –	jog –	come –
end –	put –	want –

2 Complete the text with the Past Simple form of the verbs in brackets.

Last Sunday I ¹*woke up* (wake up) at 6.30 a.m. I ² _____ (eat) a sandwich and then I ³ _____ (run) to my friend Danny's house. His dad ⁴ _____ (drive) us to a mountain called Ben Nevis. We ⁵ _____ (arrive) there at 8 a.m. We ⁶ _____ (have) a snack and then we ⁷ _____ (start) walking. We ⁸ _____ (walk) for three hours and then we ⁹ _____ (stop) for lunch. We were tired when we ¹⁰ _____ (get) to the top, but the view was fantastic!

3 In pairs, talk about what you did last Sunday. Use the text in Exercise 2 to help you.

4 Write two Past Simple sentences about you for each time expression below: one with a regular verb and one with an irregular verb.

> last night   last month   last week   last year
> this morning

My mum asked me a question last night.
I went to bed late last night.

Grammar Time

7.2

Past Simple: negative

To form negative sentences in the Past Simple, we use didn't (did not) + infinitive.
I slept last night. – I didn't sleep last night.
She laughed. – She didn't laugh.

I/You/He/She/It/We/They didn't work.
I/You/He/She/It/We/They didn't go to school.

1 Complete the sentences with the Past Simple form of the verbs in brackets.
1. We *didn't go* (not go) to the park today.
2. Liz _____ (not like) her present.
3. You _____ (not finish) your breakfast.
4. I _____ (not get up) early yesterday.
5. The game _____ (not start) at six.

2 Rewrite the sentences in the negative form.
1. We understood.
   We didn't understand.
2. She wrote to me.
3. They walked home.
4. We ate breakfast.
5. I bought a magazine.
6. He sold his laptop.

3 In pairs, correct the sentences. Use the words in brackets to help you.
1. William Shakespeare came from Canada. (England)
   William Shakespeare didn't come from Canada. He came from England.
2. J.K. Rowling wrote *The Hobbit*. (*Harry Potter*)
3. The Japanese invented chess. (karate)
4. Bill Gates started Apple. (Microsoft)
5. Leonardo Da Vinci lived in France. (Italy)
6. Albert Einstein lived in the eighteenth century. (twentieth)

4 Write five sentences about the differences between your life and your parents' lives when they were your age. Use the Past Simple.

My parents didn't go on holiday abroad.
They didn't learn English at school.
_____
_____
_____
_____
_____

7.4

Past Simple: questions and short answers

To form questions in the Past Simple, we use did + subject + infinitive.
Did I/you/he/she/it/we/they go to school?
Yes, I/you/he/she/it/we/they did.
No, I/you/he/she/it/we/they didn't.

Where did you go yesterday?
When did you see her?
What time did you get up?

1 Complete the questions with the Past Simple form of the verbs in brackets. Then match questions 1–7 with answers a–g below.
1. *Did you see* (you/see) Tom yesterday?
2. _____ (they/like) the party?
3. _____ (you/enjoy) the concert?
4. _____ (what/she/buy)?
5. _____ (they/go) to the shops?
6. _____ (what time/you/get up)?
7. _____ (where/he/stay)?

a ☐ *1* No, I didn't, but I texted him.
b ☐ I got up at six o'clock.
c ☐ Yes, they did – they really enjoyed it.
d ☐ No, they didn't. They went to the cinema.
e ☐ She bought a birthday present for her dad.
f ☐ He stayed in a hotel.
g ☐ No, I didn't. It was boring.

2 Complete the questions with the Past Simple form of the verbs below. Then, in pairs, ask and answer the questions.

| eat   get up   go   rain   wash   ~~watch~~ |

1. *Did you watch* (you) any good films last week?
2. When _____ (you) to bed last night?
3. _____ (it) yesterday?
4. _____ (you) your hair this morning?
5. What time _____ (your parents) this morning?
6. What _____ (your family) for dinner last night?

3 Imagine that you have a lifestyle blog. Write an interview with your favourite music/sports star about his/her life. Write at least five questions.

Me: When did you start playing football?
Mo Salah: I started playing football in …

132 Grammar Time

8.2

Modal verbs: *have to/don't have to, mustn't*

Modal verbs come before other verbs.
When it is necessary to do something, we use *have to*.
When it is not necessary to do something, we use *don't have to*.
When it is important not to do something (e.g. it's a bad idea or it's against the law), we use *mustn't*.

I/You/We/They	have to	get up early.
He/She/It	has to	
I/You/We/They	don't have to	worry.
He/She/It	doesn't have to	
I/You/He/She/It/We/They	mustn't	be late.

1 Read the instructions for an exam and complete the sentences below with the correct modal verb.

History exam: Room 4B, Friday 2 May, 9 a.m.

- Switch off your mobile phone.
- There are four questions. Answer three of them.
- Answer the questions with a pen, not a pencil.
- The exam ends at 11 a.m. You can leave before the end if you like.

1 You *have to* switch off your mobile phone.
2 You _____ answer all the questions.
3 You _____ answer three questions.
4 You _____ use a pen.
5 You _____ use a pencil.
6 You _____ stay until the end of the exam.

2 In pairs, write sentences about your school. Use the ideas below and *have to, don't have to* or *mustn't*.

ask the teacher questions   do a lot of homework
eat during a class   run in the corridor   shout
stand up when a teacher enters a room
study two languages   wear a uniform

In our school we have to study two languages.

3 Complete the sentences so they are true for you.
1 Every morning before I have breakfast, I have to …
2 Every night before I go to bed, I have to …
3 On Sundays, we don't have to …
4 When I'm on holiday, I don't have to …
5 At meals in our house, you mustn't …

8.4

Articles: first and second mention

The first time we mention something, we use *a* or *an* for countable singular nouns, and *some* for plural and uncountable nouns.
The second time we mention something, we use *the*.

There's *a* lake near our town. There's *an* island on the lake.
There are *some* trees on the island.
We go swimming in *the* lake. You can swim to *the* island.
The trees are very old.

1 Complete the text with *a/an*, *some* or *the*.

In my room there's ¹*a* cupboard. In ²_____ cupboard there's ³_____ red suitcase. In ⁴_____ suitcase there are ⁵_____ books. In one of the books there is ⁶_____ map. ⁷_____ map shows ⁸_____ island. ⁹_____ island is in the Pacific Ocean. On ¹⁰_____ map, in the centre of ¹¹_____ island, there is ¹²_____ big red cross – like this: **X**. ¹³_____ cross shows the location of ¹⁴_____ box. In ¹⁵_____ box there's some treasure!

2 In pairs, take it in turns to describe something in your room. Use the text in Exercise 1 to help you.

In my room there's a desk. On the desk there's a small box. In the box …

3 Choose the correct option.

Scotland is ¹*a*/ *the* small country to the north of England. In the east of the country is ²*an* / *the* amazing city – Edinburgh. ³*The* / *A* city has some ancient buildings. One of ⁴*a* / *the* buildings is a palace – Holyrood. From ⁵*the* / *a* palace, a road – the Royal Mile – goes up a hill. On top of ⁶*the*/ *a* hill there's ⁷*a* / *the* famous castle. From ⁸*a* / *the* castle there's a great view of a river – the Forth. There's ⁹*a* / *the* railway bridge over the river. ¹⁰*The* / *A* bridge is over 130 years old.

4 Write sentences about a place you know well. Use the text in Exercise 3 to help you.

Valencia is a city in the east of Spain. In the centre of the city there are some …

Grammar Time

9.2

Present Continuous for future arrangements

We use the Present Continuous to talk about arrangements. We often mention a time and/or a place.
We're meeting at six o'clock.
Dad's taking me to London on the fifteenth.
They aren't coming with us next week – they're going on holiday.
Are you coming to my party on Sunday?
Yes, I am./No, I'm not.

Time expressions
this afternoon, tonight, tomorrow, next weekend

1 Complete the sentences with the Present Continuous form of the verbs in brackets.
1. Novak Djokovic *is playing* (play) Roger Federer on Saturday. Who _____ (Rafael Nadal/play)?
2. A: What _____ (you/do) next Sunday?
   We _____ (have) a birthday party!
   B: Oh, that's a pity! We _____ (go) to a concert that evening.
3. A: _____ (you/come) to the cinema with Jake and me tomorrow evening?
   B: No, we _____ (take) our cat to the vet's.
4. A: What _____ (Jenny/do) this summer?
   B: She _____ (visit) her grandparents.
5. Ian _____ (see) the dentist this afternoon.

2 Complete your diary for the weekend with four arrangements. Use the ideas below or your own. Then, in pairs, ask and answer about your weekend.

> go swimming   go to a party   go to the cinema
> go to the hairdresser's   have lunch with …
> meet a friend   watch a football match

FRIDAY	evening	
SATURDAY	morning	
	afternoon	
	evening	
SUNDAY	morning	

A: What are you doing on Friday evening?
B: I'm going to a party! And what are you doing on … ?

9.4

Be going to for future plans

We use *be going to* to talk about intentions and plans. (These plans can change in the future.)

+	I'm going to live abroad.
	You/We/They're going to live abroad.
	He/She/It's going to live abroad.
–	I'm not going to tell him.
	You/We/They aren't going to tell him.
	He/She/It isn't going to tell him.
?	Are you/we/they going to come?
	Yes, I am./Yes, you/we/they are.
	No, I'm not./No, you/we/they aren't.
	Is he/she/it going to come?
	Yes, he/she/it is./No, he/she/it isn't.
	What are you going to do after you leave school?
	When are you going to visit us?

1 Complete the sentences with the correct form of *be going to* and the verbs in brackets.
1. I'*m going to go* (go) skiing with my family next winter.
2. The youth hostel in Venice was terrible. Next time we _____ (not stay) at the youth hostel – we _____ (find) a cheap hotel.
3. I _____ (not play) football tomorrow. I _____ (revise) for my exams all weekend.
4. A: _____ (you/see) the James Bond film this weekend?
   B: No, we _____ . We _____ (watch) the new Sherlock Holmes film.
5. They _____ (go) to New York next summer.
6. A: _____ (Tom/go) to the new shopping centre?
   B: Yes, he _____ . He _____ (buy) some new clothes.
7. We _____ (visit) my grandmother in hospital at the weekend.

2 In pairs, write five sentences about what you are going to do in the next holidays. Use the ideas below to help you.

> go to the seaside   learn a new language   meet friends
> read a lot of books   sleep until noon   watch a lot of films

In the winter holidays I'm not going to read a lot of books, but I'm going to watch a lot of films.

Irregular Verbs

🔊 10.1

Infinitive	Past Simple	Past Participle
be	was/were	been
become	became	become
begin	began	begun
break	broke	broken
bring	brought	brought
build	built	built
burn	burned/burnt	burned/burnt
buy	bought	bought
can	could	been able to
catch	caught	caught
choose	chose	chosen
come	came	come
cost	cost	cost
cut	cut	cut
do	did	done
draw	drew	drawn
dream	dreamed/dreamt	dreamed/dreamt
drink	drank	drunk
drive	drove	driven
eat	ate	eaten
fall	fell	fallen
feed	fed	fed
feel	felt	felt
fight	fought	fought
find	found	found
fly	flew	flown
forget	forgot	forgotten
forgive	forgave	forgiven
get	got	got
give	gave	given
go	went	gone
grow	grew	grown
hang	hung	hung
have	had	had
hear	heard	heard
hit	hit	hit
hold	held	held
hurt	hurt	hurt
keep	kept	kept

Infinitive	Past Simple	Past Participle
know	knew	known
learn	learned/learnt	learned/learnt
leave	left	left
lend	lent	lent
let	let	let
lie	lay	lain
lose	lost	lost
make	made	made
meet	met	met
pay	paid	paid
put	put	put
read	read	read
ride	rode	ridden
ring	rang	rung
run	ran	run
say	said	said
see	saw	seen
sell	sold	sold
send	sent	sent
set	set	set
show	showed	shown
sing	sang	sung
sit	sat	sat
sleep	slept	slept
speak	spoke	spoken
spend	spent	spent
stand	stood	stood
steal	stole	stolen
sweep	swept	swept
swim	swam	swum
take	took	taken
teach	taught	taught
tell	told	told
think	thought	thought
understand	understood	understood
wake	woke	woken
wear	wore	worn
win	won	won
write	wrote	written

Student Activities

Unit 1 — Vocabulary Activator Exercise 2

2 Turkey 4 American 6 China
3 Spanish 5 Italian

Unit 2 — Revision Exercise 9

Student B

You are a waiter in Student A's favourite restaurant. Student A is your customer.
- Say hello and ask him/her: *What would you like?*
- Ask him/her: *Anything else?*
- Take his/her order.
- Give a price. Say: *Thank you.*

Unit 3 — Lesson 3.1 Exercise 8

How healthy is your life?

Results

Mostly a: You have a very healthy life! Well done!
Mostly b: Oh dear! You haven't got a very healthy lifestyle. What can you change?

Progress Check Units 1–3 Exercise 5

Student A

You are Student B's friend and you meet him/her at a restaurant. Follow these steps.
- Greet Student B and ask how he/she is.
- Ask him/her what food he/she likes/doesn't like.
- Say what you would like to eat.
- Swap roles and repeat the role play with different ideas.

Unit 4 — Lesson 4.2 Exercises 2 and 4

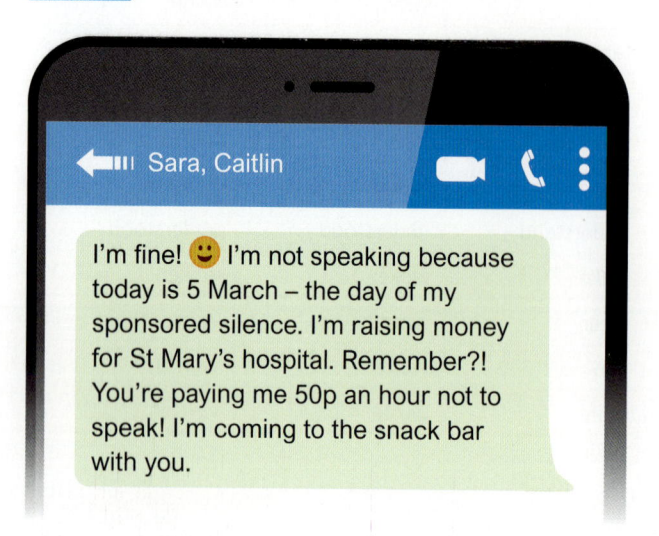

Sara, Caitlin

I'm fine! 😊 I'm not speaking because today is 5 March – the day of my sponsored silence. I'm raising money for St Mary's hospital. Remember?! You're paying me 50p an hour not to speak! I'm coming to the snack bar with you.

Unit 4 — Revision Exercise 7

Student B

Can I:	Can you:
• use your phone?	• close the door?
• sit in your chair?	• get me a drink?

Set for Life — My study routine Exercise 7

HOW SCHOOL-SMART ARE YOU?

Score

0 points for each 'never' answer
1 point for each 'sometimes' answerr
2 points for each 'often' answer

Results

12–16 points: You need some study help – fast!
7–11 points: Not bad, but you can be smarter.
0–6 points: You're already a smart student!

Unit 5 — Lesson 5.1 Exercise 6

Mia is thinking of Ed Sheeran.

Unit 5 — Lesson 5.1 Exercise 8

The Big Music Quiz

1 b 2 a 3 b 4 c
5 c 6 a 7 a 8 c

Unit 5 — Lesson 5.6 Exercise 5

Student B

1 Listen to Student A's situations. Make suggestions. Use the ideas below or your own ideas.
- study with a friend/watch YouTube videos in English
- make an omelette/eat an apple

2 Read these situations to Student A. Respond to his/her suggestions.
- It's a boring Sunday afternoon. I feel sad.
- It's my friend's birthday soon and I want to get him/her a present.

136 Student Activities

Unit 6 — Lesson 6.1 Exercise 6

SPORTS QUIZ

1 b 2 a 3 c
4 a 5 c 6 b

Unit 6 — Lesson 6.4 Exercise 7

What	Where	When
eat some crisps	at home	this morning
go jogging	at school	last night
play football	in the town centre	yesterday
run six kilometres	in the park	last week
see a tennis match	on the bus	last month
win a medal	on TV	last year

Progress Check Units 1–6 Exercise 5

Student A

Describe the photo below. Use these questions to help you.
1 What can you see in the photo?
2 Where are they?
3 What are they doing?
4 What are they wearing?
5 How are they feeling?

Unit 7 — Lesson 7.1 Exercise 4

THE HISTORY OF COMPUTERS

1 c 2 b 3 a 4 a 5 a 6 c 7 b 8 c

Unit 8 — Lesson 8.1 Exercise 4

FAST GEOGRAPHY FACTS
True or false?

1 F – The capital of Brazil is Brasília.
2 F – The word for Mexican money is *peso*.
3 F – The Japanese flag is white with a red circle.
4 T
5 T
6 F – Antarctica is south of Australia.
7 F – The Niger River is in (West) Africa.
8 T
9 F – The Pacific is the biggest ocean on Earth.
10 T

Student Activities

Unit 8 — Vocabulary Activator — Exercise 2

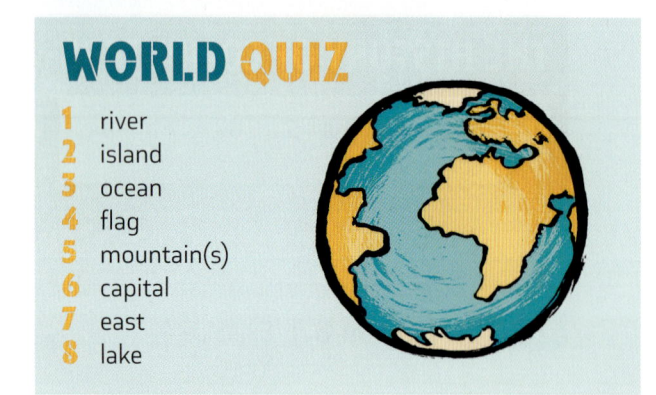

WORLD QUIZ

1 river
2 island
3 ocean
4 flag
5 mountain(s)
6 capital
7 east
8 lake

Unit 8 — Revision — Exercise 6

Student B

- Student A is explaining something to you. Use at least three of the phrases below to say you understand/don't understand.

  > I'm sorry, I don't get it.   I'm not sure I understand.
  > What do you mean?   Now I get it.   I see.   Oh, right!

- Swap roles. Explain to Student A how to attach a photo to a message, and then send the message. Use the phrases below to make sure he/she understands you.

  > Do you get it?   Do you see?   … , right?

Progress Check Units 1–3 — Exercise 5

Student B

You are Student A's friend and you meet him/her at a restaurant. Follow these steps.

- Talk with Student A and respond to what he/she says. Use the phrases below to help you.

  > I'm fine, thanks. What about you?   I like pasta.
  > I hate fish!   What would you like to eat?

- Swap roles and repeat the role play with different ideas.

Progress Check Units 1–6 — Exercise 5

Student B

Describe the photo below. Use these questions to help you.

1 What can you see in the photo?
2 Where are they?
3 What are they doing?
4 What are they wearing?
5 How are they feeling?

Progress Check Units 1–9 — Exercise 5

1 Look at some photos that show different types of holiday activities. Do you like these holiday activities? Why?/Why not?

2 In pairs, ask and answer the questions. Give reasons to explain your answers.

Do you think:
- sightseeing is interesting?
- shopping is boring?
- skiing is dangerous?
- surfing is difficult?
- hiking is cool?

3 In pairs, take it in turns to ask and answer the questions.
- Do you prefer summer or winter holidays? Why?
- What activities did you do on your last holiday?

ART

CLIL 1

Still life

Still life is a popular kind of painting for artists. Choose some objects – maybe some food or some flowers – put them on a table and paint them! Easy? Oh no! Good still life painters are talented and hard-working.

Tjalf Sparnaay is a famous still life painter today. He was born in 1954 and he's Dutch, like a lot of famous still life painters from the past. But his paintings are different. In his pictures we can see ordinary objects like bread, burgers, cola cans, fried eggs, cheese and apples. His paintings are very clever. They are like photographs. Here are two pictures of a fried egg. Which is the photo and which is Tjalf's painting?

Tjalf has got four ideas:
1 Paint pictures like very good photographs.
2 Paint ordinary things.
3 Make those things beautiful.
4 Paint very big pictures.

Tjalf's paintings are called 'Megarealism'. They're very big and very real. One painting, of a burger with salt, pepper and ketchup, is 823 x 550 cm! One look at Tjalf's paintings and you're very hungry!

1 Look at the still life paintings (A–C). Can you match the paintings with the dates (1–3)?

1 ☐ sixteenth century
2 ☐ eighteenth century
3 ☐ nineteenth century

2 🔊 10.2 Read the article. What do the paintings in Exercise 1 and Tjalf Sparnaay's paintings have in common?

3 Read the article again. Answer the questions.
1 What nationality is Tjalf Sparnaay?
2 Name three things in his paintings.
3 Why are his paintings clever?
4 What is his style of painting called?
5 How big is one of his paintings?

4 In pairs, take it in turns to choose one of the paintings from Exercise 1. Look at it for thirty seconds. Then cover the painting. How many items can you remember?

5 In pairs, discuss the questions.
1 Do you like art? Why?/Why not?
2 Who is your favourite painter?
3 What famous paintings can you name?

6 GO ONLINE Use the internet to find information about one of the artists below. Make notes about these things.
- his/her nationality
- the names of some of his/her paintings and what they show
- what you think of his/her art

Andy Warhol   Frida Kahlo   Zhou Chunya

7 SHARE IT Present your research to the class. Use your notes from Exercise 6 and the phrases below.

Frida Kahlo is from …
One of her most famous paintings is …
It shows …
I think her paintings are …

LITERATURE

CLIL 2

The Secret Garden
by Frances Hodgson Burnett

Mary loses her parents and she moves to England after living in India all of her life. She likes to explore the garden of the big house she now lives in. There is a door in the garden. She doesn't have a key for the door, but one day she finds it.

There was a strong wind that day and suddenly, it moved the plants under the robin to one side. Mary looked – and there in the wall was a door. 'The door to the secret garden!' she cried.

She felt very excited. She took the key from her coat and put it in the door. It was not easy but slowly, she turned the key. She pushed the door and it opened. She walked through and quickly shut the door behind her. She looked round excitedly. She was inside the secret garden!

It was very early spring, and there were no flowers. But there were rose trees everywhere, and rose plants climbed over the walls and the other trees in the garden. 'It's the strangest place in the world!' Mary thought.

The grass was brown, everything was brown. 'Is anything growing here? Everything looks very dead,' she thought.

Mary walked round the garden. There were little green plants in the ground. She looked at them carefully. There was grass round them and the plants couldn't grow very well. She started to pull up the grass round the plants. 'That's better,' she said.

She worked busily all morning. At midday, she went back to the house. 'I'll come back this afternoon,' she thought.

climb (v) go up
pull up (v) take out from a place
robin (n) a bird with a red front
rose (n) a type of flower

1 You are going to read an extract from a famous story called *The Secret Garden*. Look at the photo. What do you think is in the secret garden?

2 🔊 10.3 Read the story quickly and check your answers to Exercise 1.

3 Read the story again. Mark the sentences T (true) or F (false).
  1 ☐ The weather was windy.
  2 ☐ It was difficult to open the door.
  3 ☐ The grass in the garden helped the plants grow.
  4 ☐ Mary started to work in the garden.
  5 ☐ Mary decided to go back to the garden later.

4 In pairs, discuss the questions.
  1 Why does Mary shut the door quickly?
  2 What do you think makes the garden 'strange'?
  3 Do you think Mary told anyone about the secret garden? Why?/Why not?
  4 Why do you think the garden is 'secret'? Would you like to find out why?

5 (GO ONLINE) Use the internet to find information about a story for children. Make notes about these things.
  • when the author wrote it
  • who the main characters are
  • where the story takes place and what it is about
  • any film adaptations that you can watch

6 (SHARE IT) Present your research to the class. Use your notes from Exercise 5 and the phrases below.

C.S. Lewis wrote *The Lion, the Witch and the Wardrobe* in …
The main characters are a boy/girl called …
The story takes place in … It's about …
The most famous film adaptation was …

HISTORY

CLIL 3

Mummies

What is a mummy?

The ancient Egyptians buried dead people in an unusual way. They prepared the body with special oils and put it in a stone or wooden box called a sarcophagus. These bodies lasted a long time and we can look at them in museums today. The bodies are called mummies. The Egyptians also put food and valuable things with the bodies. Sometimes they put the dead person's pet there!

Why did they do this?

The ancient Egyptians believed in an afterlife. They thought that the spirit of the dead person went to another world. They needed their body and lots of their things to use in this afterlife. They needed food and drink for the journey there.

Where did they put the sarcophagus?

The ancient Egyptians put poor people in the sand, but they buried rich people in tombs. They painted the walls with pictures from their lives. Between 2628 BC and 1638 BC, the tombs of the pharaohs (the kings) were inside great stone pyramids. This was to protect them. Artists painted the sarcophagus with a picture of the pharaoh, often with expensive gold paint. Very important pharaohs had gold masks on their faces.

> **afterlife** (n) the life that some people believe people have after death
> **tomb** (n) a place people build above or below the ground to bury the dead

A s_____
B t_____
C p_____
D s_____
E m_____

1 Do you know what an Egyptian mummy is?

2 🔊 10.4 Read the article quickly and complete the labels for photos A–E.

3 Read the article again. Mark the sentences T (true) or F (false).
   1. ☐ They buried animals with the people.
   2. ☐ They thought that dead people had another life.
   3. ☐ They buried all Egyptians in tombs.
   4. ☐ They painted the bodies gold.

4 Can you name other famous tombs in the world? Who did people bury there?

5 **GO ONLINE** Use the internet to find information about one of the famous pyramids below. Make notes about these things.
   - where it is
   - when people built it
   - how big it is
   - who people buried in the pyramid

> the Great Pyramid of Giza   the Pyramid of Cestius
> Tikal Temple I

6 **SHARE IT** Present your research to the class. Use your notes from Exercise 5 and the phrases below.

> The name of the pyramid I researched is …
> It is in …
> People built it in …
> It is … metres high.
> It is a tomb for …

SCIENCE

CLIL 4

Hot-air balloons

1 ☐ The hot-air balloon isn't the fastest way to fly and it isn't the most direct. It depends on the wind. But the hot-air balloon was the first form of flying that carried people. It was a long time before aeroplanes. The first passengers were a sheep, a duck and a chicken! Then, a few weeks later, on 21 November 1783 in France, a hot-air balloon carried two people.

2 ☐ The hot-air balloon uses science in a very easy but clever way. Hot air rises in colder air because it is lighter and less dense. Think about floating on water: our body floats because water is denser than we are.

3 ☐ The hot-air balloon has three main parts. There is a balloon envelope – this holds the air. The material is nylon and has sections called 'gores'. There is a valve at the top. Under the envelope there is a burner. This uses propane gas to heat the air in the balloon. There is a wicker basket to carry passengers. Wicker is a strong and quite light material. People often use it for things like garden furniture.

4 ☐ When the pilot wants the balloon to go higher, he/she turns up the gas. This makes the air hotter, and the balloon rises. To go down, he/she opens the valve at the top of the balloon. Some hot air leaves the balloon, and it goes down. To go in the right direction, the pilot goes up or down to ride on the wind. Very clever!

1 v_____
2 e_____
3 b_____
4 p_____ g_____
5 w_____ b_____

1 🔊 10.5 Read the article. Match headings a–d with paragraphs 1–4.
   a Going up and coming down
   b The first hot-air balloon
   c The science behind it
   d The parts of the balloon

2 Complete the labels in the picture above.

3 Read the article again. Answer the questions.
   1 Who were the first passengers in a hot-air balloon?
   2 When did the first hot-air balloon carry people?
   3 Why do hot-air balloons rise?
   4 Why do hot-air balloons have wicker baskets?
   5 How do hot-air balloons go down?

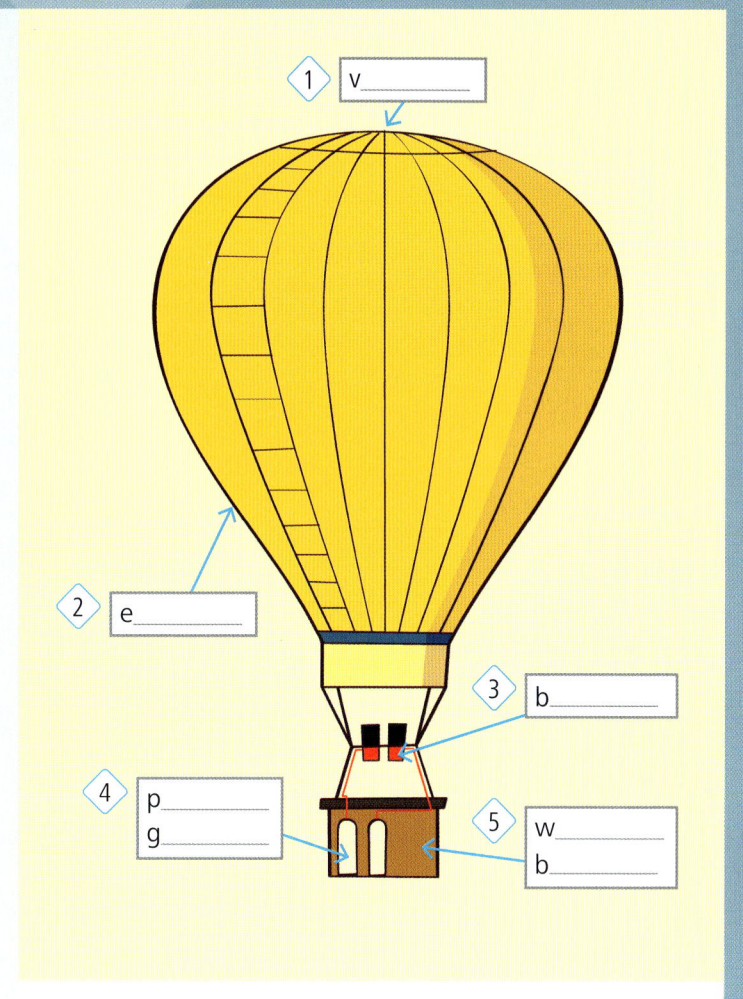

4 Would you like to travel in a hot-air balloon? Why?/Why not?

5 (GO ONLINE) Use the internet to find information about one of the airships (aircrafts that used hot gas) below. Complete the table.

The Giffard Airship   The Zeppelin LZ10
The USS Macon (ZRS–5)

Name	
When did it first fly?	
Who built it?	
In which country?	
How fast was it?	

6 (SHARE IT) Present your research to the class. Use your notes from Exercise 5 and the phrases below.

I researched the …
It first flew in …
… built it in …
… travelled at … km per hour.

Pearson Education Limited
KAO Two
KAO Park
Hockham Way
Harlow, Essex
CM17 9SR
England
and Associated Companies throughout the world.

pearsonenglish.com/widerworld2e

© Pearson Education Limited 2022

All rights reserved; no part of this publication may be reproduced, stored in a retrieval system, or transmitted in any form or by any means, electronic, mechanical, photocopying, recording, or otherwise without the prior written permission of the Publishers

First published 2022

ISBN: 978-1-292-34250-4

Set in Frutiger Next Pro
Printed in Mexico

Acknowledgements
The Publishers would like to thank all the teachers and students around the world who contributed to the development of Wider World Second Edition: Milena Aleksić, Tuğba Arslantaş, Gülşah Aslan, Mahgol Baboorian, Katarzyna Beliniak, Burcu Candan, Seri Diri, Hanna Dudich, Sema Karapinar, Nadiia Kasianchuk, Duygu Kayhan, Iryna Kharchenko, Ana Krstić, Ilknur Manav, Fulya Mertoğlu, Ivana Nikolov, Banu Oflas, Duygu Özer, Jagoda Popović, Marija Šanjević, Karmen Irizar Segurola, Elif Sevinç, Ludmila Shengel, Ayşe Sönmez, Anna Standish, Natalia Tkachenko, Pamela Van Bers, Jelena Vračar, Agnieszka Woźnicka, Münevver Yanık.

The Publishers would like to thank the following people who commented on the Wider World Second Edition content: Milena Aleksić, Mahgol Baboorian, Hanna Dudich, Izabela Kołando, Karmen Irizar Segurola, Joanna Srokosz, Anna Zając.

We would also like to thank the authors of the first edition of Wider World whose work has been the basis for creating this adaptation: Kathryn Alevizos, Carolyn Barraclough, Catherine Bright, Sheila Dignen, Lynda Edwards, Rod Fricker, Suzanne Gaynor, Bob Hastings, Jennifer Heath, Liz Kilbey, Stuart McKinlay, Sarah Thorpe, Tasia Vassilatou, Damian Williams, Sandy Zervas.

Photo Acknowledgements
123RF.com: aberration 50, adiruch 105, Aleksandr Strela 24, Alex Fagaras 115, antoshkaforever 34, arthurhidden 74, Baiba Opule 48, BlueOrange Studio 36, Bohdana Bergmannova 85, dikobrazik 69, dimaberkut 125, Dmitri Stalnuhhin 24, Edvard Molnar 29, ensup 89, erichsacco 74, freeartist 115, Gennadiy Poznyakov 67, George Tsartsianidis 50, georgerudy 48, Georgii Boronin 63, Graham Oliver 119, 137, Iakov Filimonov 81, Ian Allenden 87, 91, Igor Kardasov 17, igor terekhov 50, ira taskova 31, Jacek Chabraszewski 75, 139, Jeanette Brown 49, kakigori 53, kazitsyn 50, kubko 114, Ladislav Krajca 20, lightfieldstudios 36, 57, luckybusiness 139, Michael Fair 29, natika 24, nerthuz 50, Olga Yastremska 11, 36, opicobello 101; Pafan Julsaksrisakul 100, piksel 91, Przemyslaw Koch 89, rawpixel 69, serezniy 52, Sergey Galushko 50, shsphotography 101, sirikorn thamniyom 39, thevisualsyouneed 60, tobi 24, Valentin Valkov 89, Valentyna Zhukova 100, Viktor Moroziuk 69; **Alamy Stock Photo:** Andrey Nekrasov 142, Barry Diomede 12, 12, blickwinkel 142, CTK 77, Cultura RM 43, Dale O'Dell/ 63, Dallet-Alba 142, dpa picture alliance 100, Eric Nathan 11, Farhad Ibrahimzade 93, Frédéric de Laminne 14, Historic Collection 83, Joshua Windsor 26, Lanmas 140, Larry Lilac 142, Michael Kemp 98, Pictorial Press Ltd 77, 88, Roman Stetsyk 110, Steve Kydd 11, Stock Foundry Images 75, WENN Rights Ltd 62, 71, 114, WENN Rights Ltd/ 62, Zoonar GmbH 122; **BBC Studios:** 23, 23, 47, 73, 99, 123; **Bridgeman Images:** Leonard C. Hanna, Jr. Fund 140, Luisa Ricciarini 140; **Getty Images:** AFP 11, Alex Caparros/Getty Images Sport 14, Alex Potemkin/ E+ 41, appleuzr/DigitalVision Vectors 121, 121, 121, Barry Austin/Photodisc 84, Bettmann 77, borchee/E+ 117, bubaone/ DigitalVision Vectors 121, 121, 121, Cavan Images/Cavan 75, CSA-Archive/DigitalVision Vectors 85, Daniel Sannum Lauten/ AFP 46, Dave Kotinsky/Getty Images Entertainment 93, David De Lossy/Photodisc 84, David Madison/DigitalVision 74, Deb Perry/Moment 85, Denis Doyle/Getty Images Entertainment 19, Dobrila Vignjevic/E+ 60, Endai Huedl 108, 138, Fabio Camandona/EyeEm 12, fcafotodigital/E+ 24, Fuse/Corbis 53, Geoerge Doyle/Stockbyte 110, Halfpoint Images/Moment 125, Hill Street Studios/DigitalVision 87, Hiroyuki/Hulton Archive 63, Hispanolistic/E+ 125, Inti St Clair 69, isitsharp/E+ 76, izusek/ E+ 110, Johner Images 75, Johnny Greig/E+ 110, Jon Hicks/ Stone 95, Jose Luis Pelaez Inc/DigitalVision 72, 138, joSon/Stone 102, Kyodo News/Kyodo News Stills 93, LauriPatterson/E+ 34, Lorado/E+ 15, Margot Hartford/Design Pics 17, martin-dm/E+ 110, Maskot 60, mbbirdy/E+ 115, Miodrag Ignjatovic/E+ 86, mixetto/E+ 72, Moyo Studio/E+ 34, NurPhoto 62, Oli Scarff/ AFP 77, Patrick Smith/Getty Images Sport 14, Paul Bradbury/ OJO Images 69, Pavliha/E+ 117, Peter Dazeley/The Image Bank 97, Pollyana Ventura/E+ 12, Prasit photo/Moment Unreleased 55, Rattana Rattanawan/EyeEm 36, Rattanakun Thongbun/ EyeEm/ 24, Riot Games 63, Satoshi-K/E+ 74, Science & Society Picture Library/SSPL 88, SDI Productions/E+ 107, skynesher/ E+ 12, Suzy Spieldenner/Bongarts 14, technotr/E+ 74, Tetra Images 36, Thomas Barwick/DigitalVision 110, Tim Roberts/ Stone 105, Travelpix Ltd/Stone 113, Victor Coscaron/EyeEm 22, Vincent Besnault/The Image Bank 64, Westend61 17, Wong Sze Fei/EyeEm 110, Yuichiro Chino/Moment 88, 137; **Pearson Education Ltd:** Gareth Boden 19, 113, 119, Jon Barlow 6, 16, 18, 28, 30, 40, 42, 54, 56, 66, 68, 78, 80, 92, 94, 104, 106, 116, 118, Jules Selmes 11; **Shutterstock.com:** 34, 93, A StockStudio 110, Africa Studio 25, 36, 87, AG-PHOTO 89, Aleksandar Todorovic 117, Almix 24, Andrey_Popov 93, andreyspb21 11, Anna Frajtova 120, Anna Murashova Photo 34, axily 101, BW Folsom 24, Cynthia Farmer 39, DGLimages 113, dobrodzei 34, Dr.Margorius 140, EpicStockMedia 139, Evgeny Karandaev 24, f11photo 117, Farknot Architect 36, fizkes 105, fotolupa 65, Fresnel 74, Gerardo Vieyra/NurPhoto 62, givaga 29, GoodStudio 103, Granger 122, Have a nice day Photo 11, ifong 24, Iryna Tiumentseva 89, JethroT 29, Jill Battaglia 25, Jiri Hera 24, Karina de Carvalho 1, Ken McKay/ ITV 27, Kiselev Andrey Valerevich 64, Lana Langlois 27, Luna Vandoorne 17, MaraZe 24, 24, margouillat photo 25, Mariyana M 29, Matt Leane 112, Mike_shots 36, MikhailSh 124, Nataliia K 50, Nattika 24, New Africa 24, 25, Nickolay Vinokurov 142, nicostock 91, norikko 27, Oleksii Sidorov 67, Ollyy 53, Oscar Gonzalez/NurPhoto 62, 62, 62, ozanuysal 89, Pavlo S 2, 3, Peter Hermes Furian 109, PR Image Factory 139, Razym 75, 137, Rido 22, Rob Latour 63, RomanSlavik.com 117, Scanrail1 89, Sergey Eremin 93, Sergey Novikov 41, STX Films/StudioCanal/Kobal 141, Tomasz Warszewski 112, Tracy Whiteside 119, Tyler Olson 60, Vadym Lesyk 15, Valentyn Volkov 24, Vera Kailova 38, Versta 101, Volodymyr Krasyuk 24, William Perugini 112, 139, Wonder Life 117, Wong Yu Liang 25, YanLev 37, Yellow Cat 50; **Tjalf Sparnaay:** 140

Illustrated by Tim Bradford (IllustrationX) 79; Amber Day (IllustrationX) 33, 45, 82; The Boy Fitz Hammond 143; Carl Harrison (Beehive) 70; John Lund (Beehive) 51; Maguma AKA Marcos Guardiola Martin (IllustrationX) 35, 61, 85, 111; May Van Millingen (IllustrationX) 10, 58; Martin Sanders (Beehive) 32, 96, 118; Amit Tayal (Beehive) 9, 21, 51, 90; Rupert Van Wyk (Beehive) 8.
All other images © Pearson Education

Cover photo © *Front:* **Alamy Stock Photo:** Lenita Ouro Preto